H
936

HENRY IV: THE ESTABLISHMENT OF THE REGIME, 1399–1406

Having seized the throne from his cousin, Richard II, in 1399, Henry Bolingbroke – the first nobleman to be made king of England since the twelfth century – faced the remarkable challenge of securing his power and authority over a kingdom that was divided and in turmoil. This collection of essays, by some of the leading historians of late medieval England, takes a fresh look at the crucial but neglected first years of Henry IV's reign, examining how Henry met and overcame the challenges which his usurpation created. Topics covered include a reappraisal of the events surrounding the revolution of 1399; Henry's relations with his northern magnates; the Yorkshire rising of 1405; the 'Long Parliament' of 1406; and the nature and purpose of the king's council. As a whole, the book adds significantly to an understanding of both the character of Henry IV, and the circumstances in which he ruled.

Dr GWILYM DODD is Lecturer in History at the University of York; Dr DOUGLAS BIGGS is Associate Professor of History at Waldorf College.

YORK MEDIEVAL PRESS

HENRY IV: THE ESTABLISHMENT OF THE REGIME, 1399–1406

Edited by
Gwilym Dodd *and* Douglas Biggs

YORK MEDIEVAL PRESS

First published 2003

A York Medieval Press publication
in association with The Boydell Press
an imprint of Boydell & Brewer Ltd
PO Box 9 Woodbridge Suffolk IP12 3DF UK
and of Boydell & Brewer Inc.
PO Box 41026 Rochester NY 14604–4126 USA
website: www.boydell.co.uk
and with the
Centre for Medieval Studies, University of York

ISBN 1 903153 12 3

A catalogue record for this book is available
from the British Library

Library of Congress Cataloging-in-Publication Data
Henry IV: the establishment of the regime, 1399–1406/edited by Gwilym
Dodd and Douglas Biggs.
    p. cm.
Includes bibliographical references and index.
    ISBN 1-903153-12-3 (alk. paper)
1. Henry IV, King of England, 1367–1413. 2. Great Britain – History –
Henry IV, 1399–1413. 3. Great Britain – Kings and rulers – Biography.
I. Dodd, Gwilym. II. Biggs, Douglas, 1960–
    DA255.H46 2003
    942.04′1′092–dc21   2002151802

Typeset by Joshua Associates Ltd, Oxford
Printed in Great Britain by
St Edmundsbury Press Ltd, Bury St Edmunds, Suffolk

CONTENTS

Preface   vii

List of Contributors   viii

Abbreviations   ix

1. Introduction   1
    Anthony Goodman

2. Henry of Bolingbroke and the Revolution of 1399   9
    Michael Bennett

3. How Do You Bury a Deposed King? The Funeral of Richard II
    and the Establishment of Lancastrian Royal Authority in 1400   35
    Joel Burden

4. Henry IV and Chivalry   55
    Anthony Tuck

5. Scotland, the Percies and the Law in 1400   73
    Cynthia J. Neville

6. Henry IV's Council, 1399–1405   95
    Gwilym Dodd

7. Henry IV, the Northern Nobility and the Consolidation of the
    Regime   117
    Mark Arvanigian

8. 'They have the Hertes of the People by North': Northumberland,
    the Percies and Henry IV, 1399–1408   139
    Andy King

9. The Yorkshire Risings of 1405: Texts and Contexts   161
    Simon Walker

10. The Politics of Health: Henry IV and the Long Parliament of
    1406   185
    Douglas Biggs

Index   207

PREFACE

The reign of Henry IV has suffered from neglect over the last three decades. In spite of the great interest shown in the reign of Richard II during the 1990s and the ongoing interest in the reign of Henry V, very little material has appeared on Henry IV since the publication of John Kirby's political biography of the king in 1970. It was with a view to addressing this hiatus that we organized a colloquium on the reign in an effort to bring some new scholarship to this overlooked period.

The papers which make up this volume are the result of a three-day colloquium on the reign of Henry IV held in July 2001 at the Centre for Medieval Studies, University of York. One of our principal aims in organizing the event was to encourage as much informal debate and discussion among the participants as possible. To this end the papers were circulated in advance of the colloquium and were summarized, and then discussed in detail, during the event itself. This left us ample time for what turned out to be a series of extremely constructive and enjoyable round-table discussions, expertly chaired by our three commentators, Professors Chris Given-Wilson, Anthony Goodman and Anthony Pollard.

We should like to thank Professor Mark Ormrod for supporting us in this project and, as Director of the Centre for Medieval Studies at the time, for providing the medieval setting of the King's Manor as the venue for the conference. We would also like to thank the Department of History at the University of York for its financial assistance. Thanks are also due to Dr Craig Taylor for loading electronic versions of the draft papers on to a website that made them accessible to the participants; to Professor R.B. Dobson for advice and counsel; and to Mark Punshon for helping with general duties. And finally, we would like to thank the contributors for their papers, comments and collegiality, as well as the three commentators for helping to keep all of us on task during the colloquium and for writing the Introduction to the volume.

Douglas Biggs and Gwilym Dodd   February 2002

CONTRIBUTORS

Anthony Goodman	University of Edinburgh (*retired*)
Michael Bennett	University of Tasmania
Joel Burden	University of Newcastle upon Tyne
Anthony Tuck	University of Bristol (*retired*)
Cynthia J. Neville	Dalhousie University
Gwilym Dodd	University of York
Mark Arvanigian	California State University, Fresno
Andy King	University of Durham
Simon Walker	University of Sheffield
Douglas Biggs	Waldorf College

LIST OF ABBREVIATIONS

'Annales'	'Annales Ricardi Secundi et Henrici Quarti', in *Johannis de Trokelowe . . . chronica et annales*, ed. H. T. Riley (London, 1866)
Bennett, *Richard II*	M. Bennett, *Richard II and the Revolution of 1399* (Stroud, 1999)
BIHR	*Bulletin of the Institute of Historical Research*
BJRL	*Bulletin of the John Rylands Library*
BL	London, British Library
CChR	*Calendar of Charter Rolls*
CCR	*Calendar of Close Rolls*
CFR	*Calendar of Fine Rolls*
Chronicle of Adam Usk	Chronicle of Adam Usk 1377–1421, ed. and trans. C. Given-Wilson (Oxford, 1997)
Chrons. Rev.	*Chronicles of the Revolution, 1397–1400*, ed. and trans. C. Given-Wilson (Manchester, 1993)
CIM	*Calendar of Inquisitions Miscellaneous*
CIPM	*Calendar of Inquisitions Post Mortem*
CPR	*Calendar of Patent Rolls*
EETS	Early English Text Society
EHR	*English Historical Review*
Eulogium Historiarum	*Eulogium Historiarum*, ed. F. S. Haydon, 3 vols. (London, 1858–63)
Foedera	*Foedera, conventiones, literae, et cujuscunque generis acta publica*, ed. T. Rymer (edition as cited in text)
Given-Wilson, *Royal Household*	C. Given-Wilson, *The Royal Household and the King's Affinity: Service, Politics and Finance in England, 1360–1413* (London, 1986)
Hardyng	*The Chronicle of John Hardyng*, ed. H. Ellis (London, 1812)
Historia Anglicana	*Thomae Walsingham quondam monachi S. Albani Historia Anglicana*, ed. H. T. Riley, 2 vols. (London, 1863–64)
House of Commons	*The History of Parliament: The House of Commons, 1386–1421*, ed. J. S. Roskell, L. Clark and C. Rawcliffe, 4 vols. (Stroud, 1992)
Kirby, *Henry IV*	J.L. Kirby, *Henry IV of England* (London, 1970)
Knighton's Chron	*Knighton's Chronicle 1337–1396*, ed. and trans. G. H. Martin (Oxford, 1995)

LKLK	K. B. McFarlane, *Lancastrian Kings and Lollard Knights* (Oxford, 1972)
'Metrical History'	Jean Creton, 'A French Metrical Chronicle of the Deposition of Richard II', ed. and trans. J. Webb, *Archaeologia* 20 (1825), 1–423
POPC	*Proceedings and Ordinances of the Privy Council of England*, ed. N. H. Nicolas, 7 vols. (London, 1834–37)
PRO	London, Public Record Office
Rot. Parl.	*Rotuli Parliamentorum*, 7 vols. (London, 1783–1832)
Rot. Scot.	*Rotuli Scotiae in turri Londonensi et in domo capitulari Westmonasteriensi asservati*, ed. D. Macpherson *et al.*, 2 vols. (London, 1814–19)
Signet Letters	*Calendar of Signet Letters of Henry IV and Henry V*, ed. J. L. Kirby (London, 1978)
Somerville, *Duchy of Lancaster*	R. Somerville, *History of the Duchy of Lancaster, 1265–1603* (London, 1963)
Tout, *Chapters*	T. F. Tout, *Chapters in the Administrative History of Mediaeval England*, 6 vols. (Manchester, 1920–33)
TRHS	*Transactions of the Royal Historical Society*
VCH	*Victoria County History*
Westminster Chron.	*The Westminster Chronicle 1381–1394*, ed. and trans. L. C. Hector and B. F. Harvey (Oxford, 1982)
Wylie, *Henry IV*	J. H. Wylie, *History of England Under Henry IV*, 4 vols. (London, 1884–98)

Unless otherwise stated, all unpublished documents are in London, Public Record Office.

1

Introduction

Anthony Goodman*

Sandwiched between the more glamorous reigns of Richard II and Henry V, the reign of Henry IV has tended to be neglected by late-twentieth-century English historians. In a welcome initiative to rectify the balance in the twenty-first century, Drs Gwilym Dodd and Douglas Biggs convened a symposium of two dozen or so scholars at the King's Manor in York from 13 to 15 July 2001. The papers here published were first delivered to this informal gathering, which focused its attention on the first half of this notoriously turbulent reign.

These essays have the aim of re-evaluating both the 'revolution' of 1399 and the domestic political crises of the first fraught seven years of Henry IV's reign, which culminated with the 'Long Parliament' of 1406. The deposition of Richard II and usurpation of Henry of Bolingbroke have been a focus of scholarship in recent years. Yet it remains puzzling that a long-established ruler was ousted so deftly in favour of a noble whose various claims to the throne might be categorized as either spurious, dangerous or doubtful, and who had less experience of governing roles than comparable magnates. Moreover, the causes of political instability in the first half of Henry's reign are by no means clear-cut. Questions remain as to how far this flowed from the usurpation itself and how far from recent institutional developments and political events, or from longer-term trends. In this context, too, the impact of Henry's character and policies as king needs to be examined. In addition, the significance of the reign within the general perspective of the development of relations between crown and community needs to be reassessed.

It may well have seemed in the first months of Henry's reign that opposition to his rule in the next few years might be fomented by Richard's partisans. In the long run this was not to be the case, though the Percy revolt of 1403 was to receive support from Cheshiremen. Potential noble dissidents had perished when they precipitately launched the Epiphany Rising of 1400. It was noted with concern by the king's council that rebels had been killed without process of law by the common people.[1] Their savage reactions in different parts of southern England perhaps reflected the breadth of popular

---

* I owe thanks to Professor C. Given-Wilson and Professor A. J. Pollard for their helpful suggestions.

[1] *POPC*, I, 107ff; *Chronicle of Adam Usk*, pp. 90–1.

1

support that Bolingbroke had received, and the strength of belief that he would rule as a perfect prince. Subsequent disillusion induced a litany of discontent. The seriousness with which Henry viewed this is reflected in his personal interest in the denunciations of preachers, and harsh treatment of them. The revolution of 1399 seems to have stirred an exceptional interest of the populace in high politics, which could be exploited by Henry's newly emerging noble opponents.

Curiously, among the nobles who were to oppose Henry's rule were men who had conspicuously supported his rebellion and usurpation, had profited mightily from it and, at first, worked assiduously to make his rule a success. For instance, as Gwilym Dodd points out, Thomas Percy, earl of Worcester was one of the few magnates who worked hard on what he terms Henry's 'administrative council', and Richard Scrope, archbishop of York frequently witnessed royal charters, and so can be assumed to have counselled Henry at court. Why did some men who had known Henry personally for years, who presumably admired his undoubtedly outstanding abilities and attainments, and entrusted their own and their families' future well-being to him in 1399, turn against him within a few years?

In view of their formidable challenges, questions arise as to how Henry's rule survived intact, and why the second half of his reign was, by comparison, tranquil. Mark Arvanigian emphasizes how Henry kept a formidable basis of support among the gentry of the Lancastrian affinity and, in the context of northeast England, how he and his brother-in-law Ralph Neville, earl of Westmorland cultivated links with baronial and leading knightly families. In Henry's later years, a change of outlook among the lukewarm and potentially dissident was signalled by the earl of Northumberland's failure to raise significant domestic support for rebellion in 1408. What makes the relative ease with which Henry went on to wear the crown the more remarkable is that his health had collapsed: no other medieval English king with a tenuous physical capacity to rule did so with some success for so long. Yet this was a king who had been so hated that he had been the intended victim of attempts at assassination, an unusually drastic prescription for a reigning king. Maybe his rule came to appear more tolerable to the disillusioned and dissident because other, untainted members of his family loomed larger in it and because God had not permitted his opponents to kill him, but rather, as his physical deterioration graphically illustrated, inflicted on him a living purgatory.[2]

The authors of the following essays raise fundamental issues for the reassessment of the usurpation and of Henry's fledgling rule. The success

---

[2] A deterrent to rebellion was the increasing savagery with which Henry treated leading and vociferous opponents, and the intense use made of their remains for visual propaganda, as is pointed out by A. Dunn, 'Henry IV and the Politics of Resistance in Early Lancastrian England 1399–1413', *The Fifteenth Century III*, ed. L. Clark (forthcoming).

with which a public image of his kingship was projected and the extent to which he was willing and able to rule according to the model implicit in the deposition proceedings are central issues. As regards the development of relations between the crown and community of the realm, his dealings with parliaments (in particular, the Commons in parliament) are a crucial focus. In this context, Bishop Stubbs's theory of the existence of a 'Lancastrian constitution' is reassessed, and so is the generally accepted theory with which K. B. McFarlane replaced it, distinguished by its stress on the adversarial character of relations between king and Commons.

Extra-parliamentary adversarial politics were certainly a distinguishing feature of the period. The backgrounds to some of the domestic rebellions that helped to absorb Henry's energies, sap his resources and to force him to make heavy demands on his subjects, are re-examined. The extent to which these risings were located in the North and received support there is notable. Henry's problems with dissidence and their outcomes put the spotlight on regional institutions and society and on how his policies interacted with them.

Let us briefly review the coverage of some of the salient issues discussed in the book, starting with the events of 1399. Michael Bennett surveys the reasons for Henry's successes and their implications and consequences. Widely seen as the exemplary victim of royal injustices, Henry was able to tap into a traditional regard for baronial leaders who led armed protests against misgovernment. He and his close allies Archbishop Arundel and the earl of Northumberland shared a Biblical and providential interpretation of their joint actions, which may have been one they broadcast persuasively. This presented him as like Judas Maccabeus, a leader provided by God to the people of Israel, who by his prowess had rescued them from oppression and who governed them in peace and justice.[3] These analogies should not be dismissed as cynically self-serving and manipulative devices. As the 'Articles of Deposition' show, the architects of the revolution of 1399, like those of the Glorious Revolution of 1688, had a principled concern for what they considered to be the rightful exercise of royal power.

Anthony Tuck, focusing on Henry's international career in the 1390s, provides some of the reasons why he could be plausibly represented as a second Judas Maccabeus. The crusading expeditions he had undertaken in 1390 and 1392 to support the Teutonic Knights in their campaigns against the Lithuanians (the latter combined with a pilgrimage to the Holy Land) had introduced him widely to continental rulers and gained him a European reputation for piety, honour and prowess. His shrewdness in pursuing this agenda was reflected in his failure to participate in Richard II's Irish

---

[3] The English had already been identified as the chosen people: addressing Edward III's last parliament, Bishop Houghton asserted that England had been chosen by God as his heritage, as Israel had been: *Rot. Parl.*, II, 362.

expedition in 1394 – campaigning there does not seem to have been regarded as conducive to enhancing chivalrous reputations. Nor was campaigning in Friesland, where his eagerness in 1396 to serve was considered imprudent – a manifestation, doubtless, of his concern to assist his kinsmen of the ruling house of Hainault and Holland to assert their rights of lordship (in contrast to his failure to support actively Richard's in Ireland in 1394). Henry's wide and distinctive horizons of ambition apparently had the effects in people's minds of distancing him from Richard's increasingly unpopular policies. Despite Henry's prominent role in assisting in the punishment of his former political allies in the 'Revenge Parliament' of 1397 and his elevation in reward among the batch of new dukes, he seems to have kept his high reputation intact.

If Henry hoped that as king he would be able to burnish his international reputation, distinguishing his royal image as more like that of Edward III than of Richard, he was soon to be disappointed. Financial constraints, eventually compounded by the need at times for an unusually peripatetic royal lifestyle, in order to combat revolt, militated against the elaboration of chivalrous magnificence at court. The invasion of Scotland in 1400, grandiosely reviving the claim to the overlordship in the Edwardian tradition, and recalling the greatness of the ancient kings of Britain, soon petered out, not detectably making the desired impact on domestic opinion. Henry faced other constrictions in trying to 'brand' his kingship positively. As Joel Burden explains, his exploitation of ritual was limited by Richard's close personal identification with traditional royal cults and his appropriation of the sacred space of English monarchy. Henry drastically modified Richard's testamentary instructions for his funeral and burial in order to sever such links. The sacredness of his own rule was affirmed by propaganda that highlighted his unique anointing with the holy oil of St Thomas of Canterbury. Henry's burial (and the burial of some of his close kinsfolk) near the saint's shrine looks like an attempt to create an alternative royal cult centre to 'Ricardian' Westminster abbey. However, whatever personal reassurance Henry may have sought from the protection of St Thomas, his efforts to tweak the 'royal religion' made little discernible impression on his subjects. The image of his kingship seems to have been indelibly defined by the prophetic promise of 1399 and flawed by its failure to materialize.[4]

Though Henry's rule suffered from a crisis of expectations, that alone cannot explain the intensity and duration of his time of troubles. What other explanations can be put forward? As Professor Bennett points out, the 'Articles of Deposition' offered no new constitutional principles. Their

[4] The start of the reign seemed to promise a revival of chivalrous sports at court, when, on his return from Scotland, Henry allowed the challenges of a French and an Italian knight against Sir John Cornewall and Janico Dartasso to be held at York: 'Annales', p. 333. Henry's appropriation of the holy oil and its legend linked him with the Black Prince (near whom he was to be buried) and his ambitions in France: 'Annales', pp. 297–9.

proponents were intent on preserving the structure of royal power, not dismantling it. So one cannot argue that Henry provoked reactions by trying to evade new constitutional parameters. Did he provoke opposition because he did not adhere to the blueprint for good governmental practice implicit in the 'Articles'? Or was he simply guilty of being *rex inutile*, incapable of providing peace and justice?

Dr Dodd examines aspects of Henry's government, showing how the endorsement of large numbers of petitions from the early years of the reign with the names of small groups of councillors gives insights into the ways in which Henry used his 'administrative council' – in particular, in the settlement of difficult legal cases on which the king could not make a speedy decision just with the advice of the less technically qualified advisers who were generally to hand. He used his council in customary ways, though endorsement of petitions was a recent innovation, a means of ascertaining responsibility for decisions. This was probably considered good administrative practice, especially as the king, often absent from Westminster and its environs on pressing business elsewhere in the realm, relied heavily on his council, which for bureaucratic convenience usually met there.[5]

Dr Dodd distinguishes the normal responsibilities of the council from the counsel given personally to the king at court by nobles and household officers in attendance, both as regards answering petitions and matters of state. The evidence of witness lists to royal charters suggests that Henry frequently had a variety of magnates in his company. In normal circumstances during the reign, the Commons in parliament did not venture to lay down guidelines to police the giving of counsel at court. Their concerns on occasion focused on the composition, competences and procedures of the 'administrative council'. They wished to ascertain that measures were in place to ensure that councillors acted with probity and diligence. In 1401 they wanted to be informed about the identity and duties of councillors. The positive way in which Henry responded after the session suggests that he too was concerned to ensure their accountability. Dr Dodd's interpretation of the exchanges of Henry and the Commons on conciliar issues emphasizes their cooperation rather than confrontation, and the absence of a Commons' agenda to invade the king's prerogatives, either as part of a long-term parliamentary programme or for the pragmatic purpose of remedying defaults of government.

Light on attitudes in the Commons is shed by Douglas Biggs's examination of the composition of shire representation in Henry's early parliaments. The knights of the shire, to a high degree, were royal retainers, including a notable number of retainers of the duchy of Lancaster. The fortunes of many of them were closely bound up with those of the Lancastrian dynasty. In these circumstances, it is unlikely that the retainers would have sponsored or acquiesced in measures that discredited Henry or impaired his ability to rule.

---

[5] For variations in Henry's itineration, see Dunn, 'Henry IV and the Politics of Resistance'.

The Commons trod a fine line between being supportive and critical. If this was the case, how can we account for the unprecedented prolongation of the 'Long Parliament' in 1406, and the series of measures promoted by the Commons to define and control government, apparently downgrading the king's role in it? The culminating 'Thirty-one Articles' effectively put the crown into commission – a drastic step, which the estates of the realm had conspicuously failed to take as a corollary to the 'Articles of Deposition' in 1399. The question of whether or not relations between crown and Commons in 1406 were adversarial is crucial to the interpretation of the political and constitutional significance of events in the first half of the reign. Dr Biggs decisively rejects the argument for confrontation. In his interpretation, the key to an understanding of the prolonged crisis and the tenor of the 'Thirty-one Articles' lies in the evidence for the dramatic deterioration in Henry's health and for the turns for the worse it took during the parliamentary sessions. If, indeed, expectations arose of his imminent demise or permanent incapacitation, the measures for governing taken at the instigation of parliament can be seen as well-considered responses to a desperate crisis, which were intended to ensure the stability of the regime and to prop up Henry's apparently fading ability, not to inhibit the exercise of personal monarchy. To a large extent, this was an impressive endorsement of Henry's rule – though, as Simon Walker points out, there were misgivings in parliament about the treatment of some recent rebel leaders. On this interpretation, the constitutional significance of the 'Long Parliament' was that it showed that parliament was regarded as the natural forum to resolve a crisis in kingship, and that, on this occasion, it displayed impressive efficiency and unity in providing *ad hoc* remedies.

When the focus is turned on the provinces, the intractability of problems that confronted Henry and the defaults of his policies appear more starkly. A number of contributors throw light on the background to northern dissidence, whose scale and persistence were so notable. As Cynthia Neville points out, from the start of his reign Henry showed an appreciation that the crown needed to be assertive in order to stamp its control over the deleterious course of Anglo-Scottish relations and over the government of border society. In Professor Neville's account (complemented by that of Dr Arvanigian), in the later fourteenth century the earl of Northumberland and his son Hotspur are shown to have developed a novel degree of control over border society and its relations with the Scots. They had enhanced the judicial as well as the military and diplomatic competence of the wardenships of the marches, their tribunals encroaching on the business of the common law courts. The scope of the earl's authority was increased by royal grants of other judicial offices. Richard's abrupt curtailment of Percy officeholding led to an increase in truce-breaking that underlined the crown's regional dependence on the family. Henry saw the necessity of restoring their position. However, his invasion of Scotland demonstrated his determination to control Anglo-

Scottish relations. From the start of his reign he promoted roles in border affairs for the earl of Westmorland, who, as Dr Arvanigian shows, was a fitting instrument, because of the spread of his properties and his connections with northern barons and knights. Within a year or so of Henry's accession, as Andy King shows, he was building up the position of the royal affinity in Northumberland, by appointing retainers to offices there. Such initiatives, and then the disfavour shown by the crown in the settlement of the Percies' financial claims, posed a threat to their principal power-base in the borders – their office-holding. As Dr King demonstrates, the gentry of Northumberland were not conspicuously tied to their patronage; they were to remain largely neutral in the conflicts between Henry and the Percys, and, after the latter's overthrow, were to develop a mutually satisfactory *modus vivendi* with the crown in the running of shire affairs.

Adverse reactions to Henry's somewhat duplicitous border policies occurred in a less marginal setting – Yorkshire. The Percys had recruited heavily for their affinity among the gentry there, who consequently reaped rewards for the service they gave in support of the Percys in the borders. The erosion of the Percy position there threatened the family's historic standing in Yorkshire, and the profit and standing of substantial families there. Their participation in revolt in 1403 resulted in forfeitures that tended to destabilize local society, stoking up quarrels between magnates which, as Simon Walker explains, Archbishop Scrope saw it as part of his mission in 1405 to assuage through his mediation. For him, as for other Yorkshire gentlefolk, the aggrandizement of Westmorland in the shire, especially threatening to the interests of Thomas Mowbray, provided causes of concern. Dr Walker's chapter shows how the crown's branding of the protest movement headed by Scrope as part of Northumberland's campaign to dethrone Henry was propagandist falsehood. Scrope devised a programme of reform on traditional lines, which knitted together a variety of grievances voiced by different regional elements. He attracted particular support from clergy in York, from some local religious, from the gentry (including some connected with the duchy of Lancaster), and from citizens and inhabitants of York. The critique of government in Scrope's manifestos and Dr Walker's contextualization of it provide us with unique insights into how Henry's policies – particularly his heavy financial demands – impacted on the concerns and problems of a provincial society. In the context of frontier society the Percy hegemony may have seemed to Henry all too easily assailable, but he does not seem to have weighed carefully enough the import of the more formidably based resources and connections that the family had elsewhere, sufficient to underpin credible dynastic challenges that, even if they did not succeed, might induce wider instability.

Dr Walker remarks on resonances between complaints made in Scrope's manifestos and by the Commons in 1404. Maybe the Commons in Henry's early parliaments, despite their vociferousness, were too timid about obliging the king to accept their prescriptions. One of the demands made by Scrope was that free elections should be held for a parliament. That suggests that the Lancastrian Commons, far from being regarded as formidable watchdogs for the interest of the *res publica*, were perceived by some as barking in vain. Since they failed to narrow the gaps that opened between Henry and his subjects, Scrope undertook his hazardous assumption of a traditional extra-parliamentary role and won posthumous honour for it. He refreshed the tradition of armed protest on behalf of the estates against the oppressive policies of allegedly bad and greedy royal counsellors. That was an important constitutional achievement of Henry's reign. Scrope deserves to be heard as pronouncing a verdict on the first half of Henry's reign thath ought not to be dismissed as wholly tendentious.

These essays collectively demonstrate how complex are the issues with which the historian of Henry IV is faced. They are but a beginning of a revaluation. All participants in the symposium at which they were delivered and discussed would wish to thank the University of York for its hospitality and Gwilym Dodd and Douglas Biggs for bringing them together. And those happy few trust that what here follows is as stimulating for those who were abed.

2

Henry of Bolingbroke and the Revolution of 1399

Michael Bennett

On 30 September 1399 Henry IV ascended the throne in dramatic circumstances. The events of the day, and how they were to be recorded, had presumably been the subject of some thought over the previous weeks. The scene in Westminster Hall was carefully prepared. As the Lords and other representatives of the estates of the realm gathered, the obvious focus of attention was the throne on which Richard II had been wont to sit crowned and with all his regalia, glowering at his subjects. Draped in cloth of gold, the vacant chair mutely proclaimed the king's absence. According to the 'Record and Process', Archbishop Scrope of York recited, first in Latin and then in English, Richard's resignation of the crown. Archbishop Arundel of Canterbury then asked the assembly whether it wished, for the good of the realm, to accept the abdication, and the Lords and representatives of the estates of the realm gave it their hearty assent. It was nonetheless felt appropriate, for the sake of certainty, that a statement of the crimes and misgovernment that made Richard worthy of deposition be rehearsed and entered into the record, and that Richard be formally notified of his deposition. Henry of Bolingbroke then rose to his feet and made his formal claim to the throne. The earl of Northumberland asked the Lords individually if they gave their assent, which each then did. The 'Manner of Richard's Reconciliation' adds a lighter touch. According to this semi-official account, Henry replied by asking them to assent not merely with their mouths but with their hearts, adding that he understood well enough that some of them might have reservations.[1]

Amid the many acts of this momentous day, so carefully scrutinized by generations of historians, it is worth lingering on this moment when Henry of Bolingbroke, on the threshold of a reign, broke the tension with his self-deprecating humour. He did so again, at his coronation, when he offered to serve as his own champion, as if the king's champion might otherwise feel some discomfort in the role. One point is that there were almost certainly men

---

[1] G. O. Sayles, 'The Deposition of Richard II: Three Lancastrian Narratives', *BIHR* 54 (1981), 257–70; C. Given-Wilson, 'The Manner of King Richard's Renunciation: A "Lancastrian Narrative"?', *EHR* 108 (1993), 365–70. In general, see *Chrons. Rev.*, passim, and Bennett, *Richard II*, pp. 183–4.

who were distinctly uncomfortable with the proceedings. They could not have been otherwise. The other point, though, is that Henry, who in earlier and later years appears to have been given to self-doubt, felt supremely at ease. The tensions of the past three months in which his position had been transformed from an exile at the French court to a challenger for the crown had seemingly evaporated. Henry would have known almost all the lords, bishops and knights personally. He would have known that all but a few of them wished him well. The great majority had taken great risks either by joining, or conspicuously failing to resist, the rebellion that he had headed. He must have been aware that even some of his allies would be dismayed by his pre-emptive bid for the throne, but he probably believed, and with some justification, that his replacement of Richard was the only way to secure the aims of the movement that had coalesced around him shortly after his landing at Ravenspur. For the moment he had the courage of his convictions, and indeed the big-heartedness to encourage the waverers.

In this essay it is proposed to reconsider the significance of 1399 as an event in constitutional history, broadly defined. It will be argued that Henry of Bolingbroke was brought to power not merely by the Lancastrian affinity or indeed by a coalition of affinities, but by a broadly based movement concerned with issues of good governance, some of whom addressed such issues with a degree of political subtlety and sensitivity to legal proprieties. What actually happened in autumn 1399, especially in the lead-up to the convention of lords and other notables on 30 September, admittedly remains obscure. It is easy to imagine the complexity of both the politics and the constitutional issues, and how even much fuller documentation might miss critical points in the tortuous negotiation with the king and key parties, and of the complex interplay of so many shades of political and legal opinion.[2] The main source, the 'Record and Process', cannot be regarded as a full and accurate record of the proceedings. It leaves out too much, and, if it did not wholly invent some extra-parliamentary events, it probably misrepresented them. Yet it should not be dismissed as Lancastrian propaganda. As a formal statement of what happened it might well have had general acceptance. If it was not true that Richard had voluntarily abdicated, it was nonetheless a legal fiction that many members of the assembly would have deemed necessary. The point is that issues of constitutional principle were at stake, and widely seen to be at stake, in 1399.[3] It is thus proposed to argue for a role

[2] For the classic discussions see G. T. Lapsley, 'The Parliamentary Title of Henry IV', *EHR* 49 (1934), 423–9, 578–606; S. B. Chrimes, *English Constitutional Ideas in the Fifteenth Century* (Cambridge, 1936), esp. pp. 106–15; B. Wilkinson, 'The Deposition of Richard II and the Accession of Henry IV', *History* 54 (1939), 215–39.

[3] For recent affirmations of the importance of ideas in the politics of late medieval England see E. Powell, 'After "After McFarlane": The Poverty of Patronage and the Case for Constitutional History', in *Trade, Devotion and Governance: Papers in Later Medieval History*, ed. D. J. Clayton, R. G. Davies and P. McNiven (Stroud, 1994), pp. 1–16; J. Watts, *Henry VI*

for ideas, and indeed idealism, in the movement that led to the overthrow of Richard II, and for some rehabilitation of the notion of a Lancastrian constitutional experiment. The first Lancastrian king began his rule with some acknowledgement that the 'rules' had changed.

I

In laying claim to the crown Henry of Bolingbroke could make light of the reservations of some lords because he knew the strength of his position. Since the late 1380s he had gathered around him a select group of knights and squires who were devoted to him. As the heir of John of Gaunt, he had likewise built up relations of interest and trust with members of the broader Lancastrian affinity. In the summer of 1399 the Lancastrian machine delivered. Supplies were assembled, castles garrisoned and men mobilized.[4] Many of the lords and knights who rallied to Henry's standard in summer, and gathered at Westminster in autumn, were his father's retainers. Yet the change of regime was no mere Lancastrian putsch. It involved the active collaboration of magnates such as Archbishop Arundel and the earl of Northumberland whose factional loyalties were decidedly not Lancastrian. Furthermore, it took place with unprecedented levels of popular participation and support. All the chronicles, not least the French sources that deplored the usurpation, testify to the general enthusiasm for his cause, and stress the ease of his triumph.[5] What brought Henry to the steps to the throne was no mere rebellion but a broad-based political movement.

In 1399 Henry was able to tap a fund of goodwill that had never been available to John of Gaunt. His popularity may have been of some standing. He first won acclaim for his prowess in the lists in 1386. His reputation for chivalry grew in the following decade as he participated in tournaments abroad, a crusading expedition in Prussia, and a pilgrimage to Jerusalem.[6] According to Froissart, he was especially popular in London. At his banishment in 1398 thousands of citizens accompanied him to Dover in a

and the Politics of Kingship (Cambridge, 1996); C. Carpenter, 'Political and Constitutional History: Before and After McFarlane', in *The McFarlane Legacy: Studies in Late Medieval Politics and Society*, ed. R. H. Britnell and A. J. Pollard (Stroud, 1995), pp. 175–206.

[4] A. Goodman, *John of Gaunt: The Exercise of Princely Power in Fourteenth-Century Europe* (London, 1992), p. 373.

[5] 'Metrical History', pp. 178–9; *Chronicque de la traïson et mort de Richart Deux Roy Dengleterre*, ed. B. Williams (London, 1846), pp. 183–7, 212; 'Annales', p. 250; *The Kirkstall Abbey Chronicles*, ed. J. Taylor, Publications of the Thoresby Society 42 (Leeds, 1952), p. 78; *Chronicle of Adam Usk*, pp. 60–1.

[6] In general see Kirby, *Henry IV*, esp. chs. 2 and 3; *LKLK*, esp. part 1, chs. 1 and 2. Wylie, *Henry IV*, is a mine of information.

tumultuous display of solidarity.[7] By all accounts there was great rejoicing at his return in 1399. As news of his landing at Ravenspur spread he caught the popular imagination as a gallant knight who, unjustly deprived of his inheritance, was returning to claim his own. Yet Henry was more than a sentimental favourite. He had qualities and accomplishments that impressed not merely the populace but also the sententious poet and would-be mentor of royalty, John Gower, who as early as 1392 seemed to see Henry as England's best hope.[8] In returning to avenge the injustice done to him, Henry would prove the righter of other wrongs. Henry's personal cause could be readily associated with that of other casualties of the Ricardian regime. The early adherence to his cause of many prominent lords, knights and clerks underlined the seriousness of the movement. Two of the most notable, Thomas Arundel, the exiled archbishop of Canterbury, and his nephew Thomas Fitzalan, heir to the earldom of Arundel, joined with him on his descent on England. Their association with Henry belied any notion that his cause was limited to the recovery of his patrimony. At the very least it would involve a restoration of the dispossessed and the disinherited. In this sense the rebellion can be seen as a broad anti-Ricardian coalition.

If the leaders of the rebellion had matters to settle on their own account, it should not be assumed that they were necessarily lacking in political principle. According to Bishop Stubbs, Henry had 'a great cause to defend' as well as 'a great injury to avenge'.[9] Even if Stubbs offered little concrete evidence in support of his claim, it is at least clear what he meant by 'a great cause'. For over two centuries in England magnates and churchmen had prevailed on kings to swear to do justice, to govern according to the laws, to take counsel on important matters and to seek consent for taxation. In times of crisis they explored, and sought to establish, mechanisms to reform the administration, to call the king's servants to account, to establish conciliar and parliamentary mechanisms of restraint and accountability, and even to depose kings. Thomas Becket, England's most popular saint, owed much of his appeal to his resistance to imperious royalty. Simon de Montfort, earl of Leicester (d. 1265), who headed the baronial movement in Henry III's reign, and Thomas, earl of Lancaster (d. 1322), were the secular heroes of this tradition. The political conflicts of Edward II's reign, which resulted in Thomas of Lancaster's execution in 1322 and the king's deposition and

[7] *Chronicles of England, France and Spain by Sir John Froissart*, ed. T. Johnes, 2 vols. (London, 1842), II, 667–8.
[8] *The English Works of John Gower*, ed. G. C. Macaulay, 2 vols., EETS ES 81 and 82 (London, 1900–1); M. B. Parkes, 'Patterns of Scribal Activity and Revisions of the Text in Early Copies of Works by John Gower', in *New Science out of Old Books: Studies in Manuscripts and Early Printed Books in Honour of A. I. Doyle*, ed. R. Beadle and A. J. Piper (Aldershot, 1995), pp. 81–121 (pp. 83–4).
[9] W. Stubbs, *The Constitutional History of England in its Origin and Development*, 3 vols. (Oxford, 1874–8), III, 8.

murder in 1327, cast a long shadow over the fourteenth century. During the reign of Edward III recollection of recent bloodshed prompted restraint, and the tensions that arose were largely played out on the floor of parliament. Still, Thomas of Lancaster, like Simon de Montfort before him, lived on in popular memory as a political martyr. Miracles occurred, and his canonization was anticipated as late as 1390.[10]

The politics of Richard II's reign simply cannot be divorced from the struggles of earlier times. Richard's political education began with the tumult of the Good Parliament of 1376, in which the Commons had impeached Edward III's ministers, and the Revolt of 1381, in which peasants and townsmen had called the government violently to account. Richard detected in the English polity a spirit of rebellion and disobedience deeply rooted in the kingdom's past. In 1378 Richard II visited Edward II's tomb at Gloucester, and from the 1380s campaigned actively for his canonization. His concern to vindicate his great-grandfather, and to present him as a royal martyr, reflects his growing sense of a mission to restore the authority and majesty of the crown.[11] Richard's critics likewise positioned themselves in relation to the conflicts of Edward II's reign. In 1386 the Lords and Commons who impeached Richard's ministers and demanded the appointment of counsellors acceptable to them were conscious of earlier precedents. When Richard dismissed their demands, their spokesmen showed him documentation of their claims, including an alleged 'ancient statute', which provided for the deposition of a king by the common consent of the people and the choosing of a successor from among the royal kin.[12] Threatened with his great-grandfather's fate, Richard acquiesced in the institution of a 'continual council' to rule in his name. Its leading members included Richard's youngest uncle Thomas of Woodstock, duke of Gloucester, Richard, earl of Arundel, and Thomas Arundel, then bishop of Ely. During 1387 Richard deserted the capital, sharpening the ideological focus of the debate by securing a judicial ruling that the actions of his opponents could be construed as treason. With the political stakes raised alarmingly, Thomas of Woodstock and his colleagues looked to defend themselves, defeating an army raised in Richard's name at Radcot Bridge. After briefly contemplating Richard's deposition, they contented themselves with turning the treason charges on the king's counsellors. The Merciless Parliament of 1388 was

[10] S. Walker, 'Political Saints in Later Medieval England', in *The McFarlane Legacy*, ed. Britnell and Pollard, pp. 77–106; J. Edwards, 'The Cult of "St" Thomas of Lancaster and its Iconography', *Yorkshire Archaeological Journal* 64 (1992), 103–22.

[11] C. Given-Wilson, 'Richard II, Edward II and the Lancastrian Inheritance', *EHR* 109 (1994), 553–71. In general, see N. Saul, *Richard II* (London, 1997), passim.

[12] *Knighton's Chron.*, pp. 354–61; *Eulogium Historiarum*, III, 359–60; Saul, *Richard II*, pp. 157–8. This 'statute' was in all likelihood the so-called 'articles of accusation against Edward II': see C. Valente, 'The Deposition and Abdication of Edward II', *EHR* 113 (1998), 852–81. The continuator of the Kirkstall Chronicle, doubtless reflecting general opinion, likened Richard to Edward II: *The Kirkstall Abbey Chronicles*, ed. Taylor, p. 83.

breathtaking in the audacity of its acts and claims. The revolutionary character of its proceedings was only thinly veiled by Richard's formal acquiescence in them.[13]

It was in the crisis of 1387–8 that Henry of Bolingbroke made his debut in English politics. His father's absence in Spain made him the titular head of the most powerful affinity in the kingdom. While he played no recorded role in the political crisis of 1386, he was one of the five magnates who in December 1387 mobilized forces to defeat the army raised in Richard's name, and who in the parliament of 1388 carried the appeal of treason against the king's counsellors and friends. Henry proved less vindictive than Thomas of Woodstock, and did not serve on the new council appointed in parliament. It cannot be assumed, however, that he was any less committed to the original cause. His withdrawal from the fray may have been on his father's firm instruction. After his return to England in 1389 Gaunt, who entertained hopes for a Lancastrian succession, provided Richard with powerful support in re-establishing royal authority. It is hard to know what Henry thought. He seems to have kept his distance from the royal court, and spent substantial periods overseas in 1390–1 and 1392–3. His royal lineage was acknowledged in his participation in the ceremonies leading to Richard's second marriage, and in his assumption of the arms of St Edward the Confessor. In September 1397 he cannot have relished, and certainly soon regretted, joining the appeal of treason against Gloucester, Arundel and Warwick, his senior colleagues in 1388.[14] He must soon have become aware that there were elements at court working for the destruction of the house of Lancaster. If nothing else, Thomas Mowbray's loose talk in December 1397 made it all too clear. Henry probably feared entrapment, and saw the safest course in bringing matters to a head by accusing Mowbray of treason.[15] After holding the matter in suspense for nine months, Richard took the opportunity to rid himself of both men, exiling Henry for ten years, and then after Gaunt's death converting the banishment to life.

Henry was in an unenviable position throughout the 1390s. His own political views are in some respects irrelevant. It was a matter of what he represented. Richard showed no warmth to him. He probably never forgave him his role in the humiliation of 1387–8. In his own identification with Edward II, Richard could not fail to see Henry as the political heir of Thomas of Lancaster. Since Richard certainly viewed Henry as a possible successor,[16]

---

[13] Lapsley, 'Parliamentary Title of Henry IV', esp. p. 584; but cf. Wilkinson, 'Deposition of Richard II and the Accession of Henry IV', pp. 221–3. For more recent coverage see A. Tuck, *Richard II and the English Nobility* (London, 1973), pp. 118–26.

[14] Like his father, Henry must have been greatly disturbed by the credible rumour that Gloucester had been murdered: Goodman, *John of Gaunt*, pp. 161–2.

[15] Given-Wilson, 'Richard II, Edward II and the Lancastrian Inheritance', pp. 554–5, 563–7.

[16] In an alleged conversation at Lichfield in 1397–9 he recognized the claims only of his male cousins, Henry of Bolingbroke and Edward, duke of Albemarle. Sir William Bagot, the

he can perhaps be forgiven if, like Elizabeth I three centuries later, he found it hard to love his own winding-sheet. A London chronicler explained Richard's animosity towards his cousin in terms of some divination in which Henry was identified as his nemesis.[17] Henry's standing in the realm at large, however, was the obverse of his status in the king's affections. Where Richard looked balefully and apprehensively, an increasing number of his subjects looked in hope of deliverance.[18] The heir of six of the old earldoms – Lancaster, Hereford, Derby, Lincoln, Leicester and Northampton – and the stewardship of England, Henry would necessarily loom large in any future political landscape. Many people, even a doctor of canon law with Mortimer loyalties such as Adam Usk, saw Henry in 1399 as the hero of prophecy who would unseat Richard.[19] There must have been a sizeable body of people, too, who regarded him as having the best claim to the throne on Richard's death.

As senior prince of the blood and potentially the greatest landowner in England since the Norman Conquest, Henry was uniquely qualified to lead a movement of restoration and reform. He may well have had a genuine commitment to the principles involved. His political stance apparently caused Gaunt great concern on several occasions.[20] Henry was a man of intellect and substance, and probably identified with the political tradition associated with Thomas of Lancaster and his wife's Bohun ancestors. It is perhaps significant that in 1388, when the triumph over the court party prompted new talk about the canonization of Thomas of Lancaster, he named his second son Thomas.[21] After his accession he gave vestments depicting the life and martyrdom of Thomas of Lancaster to St George's Chapel at

source of the story, had reason to ingratiate himself with Henry, but the conversation must have seemed plausible to men who knew Richard well. If, as appears in one account, the duke of Norfolk was present at the conversation, and it indeed took place at Lichfield, it must have been Christmas 1397 or New Year 1398. This date is the more significant in that Roger Mortimer, earl of March, was then still alive. 'Annales', pp. 303–4; *Chronicles of London*, ed. C. L. Kingsford (Oxford, 1905), p. 52.

[17] *The Brut, or the Chronicles of England*, ed. F. W. D. Brie, 2 vols., EETS OS 131 and 136 (London, 1906–8), II, 589–90.

[18] According to Adam Usk, great hopes were entertained of Roger Mortimer, earl of March, but were dashed by the king's envy of his popularity even before his sudden death in Ireland in July 1398: *Chronicle of Adam Usk*, pp. 38–41, 48–9.

[19] *Chronicle of Adam Usk*, pp. 50–3; L. A. Coote, *Prophecy and Public Affairs in Later Medieval England* (York, 2000), esp. pp. 166–8; M. J. Bennett, 'Prophecy, Providence and the Revolution of 1399', forthcoming in the proceedings of the Harlaxton Symposium for 2000.

[20] It was stressed in sources more critical of Henry that he was banished in 1398 with his father's consent: *The Historians of the Church of York and its Archbishops*, ed. J. Raine, 3 vols. (London, 1879–94), II, 294.

[21] Children usually took the name of a godparent, and Henry's son was perhaps the godson of Thomas of Woodstock: *LKLK*, p. 36. The choice of name may nonetheless be significant. Interestingly, none of Henry's four sons was named Richard.

15

Windsor.[22] In 1399 Henry certainly set great store by the office of steward of England, an office previously held by Simon de Montfort and Thomas of Lancaster. Henry laid claim to the stewardship while still in exile, and after his landing at Ravenspur styled himself steward of England in official documents.[23] According to the 'baronial' tradition, it was the steward's role to take over the reins of government in times of danger, and to convene and preside over parliament in the king's absence.[24] The French chroniclers Jean Creton and the author of the *Traïson et mort* recognized this dimension to his campaign when they referred to the rebels' demand for a parliament in which Henry would be 'chief judge'.[25] In 1399 there were doubtless many English people who felt that Henry had a special responsibility to bring Richard under restraint, to take on the government of the realm, and, if necessary, to seek the consent of the estates of the realm to his deposition. In making his challenge for the crown Henry stressed that 'the realm was in point of being undone for default of governance and undoing of good laws'.[26]

In the summer of 1399 Henry led a coalition of magnates who, for all their private grievances, had the capacity to see the public issues and a readiness to embrace them. Thomas Arundel, archbishop of Canterbury, had played a major role in opposing the court in 1386–8. He had presented Richard with the parliament's demands and not-too-veiled threats in 1386, served on the 'continual council' of 1386–7, and emerged as chancellor in the regime imposed on Richard in 1388. It would be absurd to depict Arundel as some sort of ideologue of baronial rule.[27] Like almost all his contemporaries, he was a firm believer in right order in Church and state, all too keenly aware of the perils of heresy and sedition. In the early 1390s he believed that Richard had learnt his lesson, saw hopeful signs of responsible rule, and offered powerful support. Even as late as autumn 1397 he was willing to trust Richard's word. The king's actions in 1397–9, not least his own banishment and deprivation, brought home to him the need to resist the royal will. It is interesting to find him in 1398 in Florence, where his host was Coluccio Salutati, the staunch defender of Florentine liberties. This friendship, sustained thenceforward by correspondence, would suggest that Arundel by no means lacked the capacity to reflect on the purposes and forms of government.[28] Early in

---

[22] M. F. Bond, *The Inventories of St George's Chapel 1384–1667* (Windsor, 1947), pp. 44–5.

[23] *Choix de pièces inédites relatives au règne de Charles VI*, ed. L. Douët-d'Arcq (Paris, 1863), pp. 157–60; *Chrons. Rev.*, pp. 112–14; BL Add. Ch. 5829.

[24] K. W. Vernon Harcourt, *His Grace the Steward and Trial by Peers* (London, 1907), pp. 147–51; J. W. Sherborne, 'Perjury and the Lancastrian Revolution of 1399', *Welsh History Review* 14 (1988), 217–41 (pp. 222–3).

[25] 'Metrical History', pp. 133–5; *Chronicque de la traïson et mort*, ed. Williams, pp. 197–8.

[26] *Rot. Parl.*, III, 424.

[27] J. W. Dahmus, 'Thomas Arundel and the Baronial Party under Henry IV', *Albion* 16 (1984), 131–49.

[28] Salutati wrote to Archbishop Arundel in August 1399 seeking news. It is unfortunate that Arundel's reply is no longer extant. *Epistolario di Coluccio Salutati*, ed. F. Novati, 4 vols.

1399 he made common cause with Henry, notwithstanding his family's feud with the house of Lancaster. He brought along with him his nephew Thomas Fitzalan, the son and heir of the earl of Arundel, who had escaped from house arrest in England.[29] Thenceforward Archbishop Arundel was a key figure in the movement. There is a telling moment at Flint castle when, like a latter-day Becket, he dressed down the hapless Richard in such terms and at such length that Henry felt moved to intervene. He especially censured Richard's brutal treatment of the nobles who wished to curb his wantonness, observing that they were empowered to act by statute, and indeed obliged to act in times of crisis.[30] Archbishop Arundel clearly played a crucial role in setting the course and shaping the outcome of the revolution.[31]

It would be wrong to dismiss Henry's other allies as self-interested opportunists. The motives of the northern magnates, notably Henry Percy, earl of Northumberland, Ralph Neville, earl of Westmorland, and Richard Scrope, archbishop of York, have been the subject of most speculation. Northumberland and Westmorland, who was married to Henry's sister, may well have seen opportunities to consolidate their regional power-bases and to advance their interests nationally. Yet it should not be assumed that they were wholly lacking in public spirit. Both men were politically experienced. Northumberland, a veteran of Richard's regency council, was an elder statesman, and seemingly a man of some intelligence and integrity.[32] He served as intermediary, for example, between Richard and the opposition leaders in December 1387. Despite his old quarrel with Gaunt, he moved rapidly, at great personal risk, to lend support to Henry. Identifying himself as Mattathias, the patriarch of the Maccabees, he clearly saw the struggle in portentous terms.[33] The stance of Archbishop Scrope of York, who gave his blessing to the movement in its early stages, and played a prominent role in

---

(Rome, 1896), III, 360–3; D. Vittorini, 'Salutati's Letters to the Archbishop of Canterbury', *The Modern Language Journal* 36 (1952), 373–7. At the time of Arundel's sojourn in Florence, Salutati was at work on his treatise *On Tyranny*.

[29] Thomas Fitzalan was still a young man, but his name already had some political resonance. One of the Oxfordshire yeomen who allegedly conspired against Richard II in spring 1398 adopted Fitzalan's name as a pseudonym: *Oxfordshire Sessions of the Peace in the Reign of Richard II*, ed. E. G. Kimball, Oxfordshire Record Society 53 (Oxford, 1983), pp. 82–9.

[30] *Eulogium Historiarum*, III, 382. The chronicler assigns this incident to Conway, but the circumstances would indicate either Flint or Chester.

[31] In general see R. L. Storey, 'Episcopal King-Makers in the Fifteenth Century', in *The Church, Politics and Patronage in the Fifteenth Century*, ed. R. B. Dobson (Gloucester, 1984), pp. 82–98.

[32] He is described in an early record at Alnwick as 'wise', 'well-lettered' and 'eloquent': Wylie, *Henry IV*, III, 156n.

[33] *A Collection of Royal and Historical Letters during the Reign of Henry IV*, ed. F. C. Hingeston, 2 vols. (London, 1860), I, lxxxviii.

the deposition proceedings, is hardest to read.[34] Like Arundel, he was a prelate of noble birth and great learning. He clearly had the capacity to see the broader public issues. In his rebellion in 1405 he used the language of political principle, claiming that Henry had betrayed the cause. In his manifesto he presented himself and his allies as 'proctors and defenders of the republic'.[35]

In 1399 Henry and his allies had their grievances, and sought remedies to them. The rebellion, though, cannot be dismissed as simply a coalition of self-interested malcontents. A crucial point was that their personal troubles stemmed from their political positions, and contemporaries associated their private causes with the common good. After all, there were many victims of Richard's misrule, not least the hundreds of knights and other notables who had been forced to compound heavily for pardons for their support of the Appellants in 1387–8, and the inhabitants of the thirteen southern and eastern shires whose proctors had had to seal blank charters to attest their submission.[36] In the continuation of his *Vox clamantis*, John Gower presented the three senior Appellants as political martyrs, and looked to Henry very much for the deliverance of the kingdom.[37] Since in the summer of 1399 Henry sent letters far and wide to recruit support for their movement, it is a little perplexing that none are extant. According to the author of the *Traïson et mort*, they were full of 'artful fabrications' against the Ricardian regime.[38] In all likelihood, though, they would also have included appeals of a more positive nature. Thomas Walsingham and the anonymous author of *Richard the Redeless*, though using different languages, genres and idioms, presented Henry's movement very much in terms of deliverance from tyranny, the restoration of right and the reformation of government.[39] In the summer of 1399 Henry and his allies clearly rode a wave of popular discontent against Richard's misrule. Ordinary townsmen from Nottingham, a royal not a Lancastrian borough, joined the struggle for 'the general utility of the king and kingdom'.[40]

The strategy of the rebel campaign is telling. There was no march on London. There was no need to secure the capital and heartland of the kingdom. The immediate objectives were to cut Richard off from his support-bases in England, firstly by taking Bristol and then heading back north to

---

[34] P. McNiven, 'The Betrayal of Archbishop Scrope', *BJRL* 54 (1971–2), 173–213 (pp. 177–8).

[35] *Historians of the Church of York*, ed. Raine, II, 292–304.

[36] C. Barron, 'The Tyranny of Richard II', *BIHR* 41 (1968), 1–18; Bennett, *Richard II*, pp. 127, 130.

[37] *The Major Latin Works of John Gower: 'The Voice of One Crying' and 'The Tripartite Chronicle'*, ed. E. W. Stockton (Seattle, 1962), pp. 300–10.

[38] *Chronicque de la traïson et mort*, ed. Williams, pp. 180–3.

[39] 'Annales', pp. 240, 242; *Mum and the Sothsegger*, ed. M. Day and R. Steele, EETS OS 199 (London, 1936), pp. 1–26.

[40] *Records of Borough of Nottingham, 1155–1399*, ed. W. H. Stevenson (London, 1882), pp. 358–61.

Chester. After the duke of York, the keeper of the realm, had thrown in his lot with them, Henry and his allies were able to assume responsibility for the government of the realm. The crucial task was to secure the king's person. Richard had returned from Ireland, jettisoned one army in south Wales and was holed up at Conway castle. With his military position hopeless, Richard surrendered, banking on finding some later opportunity to turn the tables on his opponents. As he told Creton, he would then flay them alive.[41] The immediate concern of Henry and Archbishop Arundel was for Richard to accede in their taking control of the kingdom preparatory to the convening of a parliament that would do justice and reform the realm. The intention throughout was to involve the wider political community in the legitimation of a new settlement. On 19 August writs were dispatched from Chester in Richard's name summoning the Lords and Commons to Westminster at Michaelmas. The Londoners who sent a delegation to Henry and his allies congratulated them on securing England in less than a month, and petitioned for Richard's immediate execution.[42] Adam Usk likewise wrote of Henry's 'having gloriously, within fifty days conquered both king and kingdom'.[43] Henry's glorious conquest was largely achieved without bloodshed. It was in this sense England's first 'glorious revolution'.

II

The rebellion against the Ricardian regime in the summer of 1399 had broad appeal. Henry's bid for the throne, though, went beyond the stated aims of the movement, and it is a moot point whether his succession was so widely supported. In 1402 Louis, duke of Orleans, who had assisted him prior to his departure from France, was the first of his former allies to profess dismay at his usurpation and accuse him of bad faith.[44] In 1403 the Percies alleged that Henry had sworn an oath that his private aims went no further than recovering his inheritance.[45] In his manifesto of 1405 Archbishop Scrope repeated the allegation. If, as seems probable, Henry did take an oath that he had no designs on the throne, Northumberland was in a position to testify to this oath in his negotiations with Richard at Conway. After all, Richard would not have willingly surrendered without assurances that he would be allowed to keep his life and his crown. To all appearances, Northumberland participated fully in the proceedings of 30 September. In retrospect, if not at

[41] 'Metrical History', p. 40.
[42] 'Metrical History', pp. 176–7; *Chronicque de la traïson et mort*, ed. Williams, p. 212.
[43] *Chronicle of Adam Usk*, pp. 60–1. See the similar comments of Thomas Walsingham: 'Annales', p. 250.
[44] *The Chronicles of Enguerrand de Monstrelet*, ed. and trans. T. Johnes, 2 vols. (London, 1849), I, 16–23.
[45] Sherborne, 'Perjury and the Lancastrian Revolution of 1399', pp. 219–21.

the time, he may have come to feel especially compromised by the failure to honour the undertakings he had given in good faith to Richard.

It would be misleading, though, to present Henry as betraying the movement by his private designs on the throne. From the outset there was an intention to effect a transfer of power by bringing Richard under constraint and reforming his government. It might have appeared an option in some quarters for Richard to remain king for the rest of his life, but to surrender the reins of government to some conciliar body or vice-regal figure. The kingdom of Scotland furnished recent examples of this sort of arrangement, including David II's acceptance of Robert the Steward as his heir and lieutenant, Robert II's cession to the future Robert III in 1384, and Robert III's own delegations to his brother and son through the 1390s.[46] Of course, none of the precedents were English, or especially auspicious. In 1399 the duke of Albany, Robert III's eldest son and lieutenant of the realm, was murdered. The major problem was Richard himself. In August 1399 he may have indicated his readiness to submit to conciliar rule, or to relinquish the 'rule' of the kingdom to a lieutenant. Even in the best of times, as Henry and Archbishop knew from painful experience, Richard simply could not be trusted. In any event Henry would scarcely have been willing to accept a vice-regal role without formal designation as heir to the throne.

There could have been no settlement in 1399 without agreement on the succession. Richard was thirty-three years old, and childless. A number of actions, most notably his second marriage in 1396 to a six-year-old French princess, suggest that he was reconciled to his lack of issue.[47] From as early as the mid-1380s, though, Richard seems to have sought political advantage by mixing messages with regard to the succession. According to common law rules of inheritance his heir was Roger Mortimer, earl of March. Although the evidence is confused, Richard may actually have designated him his heir in parliament in 1385. If he did, though, he showed no inclination to confirm this status by showing him royal favour or even acknowledging his bloodline. In the 1390s Richard was more inclined to accord honour to his kinsmen in the male line, especially the dukes of Lancaster and York and their sons. In 1376 Edward III had laid down an order of succession in which the crown would pass, in the event of Richard's death without issue, to John of Gaunt and his male heirs, effectively sidelining the claims of the daughter of the late Lionel, duke of Clarence, and her son, the earl of March.[48] If it were not for his suspicions of Gaunt and his general animus to the house of Lancaster, Richard might have been generally well-disposed to reinstating this entail. The earl of March's sudden death in June 1398, leaving as his heir an infant

[46] B. Webster, *Medieval Scotland: The Making of an Identity* (London, 1997), pp. 96–7.
[47] Bennett, *Richard II*, p. 57.
[48] M. J. Bennett, 'Edward III's Entail and the Succession to the Crown, 1376–1471', *EHR* 113 (1998), 580–609.

son, highlighted the continuing uncertainty with respect to the succession. Henry's banishment two months later compounded the confusion. Earlier in the year popular opposition to the Ricardian regime had found expression in the rapturous reception accorded March at the Shrewsbury parliament. In November it found expression in the lamentations associated with Henry's departure into exile.

In 1399 Henry may have been widely seen as Richard's heir. Descended from the royal line on both sides, he had an impeccable royal pedigree. He was Richard's closest male heir, and indeed his closest adult heir. The members of the Lancastrian affinity who rallied to him on his return doubt-less regarded him in his light. In the broader coalition that gathered under Henry's leadership there were probably other views. The Percies were later to champion the Mortimer cause, but their position in 1399 is hard to read. A key point is that from the outset the allies were giving thought to the issue of the succession. Henry's oath at Doncaster was designed to secure the broadest possible support for the movement by disavowing any clearly treasonable intent, but it clearly reflects the salience of the succession prob-lem. According to the Dieulacres chronicle, the earliest account, Henry swore that he did not seek the crown, but added, in a striking equivocation, that he was ready to step aside if anyone were found worthier.[49] It was likewise all very well for him to say that he would be content with the duchy of Lancaster. There was little prospect of his becoming duke if Richard remained king. Henry's campaign to recover his inheritance assuredly involved the recovery of his rightful place in the succession.[50]

As he made his triumphal progress towards the capital, Henry grew ever more confident of the rightness of his cause. Walsingham marvelled at how rapidly Henry pacified and unified the realm, and saw it as 'a clear miracle of God'.[51] Henry had good cause to believe that his success was providential, and, as he and his confidants said on a number of occasions, that God had blessed his cause. There was probably a broad consensus that Richard should no longer have the government of the realm. In the elections of 1399 the counties and boroughs returned eleven per cent of the members who had served in Richard's 'great parliament' of 1397–8. Even more telling is the fact that thirteen per cent were actually veterans of the Merciless Parliament of 1388.[52] Such men can have had no illusions about Richard's willingness to accept conciliar restraint, and must have been generally predisposed to his removal. Many people already saw Henry as his successor. According to Philip Repton, Henry was hailed not merely as a hero but as a king: 'All the

---

[49] M. V. Clarke and V. H. Galbraith, 'The Deposition of Richard II', *BJRL* 15 (1931), 100–37; Sherborne, 'Perjury and the Lancastrian Revolution of 1399', p. 221.

[50] *Chronicle of Adam Usk*, pp. 64–7; *Hardyng*, pp. 353–4; *Scotichronicon by Walter Bower, Vol. VIII: Books XV and XVI*, ed. D. E. R. Watt (Aberdeen, 1987), pp. 20–1.

[51] 'Annales', p. 250.

[52] *House of Commons*, I, 209.

people were clapping their hands and praising God with one voice, going forth, as the sons of Israel did to meet Christ on Palm Sunday, crying out to Heaven for you, their anointed king, as if you were a second Christ, ' "Blessed is he that cometh in the name of the Lord, our king of England".'[53]

Once in the capital deliberations began as to the best approach to effect the transfer of power. The assumption seems to have been that Richard would be removed. Discussion focused on ways and means, and a committee of lawyers was appointed to review the precedents and make recommendations. As in 1327 the safest approach was to contrive an abdication and to reinforce it with a deposition 'by the authority of the clergy and people'. Richard's abdication, 'with cheerful countenance', was probably a fiction, albeit a necessary one. Yet Richard was a past master at duplicity, and it is perfectly probable that for tactical reasons he did agree at some stage to abdicate. Henry and his allies clearly resolved to deny Richard the opportunity to declare his position in public. After protracted negotiations in the Tower of London, Richard seems to have agreed to resign, and an instrument recording his abdication was then read to the Lords and Commons who had gathered at Westminster Hall for the parliament called in Richard's name. The assembly then proceeded, after drawing up a schedule of Richard's misdeeds, to depose Richard, and the next day Sir William Thirning, the chief justice, went to Richard and speaking on behalf of the estates and the people renounced homage and allegiance. Throughout the proceedings some care was taken with respect to legal forms and precedent. The men who organized the change of regime, for example, were clear that the assembly was not a parliament. The parliament summoned by Richard ceased to exist with his abdication, and indeed parliament, as the king's court, had no jurisdiction over the king. It was an assembly of the estates of the realm that approved the deposition, but an assembly, it needs to be said, held in parliament time, and comprising the magnates and the representatives of the people who, together with the king, constituted a parliament. The real point is that there was no strictly legal way to put on trial and depose the king. It seemed wisest to proceed, as in 1326–7, on the fiction of an empty throne. Given that no better solution was found in 1688–9, the men of 1399 do not deserve the condescension of posterity.

This assembly of the estates of the realm likewise heard and approved Henry's challenge for the throne. It is likely that just as there seemed no practical alternative to the removal of Richard there was no serious alternative to Henry as his successor. Adam Usk, who served on the advisory committee, gives the impression that the key issue to resolve was the exact nature of Henry's title. He mentions that there was an examination of a claim that Edmund 'Crouchback', the first earl of Lancaster, was the eldest the son of Henry III, in which case Henry would have had a stronger hereditary title

[53] *Chronicle of Adam Usk*, pp. 138–9.

than Richard himself. Though there is some evidence that John of Gaunt promoted this legend in the 1390s, and it might have served as a convenient fiction in 1399, it cannot be assumed that Henry would have been disappointed when the expert committee dismissed it out of hand.[54] What was important to Henry was his impeccable royal lineage. His reference in his challenge to descent from Henry III is better seen as a shorthand reference to his double royal bloodline than as a desperate evocation of the Crouchback legend. As Richard's heir in the male line, and as his closest adult kinsman, he had an exceptionally strong claim to the succession by hereditary right. It was a title, too, that had been vindicated by his God-given success in arms. There was some concern, though, that a title based on conquest would threaten other people's legal rights. After his challenge Henry was quick to reassure the assembly that it was not his intention to dispossess anyone, except those who 'have acted contrary to the good purpose and common profit of the realm'.[55]

In making his bid for the throne Henry seems to have set considerable store on the assent of the people. The manner in which he made light of the reservations of some of the magnates, and offered to serve as his own champion, attests to his blithe confidence. After Henry's acclamation, Archbishop Arundel preached a sermon on the text, 'A man shall rule over my people' (I Samuel 9. 17). Richard and Henry were very much the same age, but the former was dismissed as still a child, lacking in moderation, reason and resolution. In contrast to Richard, Henry was a family man, with four sons and two daughters, and the archbishop's sermon played on this point. John Gower wrote a Latin poem in which he presented the character and actions of the royal cousins, point by point, as opposites.[56] All in all, the speeches and writing of the time placed unwonted emphasis on Henry's eligibility and popularity. Indeed, his critics alleged that he was raised to the throne by the mob. Historians have wasted a great deal of ink on whether Henry sought, or indeed consciously avoided, a parliamentary title. It is clear that the assembly in Westminster Hall was not a parliament, and that Henry would have firmly believed that his title was grounded in hereditary right and that he had been raised by God to the royal dignity. Still, the role of the people, broadly defined, was much more extensive in 1399 than the customary acclamations at coronations. Henry's claim was accepted by the estates of the realm as well as by popular acclaim, and, when the estates of the realm reconvened as Henry's first parliament, immediate steps were taken to ratify the Lancastrian succession. The events of 1399 need to be seen in the context of an increasing tendency to regard parliament and 'the estates

---

[54] *Chronicle of Adam Usk*, pp. 64–7. For Lancastrian interest in the legend see *Hardyng*, pp. 353–4; *Scotichronicon VIII*, ed. Watt, pp. 20–1; A. Gransden, *Legends, Traditions and History in Medieval England* (London, 1992), p. 295.

[55] *Chrons. Rev.*, p. 186.

[56] *The Major Latin Works of John Gower*, ed. Stockton, p. 325.

of the realm' as synonymous, and to identify parliament as the assembly of the nation.[57]

The men who drew up the 'articles of deposition' sought primarily to demonstrate Richard's unworthiness to be king, but they were by no means unaware of the larger principles. They made a point of affirming the laws, conventions and expectations that Richard had allegedly broken, flouted or disappointed. They began with a reiteration of the coronation oath and made reference to Magna Carta. They assumed the king's obligation to govern according to the law, to take advice from the great men of the realm and to seek the common good. They affirmed the special status of parliament in respect of legislation and grants of taxation, and as a forum for seeking redress. They did not seek to limit the king's freedom, but stressed that the royal prerogative did not all allow him to flout the laws made in parliament. The charge that Richard had asserted that the laws were in his breast or his mouth is especially significant. Superficially it provides another instance of the king's lack of discipline, petulance and folly. Yet it also reflects a concern to reject a conception of princely power that was held to be repugnant to the English political tradition, and to reaffirm the principle that the king was subject to the law, and not, as in Roman law, the source of law. As early as 1401 Richard was presented as the prime example of a king punished by God for disregarding the laws. Princes who scorn the law, Philip Repton reminded Henry, 'shall be confounded – of which we have seen a striking example, as in a mirror, during these last two years in the case of King Richard, an image which will forever be indelibly impressed upon the memory of the whole world and of future ages'.[58]

It is true that the men of 1399 offered no new constitutional doctrine. There was no claim that parliament had the power to depose the king or confer the crown on another. There were no grand theoretical statements about the limitations of the monarchy. It was generally assumed that the king had a right to rule, and that his prerogatives should remain intact. The Commons probably needed little urging to petition in parliament that Henry should be as free in his regality as his ancestors. Nonetheless the fact that there was no formal reordering of the constitution should not detract from the enormity of the whole proceeding. A rebellion involving a broad section of the population had culminated in the king's abject surrender. With the king a captive, and his crown effectively in commission, a parliament had been summoned in his name to make provision for the kingdom. Assembling on 30 September, the Lords and Commons confronted and out-stared the empty throne. As representatives of the estates of the realm, they received Richard's abdication, and set about a process of deposition. They then heard Henry's challenge for the throne, and acclaimed him as king. Reconvening as Henry's first

---

[57] Chrimes, *English Constitutional Ideas*, pp. 106–16.
[58] *Chronicle of Adam Usk*, pp. 140–1.

parliament, they continued to concern themselves with weighty and contentious matters. In requesting that Henry should be as free as his ancestors, the reference to Richard's abuse of a like request seemed to imply that it was in some measure provisional. If Henry did not owe his crown to parliament, he certainly sought parliamentary endorsement of the new dynasty.[59]

In assessing the achievement of 1399 it is necessary to take seriously the role of ideas. In presenting Henry to the people Archbishop Arundel delivered a sermon on the text: 'It behoves us to make provision for the kingdom' (I Maccabees 6. 57). This text may well have been the motto of the revolution. He glossed it to indicate that Henry wished 'to be counselled and governed by the honourable, wise and discreet persons of his realm, and by their common counsel and assent to do the best for the government of himself and of his realm; not wishing to be governed by his own whim, nor by his wilful purpose or singular opinion, but by common advice, counsel and assent'.[60] As Stubbs fairly observed, there was some 'recognition of formal principles of government – principles which all parties recognised, or pretended, when it was convenient, to recognise'.[61] The 'Record and Process' was drawn up and promulgated, it must be assumed, with the consent of Henry IV, Archbishop Arundel and other key figures. As Douglas Biggs has argued, it implies more in the way of constitutional ground-rules than it explicitly states. Interestingly, this point has been well made in respect of the formal statements in the Glorious Revolution of 1688–9. Lois Schwoerer, for example, has argued persuasively that the Bill of Rights was a minimalist statement on which a significantly large section of the political nation could agree.[62] It was not the alpha and omega of a revolution in which more radical contractual ideas of government were salient in the thinking of the time.

III

In autumn 1399 Henry of Lancaster was the all-conquering hero, who obliged the people by specifically not pressing the notion that he ruled by conquest. He began his rule on a note of blithe optimism. Indeed, the earliest opposition

---

[59] E. F. Jacob, *The Fifteenth Century, 1399–1485* (Oxford, 1961), p. 23; P. McNiven, 'Legitimacy and Consent: Henry IV and the Lancastrian Title', *Mediaeval Studies* 44 (1982), 470–88 (pp. 474–5, 481–2).

[60] *Rot. Parl*, III, 415.

[61] Stubbs, *Constitutional History*, II, 512.

[62] D. Biggs, 'Henry IV and his Parliaments: Opposition or "Lancastrian Constitutionalism"?', unpublished conference paper, International Congress on Medieval Studies, Kalamazoo, 1996; L. G. Schwoerer, 'The Bill of Rights: Epitome of the Revolution of 1688–89', in *Three British Revolutions: 1641, 1688, 1776*, ed. J. G. A. Pocock (Princeton, NJ, 1980), pp. 224–43.

he had to face was seemingly from members of his own retinue, who clamoured for sterner punishment to be meted out to the leaders of the Ricardian regime. Henry's magnanimity was shown to be misconceived when, early in 1400, a group of Ricardian lords conspired against his rule. The execution of the ring-leaders and the death of Richard himself shortly afterwards did not bring stability. Henry found it impossible to put the circumstances of his accession behind him, and throughout his reign was beset by criticism, conspiracy and rebellion. The Percies, his former allies, turned against him, challenging both his manner of rule and his right to be king. Rumours that Richard was still alive and would come again encouraged popular dissent. In 1402 the duke of Orleans warned Henry, 'God may have dissembled with you, and have set you on a throne, like many other princes, whose reign has ended in confusion.'[63] At one point the king found himself declaring that he did not seize the crown, but was 'properly elected'.

It is possible to view Henry's problems as reflecting the dubious circumstances of his accession. From the outset Henry found himself under pressure to reward the men who had raised him to the throne. He granted Northumberland and his son, Harry Hotspur, a share of Richard's treasure, and expanded his retinue through grants of annuities.[64] Even in his first parliament Henry's generosity to his friends led to a call that his largesse be limited. At the same time, alongside a ban of the wearing of lords' badges, the use of the king's badge was limited to retainers actually attendant on the king.[65] Criticism of the royal retinue soon became almost as strident as it had been in Richard's last years. The anonymous author of *Richard the Redeless* had attributed Richard's loss of his realm to the depredations of his livery of the white hart. In *Mum and the Sothsegger* the same poet was concerned to have this point brought home to Henry IV. Henry found himself assailed from all quarters. In 1401 Philip Repton, his confessor, admonished him for his failure to bring law and justice to the land.[66] In March 1402 a Hertfordshire woman claimed that since his accession there had not been 'seven days' good and seasonable weather'.[67] In addition to the people who held that Henry was irremediably tainted by regicide, there were others who believed reports that Richard was still alive and would regain the crown. A number of

---

[63] *The Chronicles of Enguerrand de Monstrelet*, ed. and trans. Johnes, I, 20.

[64] A. L. Brown, 'The Reign of Henry IV', in *Fifteenth-Century England 1399–1509*, ed. S. B. Chrimes, C. D. Ross and R. A. Griffiths (Manchester, 1972), pp. 1–24 (p. 24); D. Biggs, 'The Reign of Henry IV: The Revolution of 1399 and the Establishment of the Lancastrian Regime, 1399–1406', in *Fourteenth Century England I*, ed. N. Saul (Woodbridge, 2000), pp. 195–210; D. Biggs, 'Sheriffs and Justices of the Peace: The Patterns of Lancastrian Governance, 1399–1401', *Nottingham Medieval Studies* 40 (1996), 149–66.

[65] *Rot. Parl.*, III, 428; *Chronicles of London*, ed. Kingsford, p. 61.

[66] The letter achieved some circulation. It was included by Adam Usk in his chronicle prior to his departure for Rome early in 1402. *Chronicle of Adam Usk*, pp. xlvi–xlvii, 136–43.

[67] *Select Cases in Court of King's Bench under Richard II, Henry IV and Henry V*, ed. G. O. Sayles, Selden Society 88 (London, 1971), pp. 122–5.

Franciscan friars preached against the king. Dr William Frisby, a Franciscan friar, openly challenged Henry. He made the telling point that if Richard were alive he was the true king, and if he were dead Henry, as a regicide, forfeited whatever title he had to the crown.[68]

It is a measure of the revolution that more was expected of Henry than Richard. The point can be made most clearly in respect of the royal finances. In 1399 Henry promised to 'live of his own'. It was assumed that the Lancastrian patrimony, along with the residue of Richard's hoard, would provide cheap government. Henry soon found himself embarrassed financially. The expedition to Scotland, the revolt in Wales and the resumption of hostilities with France made it necessary for him to call on parliament and convocation. His requests were generally met, though seldom with good grace. When in 1401 he asked his second parliament for a subsidy, the Commons responded by requesting that he first redress their grievances.[69] In the same session the Commons unsuccessfully petitioned that the king's chief officers and councillors be named and sworn in parliament. In 1404 the grant of a subsidy was made conditional on the appointment of special treasurers to oversee disbursements. Henry felt constrained to agree to ordain his council in parliament 'for the ease and comfort of his whole realm', and to concede to the council oversight of the expenditure of a grant of taxation.[70] The Commons ordained in 1406 that he should 'undertake to submit all warrants involving expenditure to the council for its endorsement', and that the councillors should swear to observe articles drawn up 'for their guidance'.[71]

In 1399 Henry presented himself as the champion of the concerns dear to the hearts of the Commons, and seems to have regarded parliament as the natural forum for the reformation of the kingdom. He saw himself as making a break with the immediate past. In his annulment of Richard II's treason act, he noted that the definition of treason had been extended so broadly that no one was able to speak or act for fear of the penalties. He wished, he said, to act in quite a different manner.[72] Over the following years Henry continually reassured the Lords and Commons that they might speak freely in parliament. Indeed, the assertiveness of the Commons in Henry's parliaments is in marked contrast to their timidity in the late 1390s. If Stubbs was perhaps too prone to invest power-play in parliament with great constitutional significance, the author of *Richard the Redeless*, who penned a remarkable satire of the cravenness of the Commons of 1397–8, had clear expectations of parliament

---

[68] *Eulogium Historiarum*, III, 389–94. P. McNiven, *Heresy and Politics in the Reign of Henry IV: The Burning of John Badby* (Woodbridge, 1987), p. 97.

[69] *Rot. Parl.*, III, 458; *LKLK*, p. 89.

[70] *LKLK*, pp. 88–90.

[71] *LKLK*, pp. 97–9.

[72] *Rot. Parl.*, III, 423; G. Dodd, 'Conflict or Consensus: Henry IV and Parliament, 1399–1406', in *Social Attitudes and Political Structures in the Fifteenth Century*, ed. T. Thornton (Stroud, 2000), pp. 118–49.

and its elected members. Sir Arnold Savage and Sir John Tiptoft, who served as speakers in Henry's parliaments, sought to consolidate new understandings of the role and rights of the House of Commons. The knights and gentry were growing in social weight and confidence, and showing themselves ever more capable of independent action, especially at the time when the ranks of the nobility seemed somewhat depleted. They must have been emboldened by their relations with the king. A great many were royal retainers, and Henry, like his royal predecessor, was criticized for seeking to pack parliament. Their 'corporate complicity in the downfall of Richard II' must have given the knights and squires associated in the revolution of 1399 a clear sense of partnership with the king in the government of the realm.[73] The loyalty of such men to the new order was beyond question, but it did not prevent their speaking their minds.[74] Generally speaking, Henry dealt patiently with their demands. In 1406 he declared, in exasperation, that 'kings were not wont to render account', but nonetheless conceded the point.[75]

If the notion of a Lancastrian constitutional experiment has fallen out of favour among historians, some contemporaries believed that Henry had made a covenant with the people. In spring 1402 men were arrested for saying that he had not kept his covenant with the Commons. They claimed that despite his promise that the people would be quit of all save war-taxation, he had raised taxes, and not for the profit of the realm but for the benefit of his lords and knights.[76] In May there were reports of preachers alleging that the king had not kept the oaths made on his arrival in England, at his coronation and to his parliament. Interestingly, Henry does not actually deny this covenant. In fact, he responded by specifically instructing the sheriffs and other officials to make proclamation throughout the land that it was, is and always would be his intention to observe and safeguard the public interest and the common good, and the laws and customs of the realm.[77] A number of Henry's closest counsellors and allies likewise professed to the nobility of the cause in 1399. One of Henry's staunchest critics was his own confessor, Philip Repton, abbot of Leicester. He had joined Henry in the Midlands, and presumably participated fully in the revolution. In a letter to the king in 1401 he asked Henry to recall 'his miraculous entry into England' and his rapturous reception by the people who praised God 'in the hope of good government for the kingdom', and admonished him to live

---

[73] Dodd, 'Conflict or Consensus', pp. 118–49.

[74] A. J. Pollard, 'The Lancastrian Constitutional Experiment Revisited: Henry IV, Sir John Tiptoft and the Parliament of 1406', *Parliamentary History* 14 (1995), 103–19; Dodd, 'Conflict or Consensus', pp. 139–40.

[75] *LKLK*, pp. 97–9.

[76] *Select Cases in Court of King's Bench under Richard II, Henry IV and Henry V*, ed. Sayles, pp. 122–5.

[77] *Foedera*, 20 vols. (London, 1725–35), VIII, 255–6; *CPR, 1401–5*, pp. 126–9.

up to the ideals and expectations. In a letter written when relations between the former allies had decidedly soured, the earl of Northumberland signed off as 'your Mattathias', an allusion to his role as elder statesmen of a movement akin to the freedom struggle of the Maccabees.[78] At the time of his rebellion in 1403 Hotspur stated bluntly that he had risen against Richard because he was a bad king, and was in rebellion again because he had likewise found Henry wanting.[79] In 1405 Archbishop Scrope drew up a manifesto against Henry in which he and his allies presented themselves as 'proctors and defenders of the republic against Henry in the court of our lord Jesus Christ'.[80]

It is easy to present the first Lancastrian king as a ruthless usurper, a man of action who made promises he did not mean to keep, but in fact he was cautious, thoughtful, probably well-read and seemingly very scrupulous.[81] Even before his accession Henry had had to face great moral dilemmas in political life, most notably over the winters of 1387–8 and 1397–8. Once he was king, there was no honourable escape, no withdrawal into private life, though abdication may have been contemplated. What is interesting is the degree to which the king's conscience became public property. The admonition of Philip Repton, his confessor, the debate with Dr Frisby over his title to the throne, the denunciation by William Norham, and the resistance and martyrdom of Archbishop Scrope, are all recorded in chronicles that are too often uncritically labelled 'Lancastrian'.[82] They all assume a responsiveness to issues of political principle, not least from Henry himself. Since Repton's letter was written after a long discussion with Henry, it assumes much common ground. In asking Henry to remember what moved people in the summer of 1399, he had every reason to assume that was how Henry remembered it as well. When he claimed that exaltation had now given way to desolation, and that 'in the place of the law, *tirannica uoluntas* now suffices', the words 'tyrant will' were intended to sting.[83]

Of course, the settlement of 1399 did not resolve the problem of how the king's will might be constrained. Kings were required to take the coronation oath, and Henry IV seems to have given other undertakings. As John Watts has made plain, however, the king was expected, after taking to counsel, to exercise his will, and in Henry VI's time there seemed no legal way of limiting this prerogative.[84] In the circumstances of 1399, though, the notion

---

[78] *Royal and Historical Letters during the Reign of Henry IV*, ed. Hingeston, I, lxxxviii.
[79] *Eulogium Historiarum*, III, 396.
[80] *Historians of the Church of York*, ed. Raine, II, 294.
[81] John Capgrave memorably describes him discussing with learned clerks the finer points of moral questions: *Johannis Capgrave Liber de Illustribus Henricis*, ed. F. C. Hingeston (London, 1858), pp. 108–9.
[82] *Chronicle of Adam Usk*, pp. 136–43; *Eulogium Historiarum*, III, 390–3, 405–8; 'Annales', pp. 161–2, 403–5.
[83] *Chronicle of Adam Usk*, pp. 136–7.
[84] Watts, *Henry VI*, passim.

that the king was fully representative of the kingdom cannot have seemed especially compelling. In assuming responsibility for the governance of the realm in July 1399, Henry and his allies believed that in certain circumstances the steward, the leading magnates and churchmen, and representatives of the estates of the realm, might represent the kingdom against the king. They would have regarded it as axiomatic that the 'common good' could be best discerned in the king in parliament. Finally, there was the old sore, not documented but doubtless voiced in 1399 as in 1327, *vox populi, vox Dei.*[85] When Philip Repton warned Henry of the possible loss of his kingdom, he was justifying revolt, but reminding him that God's providence was a living force. The Bible and British history provided innumerable examples of tyrants who, once their divine mandate to rule was forfeited, were overthrown by their own people.

Henry clearly did not enjoy his kingship. The gallant knight of the 1390s became in the following decade a sort of 'leper king'. For all his chivalric reputation and his real qualities of mind, he found himself diplomatically isolated and without the means to maintain an honourable court.[86] He eschewed ceremonial display, and showed no inclination to maintain that carapace of regal splendour that Richard had assembled. His style of kingship doubtless reflected his personality and circumstances, including increasing financial stringency. It was also a political statement, an implicit contrast between Richard's lofty conception of monarchy and his own. It is particularly noteworthy that he neglected the sacral dimension of his kingship. Although he was the first king to be consecrated with the holy oil of St Thomas of Canterbury, he made surprisingly little of this fact. He discontinued Richard's participation in the liturgy at Westminster Abbey and his practice of regular crown-wearings.[87] When he came to choose his burial-site a number of considerations militated against the royal mausoleum at Westminster. His decision to seek a resting-place at Canterbury close to the shrine of Thomas Becket, a national rather than a royal site, is perhaps his final testimony to his conception of his place in English history.

IV

In the late nineteenth century Bishop Stubbs made 1399 a central event in his constitutional history of England. It is easy to parody his views. He did not claim that Henry IV sought to rule with a parliamentary title as a constitu-

---

[85] E. Peters, 'Vox populi, vox Dei', in *Law in Medieval Life and Thought*, ed. E. B. King and S. J. Ridyard (Sewanee, 1990), pp. 91–120.

[86] Brown, 'Reign of Henry IV', p. 11.

[87] Perhaps he did not want to repeat the experience of 1399. According to Adam Usk, as a result of his anointing 'his head was so infected with lice that his hair fell out, and for several months he had to keep his head covered'. *Chronicle of Adam Usk*, pp. 242–3.

tional monarch. He did not see the revolution as the triumph of 'constitutionalism' over 'absolutism'. Stubbs expressly stated that the change of
regime was not 'the pure and legitimate result of a series of constitutional
workings'. In his account of the overthrow of Richard II he continually
acknowledged the role of chance, personal factors, and private interests. He
nonetheless believed that 'public causes' were at stake in 1399, that the
revolution was more than a partisan coup, and that the new regime saw the
'trial and failure of a great constitutional experiment'.[88] More modern
scholars have tended to be more cynical, not least because they have been
rightly sceptical of projecting back to 1399 later conceptions of parliamentary
monarchy. To deny that Henry and his allies sought constitutional outcomes
that even the leaders of the Glorious Revolution of 1688–9 refused to
countenance, however, is not to assert that the men of 1399 were wholly
devoid of political convictions, however crude and lacking in coherence, and
however inconsistently and imperfectly applied.

The magnates and churchmen of late medieval England were quite capable
of distinguishing between forms of government in which the king ruled
according to his will and in which the king ruled according to the law. This
distinction formed the analytical centrepiece of the *Song of Lewes*, written to
commemorate Simon de Montfort's victory in 1264.[89] It is true that the
political struggles of the fourteenth century, for all their bitterness, were
largely conducted and concluded in ways that discouraged ideological
elaboration. There was a focus on law and custom, and on teasing out the
implications of 'mixed monarchy', rather than a return to first principles.
What that does not mean is that the men who resisted Richard II could not
have acted from conviction. Ricardian politics were informed by an awareness of the issues and outcomes of earlier conflicts. In 1397–8 Richard turned
the tables on his opponents of 1387–8, and secured the repeal of the
proceedings of the parliament of 1388. He also worked to reverse parliamentary acts dating back to Edward II's time, annulling the sentences of 1321 and
1327 against Hugh Despenser and allegedly scheming to reinstate the verdict
of 1322 against Thomas of Lancaster.[90] Conversely, the revolution of 1399
reinstated the legislation of 1388, and one chronicler noted how comparisons
were drawn between Richard and Edward II. Behind this settling of scores,
there was a real conflict of ideas. Richard allegedly claimed that he was the
source of law, not subject to it, and assiduously and imaginatively cultivated
the material and ideological props to his high conception of kingship. He
certainly believed that the English political tradition was blighted by

[88] Stubbs, *Constitutional History*, III, 5–6.
[89] *The Song of Lewes*, ed. C. L. Kingsford (Oxford, 1890), pp. 42–54; M. Prestwich, *English Politics in the Thirteenth Century* (London, 1990), pp. 12–13.
[90] *Rot. Parl.*, III, 360–8; Given-Wilson, 'Richard II, Edward II and the Lancastrian Inheri-
tance', p. 560; Bennett, *Richard II*, p. 119.

disobedience, readily called to mind the humiliations to which he and his forebears had been subject, and expressed a fierce resolve to root out opposition and restore due obedience. Richard's opponents held that kings were subject to the law, that their will could be constrained, and that there were statutes. Archbishop Arundel is on record as having said as much to Richard's face in 1386 and 1399.

If Stubbs, like his Whig forebears, saw the history of the constitution too much in terms of the history of parliament, he was not wrong in seeing the revolution of 1399 as an important landmark. More capacious understandings of 'constitutional history' increase rather than diminish its significance. The high level of popular mobilization and the generally public nature of the proceedings made the experience deeply educative. It reflected in some wise the growth in size, complexity and ambition of the political nation, broadened conceptions of the 'public good', and contributed materially to the entrenchment of 'a system of government in which crown and subjects shared responsibility' in England.[91] Above all, key elements of a 'constitutional' tradition were affirmed by a newly enlarged ruling class. Richard's deposition represented an early and significant reverse to the trend that over the next three centuries would largely destroy 'mixed monarchy' on the European mainland. In the 1460s Sir John Fortescue had Richard pre-eminently in mind when he wrote that certain kings of England were drawn to the Roman law, especially the maxim 'that what pleases the prince has the force of law', which seemed to give them the authority to 'change laws at their pleasure, make new ones, inflict punishments, and impose burdens on their subjects, and also determine suits of parties at their own will and when they wish'.[92] Fortescue's conviction that the kings of England were obliged to rule 'politically' as well as 'regally' was well founded. Richard would have had it otherwise.

The issue remains whether Henry IV saw himself as a king of a more political sort. At times Stubbs appears agnostic on this point, acknowledging the elusiveness of Henry's personality. He recognizes that Henry had 'a great injury to avenge', but nonetheless states that Henry was 'consistent in political faith', and that he could not, without discarding all the principles that he had ever professed, 'even attempt to rule as Richard II and Edward III had ruled'.[93] It must be confessed that there is no compelling evidence for Stubbs's view of Henry. All that it is possible to do is to make a connection between Henry's participation in the crisis of 1387–8, his role in the overthrow of Richard II and certain features of his kingship. Still, it is possible to

[91] The phrases are from G. L. Harriss, 'Political Society and Growth of Government in Late Medieval England', *Past and Present* 138 (1993), 28–57 (pp. 34, 57).
[92] Sir John Fortescue, *De laudibus legum Anglie*, ed. S. B. Chrimes (Cambridge, 1949), pp. 78–81.
[93] Stubbs, *Constitutional History*, III, 6, 8.

learn something about the man from the company he kept and the expectations they had of him. His colleagues and well-wishers included statesmen
like Archbishop Arundel and the earl of Northumberland, and moralists like
Philip Repton and John Gower. Supporters of the Lancastrian revolution
included wise heads like Richard, Lord Scrope of Bolton and John, Lord
Cobham.[94] A veteran of the councils of the late 1380s, imprisoned for life by
the vindictive Richard II in 1397, Lord Cobham addressed the parliament in
1399. In his speech he identified a key problem in 'mixed monarchy': the king
who fails to take counsel and cannot inspire trust. After talking at length
about the evils of Richard's reign he noted how under his rule the English
had sunk to a condition worse than the heathens, who at least were truthful,
because through fear of loss of possessions, exile or even death they had not
dared to speak or act according to the truth.[95] Henry set himself to rule in a
manner very different from Richard. His successes and failings need to be
measured in relation to the expectations he had raised, and indeed the high
standards that he seems to have set himself.

[94] C. Given-Wilson, 'Richard II and the Higher Nobility', in *Richard II: The Art of Kingship*, ed.
A. Goodman and J. L. Gillespie (Oxford, 1999), pp. 107–29 (pp. 112–14).
[95] *Chrons. Rev.*, pp. 204–5.

3

How Do You Bury a Deposed King?
The Funeral of Richard II
and the Establishment of Lancastrian
Royal Authority in 1400

Joel Burden

INTRODUCTION

The deposition of Richard II in 1399 has generated much historical interest, but seldom has this extended on to the symbolic plane through analysis of either the coronation of Henry IV or the funeral of Richard II. Some historians have discussed the introduction of a special consecration oil at the coronation of Henry IV, although the story in fact failed to fire the imagination of Lancastrian chroniclers, only two of whom made mention of it in their accounts of Henry's usurpation.[1] By contrast, descriptions of Richard II's funerary celebrations in London and King's Langley were integral to most contemporary narrative accounts of the king's deposition, perhaps in part because they represented an obvious end point for moralistically tinged versions of Richard II's fall.[2]

The underlying contention of this discussion is that the royal rituals of Henry IV's accession were not simply 'due processes' determined by an unthinking tradition, but rather they were events that manifested a variety of aspects and features that both responded to, and also addressed, the peculiarities of the political contexts in which they occurred. Ritual is interpreted here as a dynamic way of behaving within a given situation, despite its tendency to provoke an opposite impression among its participants and spectators that it is resistant to change and detached from the

---

[1] W. Ullmann, 'Thomas Becket's Miraculous Oil', *Journal of Theological Studies* 8 (1957), 129–33; T. A. Sandquist, 'The Holy Oil of St Thomas of Canterbury', in *Essays in Medieval History Presented to Bertie Wilkinson*, ed. T. A. Sandquist and M. R. Powicke (Toronto, 1969), pp. 330–44; C. Wilson, 'The Tomb of Henry IV and the Holy Oil of St Thomas of Canterbury', in *Medieval Architecture and its Intellectual Context: Studies in Honour of Peter Kidson*, ed. P. Crossley and E. Fernie (London, 1990), pp. 181–90. See 'Annales', pp. 297–300 (*Chrons. Rev.*, pp. 201–2); *Eulogium Historiarum*, III, 379–80, 384.

[2] *Historia Vitae et Regni Ricardi Secundi*, ed. G. B. Stow (Philadelphia, 1977), pp. 166–7 (*Chrons. Rev.*, pp. 241–2); *Chronicle of Adam Usk*, pp. 88–91.

currents of contemporary political life. Of course, as a mechanism for legitimating royal authority, the power of a royal ritual occasion such as a coronation was located in its representation of normative appearances, rather than its safeguarding of normative principles or practices. In this sense, it can be observed that while rituals are indisputably tied up with notions of tradition, such traditions are themselves not static but continually reinvented or reproduced.[3]

Precisely because royal rituals were dynamic public occasions they demand analysis as part of the fabric of medieval politics. However, they need to be studied 'in action' rather than 'in the abstract' if they are to be understood in relation to their particular performative contexts.[4] In practical terms this means placing an increased emphasis on the study of narrative and administrative source evidence alongside the prescriptive ritual texts that have traditionally tended to shape our modern understanding of medieval royal ritual. It also means that historians need to pay much greater attention to the actual mechanics of how meaning in performance was communicated to participants and spectators. In order to do this it is necessary to recognize that ritual does not weave its magic primarily through the written word, but rather through the impact of images, actions, sounds, gestures and spoken words on the full range of the human senses. This throws up a range of analytical challenges, which it is beyond the scope of this article to discuss in detail, but some attention will be given to developing a more contextualized analysis of the funeral of Richard II, paying close attention to the striking visual dimensions of that ritual occasion.[5]

In common with other usurpers, Henry IV needed at the outset of his reign to address the problem of establishing a credible and independent royal identity of his own. However, although the king was successful militarily in maintaining his position on the throne, it was perhaps not until the reign of Henry V that the Lancastrian dynasty finally managed to attract broad-based loyalty within England on its own terms. Ultimately, Henry IV failed in this regard because he was unable to frame his exercise of kingship in a wholly positive vein. Crucially, Henry did not succeed in an attempt to persuade the parliamentary Lords in September 1399 to recognize his right to rule on the basis of a superior hereditary claim to the throne.[6]

Interestingly, although Henry's unsuccessful hereditary claim was highly dubious as a legal basis for taking the throne, his preparedness to advance such a flimsy argument was perhaps an indication of his sharp political

[3] J. F. Burden, 'Rituals of Royalty: Prescription, Politics and Practice in English Coronation and Royal Funeral Rituals c.1327 to c.1485' (unpublished D. Phil. thesis, University of York, 1999), pp. 12–18.
[4] Burden, 'Rituals of Royalty', pp. 21–3.
[5] Burden, 'Rituals of Royalty', pp. 72–113.
[6] G. T. Lapsley, 'The Parliamentary Title of Henry IV', *EHR* 49 (1934), 423–49, 577–606; *Chrons. Rev.*, pp. 41–4.

instincts rather than his political naivety. Henry must have foreseen that the unorthodox circumstances of his accession and the final accepted basis of his claim to the throne (reflected in the parliamentary record of the deposition) locked the new king into an uncomfortable and oppositional relationship with his deposed predecessor.[7] In essence, Henry's exercise of kingship rested primarily and somewhat negatively on a widespread perception of Richard II's gross failings as a king, rather than more positively on any notion of Henry's own better claim. As the saviour of England from the clutches of a 'royal tyrant and oppressor', Henry IV's cross to bear was that the measure of his success would always be the yardstick of Richard's remembered failure.

Unsurprisingly, public events aimed at cementing the authority of Henry IV at the outset of his reign were shaped and orchestrated in relation to the spectral presence of Richard II. As will be discussed, this was particularly clear-cut in the Lancastrian-sponsored funeral of Richard in 1400. Although the funeral was ostensibly a public act of closure on the royal life (if not the reign) of Richard II, it was nevertheless framed in conformity with a Lancastrian agenda that recognized the continued potency of a Ricardian threat to the new regime. Henry IV's own coronation on 13 October 1399 likewise offers the impression that its more dynamic features were con-ceived as a direct response to issues of particular importance at the end of the reign of Richard II. Henry broke with tradition in choosing to be crowned on a Monday rather than a Sunday, a change that allowed his coronation to coincide with the feast of the Translation of St Edward the Confessor. Of course, the Confessor was the royal saint most intimately connected with the coronation service owing to a general (though erro-neous) belief that the coronation regalia had belonged to the Anglo-Saxon king.[8] However, if coronation on the feast day of the Confessor attached some much-needed aura to Henry IV's sudden elevation, it also carried with it a beautiful and pointed irony that would not have been lost on contemporary observers. It was St Edward the Confessor, after all, who had emerged above all other saints as Richard II's personal patron and protector during the 1390s.[9]

The usage of a new consecration oil associated with St Thomas Becket was certainly the most striking innovation in the coronation of Henry IV. This alteration in traditional consecration procedures followed within coronation rituals was symbolically very significant and provides an excellent example of the way in which change could simultaneously be engineered as both a defensive reaction and a proactive response to the

---

[7] *Rot. Parl.*, III, 422–3 (*Chrons. Rev.*, p. 186). See P. Strohm, *Hochon's Arrow: The Social Imagination of Fourteenth-Century Texts* (Princeton, 1992), pp. 75–82.

[8] D. A. Carpenter, *The Reign of Henry III* (London, 1996), pp. 427–61.

[9] N. Saul, *Richard II* (London, 1997), pp. 311–15.

current political climate. The new holy oil of St Thomas first made an appearance in royal circles during the reign of Edward II, but it was the rediscovery of the oil by Richard II and his subsequent failure to secure re-anointment with the oil in the late 1390s that lent a particular piquancy to Henry IV's own anointing with the oil in 1399.[10] At the crudest level, Henry's invention of a new tradition of royal anointing was no more than a wonderful piece of medieval one-upmanship that allowed him to claim access to a 'super-anointed' status that his deposed predecessor had been denied. More interesting, though, is the notion that Henry may in fact have acted or been reacting in direct response to a heightening of debate on issues of sacrality and anointing that was prompted by Richard's dissenting to the full implications of his enforced abdication. Certainly, two of the best sources for the abdication in the Tower on 28–29 September 1399 seem to suggest that while Richard was perhaps receptive to the idea that he might abdicate the actual exercise of his kingship, he prevaricated over the terms of this resignation with specific regard to the abdication of his anointed royal status.[11]

If Henry's introduction of a new coronation oil looked backwards towards debate at the close of the previous reign, it also set out an entirely new Lancastrian stall in terms of establishing a holy royal relationship with the Canterbury cult of St Thomas Becket. Henry's identification with this new royal saint was not restricted to his consecration with St Thomas's oil, although this event was sufficiently seminal for it to be referenced many years later in the iconographical imagery painted on the king's tomb tester.[12] Interestingly, Henry developed the new royal relationship with St Thomas through the establishment of a new royal dynastic mausoleum at Canterbury Cathedral where he was duly buried in 1413.[13] In this respect at least, Henry's approach to change was constructive, forward-looking and remarkably in touch with the mood of continental Europe, where a number of other new royal dynastic mausolea were being established around this time. In a sense, it was Henry's misfortune to be succeeded by a conspicuously traditionalist king who scuppered his father's more imaginative ideas on dynastic memor-ialization by reverting quickly and publicly to a pre-eminent reverence towards the old royal cult of St Edward the Confessor. This was reflected

---

[10] *English Coronation Records*, ed. L. G. Wickham Legg (London, 1901), pp. 69–76, reproduces a letter from Pope John XXII to Edward II on re-anointment with the oil (not then associated with Becket).

[11] 'Annales', p. 287 (*Chrons. Rev.*, pp. 188–9); 'The Manner of King Richard's Renunciation', in *Chrons. Rev.*, pp. 162–4.

[12] Wilson, 'The Tomb of Henry', pp. 181–90.

[13] C. Wilson, 'The Medieval Monuments', in *A History of Canterbury Cathedral*, ed. P. Collinson, N. Ramsey and M. Sparks (Oxford, 1995), pp. 451–510 (pp. 498–506). Henry IV's half-brother, John Beaufort, earl of Somerset (d. 1410) and his second son, Thomas, duke of Clarence (d. 1421), were also buried at Canterbury.

most particularly in Henry V's reburial of Richard II at Westminster Abbey at the very outset of his reign and his own magnificent burial within the abbey at its end.[14]

EVENTS

The events of Richard's II's death and burial can be reconstructed through analysis of contemporary administrative records and narrative accounts. The deposed king was removed from the Tower of London after several weeks of imprisonment in late October 1399. By Christmas he was in custody at Henry IV's castle of Pontefract in Yorkshire, a secure place that fitted the parliamentary Lords' recommendation that Richard be kept in a 'secret location' staffed with trusted Lancastrian servants.[15] In the records of a council meeting held on or around 8 February 1400, there survives an intriguing minute that can be read as a veiled recommendation to Henry IV that he should terminate his predecessor's life. The council recommended that Richard should be kept securely if he was still alive, but that if the deposed king no longer lived, then his body might be shown openly to the people so that they would know that he was dead.[16] Official records provide no firm clues regarding the manner of Richard II's death, but surviving Exchequer accounts pertaining to arrangements for the carriage of Richard's corpse from Pontefract to London indicate that the king was known or expected to be dead by 17 February 1400.[17]

The main narrative sources for the deposition events provide wildly different versions of Richard II's demise. Most sources cite starvation as the cause of Richard's death, although opinions were clearly divided on the issue of whether starvation was enforced or voluntary.[18] In reality, it seems probable that the circumstances of his death were sufficiently obscured from view to leave contemporary commentators guessing at the truth. The author of the *Vita Ricardi Secundi* encapsulates this sense of a rumoured environment by recording both versions of the starvation story.[19] Meanwhile, Froissart's account offers the revealing statement that while the writer knew for certain

---

[14] P. Strohm, *England's Empty Throne: Usurpation and the Language of Legitimation, 1399–1422* (London, 1998), pp. 87–111; W. H. St John Hope, 'The Funeral, Monument and Chantry Chapel of King Henry the Fifth', *Archaeologia* 65 (1913–14), 145–86; C. Allmand, *Henry V* (London, 1992), pp. 180–2.

[15] 'Annales', p. 313; *Rot. Parl.*, III, 426; Saul, *Richard II*, p. 424.

[16] *POPC*, I, 111–12. Strohm, *England's Empty Throne*, p. 104, has a more accurate transcription from BL MS Cotton Cleopatra F III, fol. 9b (now 14b).

[17] *Issues of the Exchequer: King Henry III to King Henry VI*, ed. F. Devon (London, 1837), pp. 275–6.

[18] Saul, *Richard II*, pp. 425–6; *Chrons. Rev.*, p. 51.

[19] *Historia Vitae*, ed. Stow, p. 166 (*Chrons. Rev.*, p. 241).

that Richard was dead, he could shed no light on the actual circumstances of his death.[20]

Richard II's death was probably prompted by a heightening of political instability in the aftermath of the Epiphany Rising of January 1400.[21] The political profile of the leading conspirators in the rising was staunchly pro-Ricardian, despite their ostensible support for a pseudo-Richard II in the person of the deposed king's confessor, Richard Maudeleyn. The extent to which the conspirators formed a Ricardian inner circle is reflected in the fact that they included in their number several executors of the king's will of 1399, a couple of other leading luminaries of Richard's post-1397 court, and a number of pro-Ricardian clerics such as the abbot of Westminster and the newly deprived archbishop of Canterbury.[22]

The political instability that formed the backdrop to the death of Richard II created a pressure for a public and high-profile funeral for the deposed king. In keeping with the recommendations of the council, the Lancastrian government therefore eschewed the option of burying Richard quietly in the north. Instead, very public funeral exequies were staged for the deposed king in London prior to the final interment of Richard's remains at the Dominican friary of King's Langley in Hertfordshire. The main narrative sources for Richard II's funeral in March 1400 manifest clear differences in their detailing and emphases. Nonetheless, these sources do offer a broadly homogeneous impression of the ritual arrangements organized for the exequies and burial of the king. The examination of narrative sources in conjunction with some surviving financial accounts in the Exchequer records enables a cautious reconstruction and assessment to be undertaken of the form and character of Richard II's funeral. Exchequer records reveal that Richard II's corpse was moved to London in the immediate aftermath of the king's death at Pontefract in mid-February 1400. Payments totalling £80 were paid in two instalments to the Keeper of the Wardrobe, Thomas Tuttebury, to cover expenses incurred in the carriage of Richard's body to London.[23] Clearly, the cortège had reached London by 6 March, since a requiem service was celebrated on that day in the presence of the royal corpse at St Paul's Cathedral.

[20] *Chronicles of England, France and Spain by Sir John Froissart*, ed. T. Johnes, 2 vols. (London, 1842), II, 708.
[21] Wylie, *Henry IV*, I, 91–111; D. Crook, 'Central England and the Revolt of the Earls, January 1400', *Historical Research* 64 (1991), 403–10.
[22] The executors were Thomas Merks, bishop of Carlisle; Edward of York, earl of Rutland; Thomas Holland, earl of Kent; John Holland, earl of Huntington; and Richard Maudeleyn. Other leading courtiers involved were John Montagu, earl of Salisbury and Edward, Lord Despenser. See *A Collection of Wills . . . of the Kings and Queens of England*, ed. J. Nichol (London, 1780), pp. 191–201, printed in translation in J. Harvey, *The Plantagenets* (New York, 1959), pp. 222–7.
[23] E 403/564; *Issues of the Exchequer*, ed. Devon, pp. 275, 277, dated 17 February and 6 April.

The interlude of over three weeks that separated the death and burial of Richard II would normally have demanded the evisceration and embalming of his corpse. Government records in fact provide no evidence that measures were taken for the preservation of Richard's corpse. However, a description of the appearance of the corpse in the *Annales Ricardi Secundi et Henrici Quarti* indicates that such measures must have been taken by the time the funeral cortège reached the abbey of St Albans. Walsingham recounts in the *Annales* that at every place where Richard's cortège stopped for the night on its journey to London the body of the king was exhibited '. . . or at least that part of his body by which he could be recognised was exhibited, namely from the base of his forehead down to his throat'.[24] This probable eye-witness description preserved in the *Annales* text is supported by further descriptions of the appearance of Richard's corpse contained in several continuations of the *Brut* chronicle.[25] The *Brut* continuations also provide additional information suggesting that the corpse was bound tight in waxed linen cloth.[26]

The various narrative descriptions of the appearance of Richard II's corpse at different stages of the funeral celebrations strongly suggest that a funeral effigy was not used. Indeed, no reference to the use or later existence of a funeral effigy of Richard II can be found in any of the chronicle sources or among the records of the royal government or Westminster Abbey. In essence, a royal funeral effigy was a life-sized representation of a dead king or queen that was manufactured specifically for purposes of display at royal funeral celebrations. They should not be confused with tomb effigies, although there were often notable iconographical and stylistic similarities between the two forms of representation. Unlike tomb effigies, funeral effigies were not constructed as permanent monuments to the deceased. Typically, they were manufactured within a few days of a king or queen's death, and as far as we can tell, their function ceased with the completion of the funeral celebrations. The absence of any mention of a funeral effigy in 1400 is certainly significant, since effigies had clearly been used in the funerals of both Edward II and Edward III, and also in the funeral of Richard's first queen, Anne of Bohemia.[27]

Descriptions of Richard II's funeral preserved in the narrative accounts of contemporary writers tend to concentrate attention on the events that took place in London. Furthermore, virtually all of these sources represent the

---

[24] 'Annales', p. 331 (*Chrons. Rev.*, p. 229).

[25] *The Brut, or the Chronicles of England*, ed. F. W. D. Brie, 2 vols., EETS OS 131 and 136 (1906–8), II, 360, 546; *The Great Chronicle of London*, ed. A. H. Thomas and I. D. Thornley (London, 1938), p. 83.

[26] *Brut*, ed. Brie, II, 360.

[27] W. H. St John Hope, 'On the Funeral Effigies of the Kings and Queens of England', *Archaeologia* 60 (1907), 530–3, 544; P. Lindley, 'Edward III', and 'Anne of Bohemia', in *The Funeral Effigies of Westminster Abbey*, ed. A. Harvey and R. Mortimer (Woodbridge, 1994), pp. 31–9.

celebration of exequies for Richard at St Paul's Cathedral as the central focus of the London celebrations. According to the *Annales* account, there were two days of services at the cathedral. Henry IV attended on both days, while prominent members of the nobility and the citizenry of London attended only on the second day.[28] The slightly fuller account given in Walsingham's *Historia Anglicana* reiterates the point that Richard's body was publicly displayed at the religious services; firstly after the office of the dead, then on the following day after the mass, and finally at the exequies attended by Henry IV and the London citizens.[29] Chronicles in the *Brut* tradition support the view that there were two days of funerary celebrations in London, but on the second day these celebrations are reported to have taken place at Westminster Abbey rather than St Paul's.[30] Among the pro-Ricardian French chronicles, both Creton's account and the *Traïson et mort* place all the liturgical action at St Paul's, while the latter adds that Richard's corpse remained at the cathedral for two days in order '. . . to shew him to the people of London, that they might believe for certain that he was dead'.[31] Adam of Usk records that Richard's face remained uncovered during the religious rites celebrated at St Paul's, while the perhaps more fanciful account given by Froissart suggests that Richard's corpse was displayed at Cheapside on a canopied litter with the king's face uncovered.[32] Here, Froissart asserts, the royal corpse was viewed by upwards of 20,000 people in a period of just two hours.

The French chronicles are the only sources for the funeral of Richard II that describe the composition and visual character of the king's cortège. The fullest information is contained in the *Traïson* text, which says that Richard was brought to St Paul's 'in the state of a gentleman'.[33] Nonetheless, the writer proceeds to describe the appearance of the cortège in terms not altogether inappropriate for a king. Accordingly, the funeral hearse is described as having been entirely covered in black cloth and incorporating four banners, two with the arms of St George and two with the arms of St Edward the Confessor. The *Traïson* text adds that one hundred mourners clad in black and carrying torches accompanied the hearse in London. These mourners were met by a further thirty mourners who were Londoners, all of whom were dressed in white robes and also carried torches.[34]

Jean Creton, though he did not believe that Richard II was really dead, recorded that a surrogate corpse was nevertheless carried through London

---

[28] 'Annales', p. 331 (*Chrons. Rev.*, p. 229).
[29] *Historia Anglicana*, II, 246.
[30] *Brut*, ed. Brie, II, 360, 546; *Great Chronicle*, ed. Thomas and Thornley, p. 83.
[31] 'Metrical History', p. 220 (*Chrons. Rev.*, p. 244); *Chronicque de la traïson et mort de Richart Deux Roy Dengleterre*, ed. B. Williams (London, 1846), p. 261.
[32] *Chronicle of Adam Usk*, pp. 94–5; *Chronicles*, ed. Johnes, II, 708–9.
[33] *Traïson*, p. 261.
[34] *Traïson*, p. 261.

'. . . accompanied by the sort of pomp and ceremony that befits a dead king'.[35] Creton adds that 'Duke Henry' and his kinsmen were prominent among the mourners, with the Lancastrian king even carrying the funeral pall behind the hearse.[36] Exchequer records contain references to payments, which perhaps provide some further oblique confirmation of Henry IV's interest and involvement in the funerary events in London. A payment of 25 marks is recorded to Henry IV's almoner for distribution among 'certain religious persons' for singing a thousand masses for Richard's soul. Meanwhile, a second payment of a pound is recorded to Henry's confessor to cover the costs of disbursements to paupers and cripples at the exequies in St Paul's.[37]

Most of the sources mentioning Richard II's burial simply record that the king was interred in the house of the Dominican Friars at King's Langley. John Gower describes the interment as solemn, but 'without the honour of praise', adding somewhat acidly (and implausibly) that the corpse was buried at Langley for want of anywhere else willing to receive it.[38] Two chronicles written by Thomas Walsingham, the monastic historian at St Albans, provide the only real details relating to Richard's interment. In this instance, Walsingham's notorious anti-Ricardian attitude must be set against his excellent access to information, since it was the abbot of St Albans who presided over the burial rituals.[39] According to the *Annales* account, Richard's body was brought to King's Langley in the 'dead of night' straightaway after the completion of the exequies for the deposed king in London. On the following day, the abbot of St Albans conducted the last funeral rites over the king with the assistance of the bishop of Chester [*sic*] and the abbot of Waltham '. . . and thus without ceremony and almost unattended, was this royal corpse committed to the grave'.[40] The description of the burial contained in the *Historia Anglicana* amplifies the foregoing impression that the interment was an unceremonious affair by adding that Richard was buried without the presence of nobles or any other crowd of people. Indeed, after the completion of the service the officiating clerics did not even tarry at King's Langley for the usual celebratory meal.[41]

---

[35] Creton, p. 220 (*Chrons. Rev.*, p. 244).

[36] Creton, p. 220 (*Chrons. Rev.*, p. 244).

[37] *Issues of the Exchequer*, ed Devon, p. 276; E 403/564, 20 March 1400.

[38] John Gower, 'Cronica Tripertita', III, ll. 453–4, in *The Complete Works of John Gower*, ed. G. C. Macauley, 4 vols. (Oxford, 1899–1902), IV, 341.

[39] See G. B. Stow, 'Richard II in Thomas Walsingham's Chronicles', *Speculum* 59 (1984), 68–102; A. Gransden, *Historical Writing in England II: c. 1307 to the Early Sixteenth Century* (London, 1982), pp. 136–44.

[40] 'Annales', p. 331 (*Chrons. Rev.*, p. 229).

[41] *Historia Anglicana*, II, 246.

ANALYSIS

Richard II's burial at King's Langley contravened the king's stated lifetime intention to be buried in the shrine chapel of St Edward the Confessor in Westminster Abbey. Arrangements for the construction of a lavish double tomb for Richard and his first queen, Anne of Bohemia, were set in motion a few months after Anne's death in 1394.[42] At the deposition of the king, work was virtually finished on the marble tomb-chest with its gilt-copper fittings and its magnificent cast metal effigies of Richard and Anne. Two indentured contracts drawn up with the head masons and coppersmiths commissioned to oversee work on the tomb are preserved among the royal records of the reign.[43] These reveal the keen personal interest Richard exercised as a royal patron in the aesthetic detailing of the tomb. Indeed, it is striking that the terms of Richard II's will of April 1399 indicate that he maintained his commitment to be buried beside Anne of Bohemia, despite contracting a second marriage to Isabelle of France in 1396:

> . . . we [Richard] have chosen a royal burial in the church of St Peter at Westminster among our ancestors kings of England of famous memory; and in the monument which we have caused to be erected as a memorial for us and for Anne of glorious remembrance once queen of England our consort.[44]

During the second half of his reign, Richard II's patronage towards the monastic community at Westminster extended far beyond the king's expressed intention to be buried within the abbey church. Indeed, Richard's identification with the abbey amounted to a public commitment to the Benedictine house as a focal point of his kingship.[45] The king's lavish bequests were made in recognition of Westminster's privileged role as a coronation church, as well as its developing importance as a royal dynastic mausoleum.[46] The more conventional aspects of Richard's interest in West-minster Abbey as a royal space also merged with other interests in the monastic house that were more peculiar to the king. In particular, it is noteworthy that Richard exercised an unusually strong personal devotion

[42] P. Binski, *Westminster Abbey and the Plantagenets: Kingship and the Representation of Power, 1200–1400* (London, 1995), pp. 200–2; R. A. Brown, H. M. Colvin and A. J. Taylor, *A History of the King's Works: The Middle Ages*, 2 vols. (London, 1963), I, 487–8.

[43] *Foedera*, 10 vols. (The Hague, 1739–45), III(iv), 105–6.

[44] *Collection of Wills*, ed. Nichols, p. 192 (Harvey, *Plantagenets*, p. 222).

[45] See N. Saul, 'Richard II and Westminster Abbey', in *The Cloister and the World: Essays in Medieval History in Honour of Barbara Harvey*, ed. W. J. Blair and B. Golding (Oxford, 1996), pp. 196–218.

[46] Saul, 'Richard II and Westminster Abbey', p. 205, referencing Westminster Abbey Muniments 9473; *Westminster Chron.*, pp. 372–3, 414–17; *Chronicle of Adam Usk*, pp. 90–1.

towards the Westminster cult of his Anglo-Saxon predecessor, St Edward the Confessor.[47]

It would seem that the Lancastrian decision to bury Richard II at the Dominican friary at King's Langley represented a major departure from the publicly stated intentions of the dead king. Clearly, the Dominican house was not as obscure a royal burial site as was sometimes suggested by later Yorkist commentators.[48] In fact, Richard had himself arranged the reinterment of his elder brother Edward's remains at the friary in 1388–9, and he remained a frequent visitor at the adjacent royal palace throughout his lifetime.[49] Nevertheless, Richard's burial at King's Langley lacked the clear-cut royal connotations that would have attached to burial at Westminster Abbey. Additionally, as well as contravening Richard's express lifetime wishes, the King's Langley burial established a somewhat ridiculous situation in which the monks of Westminster were required to celebrate obits for the dead king at his completed but empty tomb.[50]

The reluctance of Henry IV to allow Richard II to be buried at Westminster Abbey undoubtedly responded to a perceived danger that Richard's corpse could become a dangerous focus of memory within an environment that was redolent with Ricardian associations. More particularly, this reluctance would have been prompted by the awkward aesthetic connotations that stemmed from the unprecedented extent to which Richard had succeeded in stamping his symbolic 'presence' within the abbey. During his reign, Richard II had exercised a literal presence in Westminster Abbey through his frequent use of the abbey church as a venue for worship.[51] Indeed, in the 1390s, the monastery was increasingly drawn into the orbit of Richard II's Westminster-based court – a situation exemplified in the controversial burial of loyal members of the royal household in previously exclusive royal and monastic

---

[47] See Saul, *Richard II*, pp. 311–15.

[48] *Hardyng*, p. 357.

[49] E 403/564. See *Issues of the Exchequer*, ed. Devon, p. 248, dated 15 May 1392, for a payment relating to the tomb. However, R. G. Davies, 'Richard II and the Church', in *Richard II: The Art of Kingship*, ed. A. Goodman and J. L. Gillespie (Oxford, 1999), pp. 83–106 (p. 88), suggests that the priory had a very difficult time during Richard's reign because until April 1399 the king perverted the terms by which his grandfather's will had settled estates on the house. On other contemporary royal tombs at King's Langley, see J. Evans, 'Edmund of Langley and his Tomb', *Archaeologia* 46 (1881), 297–328; H. C. Baker, 'The Royal Tomb at King's Langley', *Transactions of the Monumental Brass Society* 11 (1969–74), 279–84. See Saul, *Richard II*, pp. 469–74, for Richard's itinerary.

[50] Richard's will ordained the transfer of property to the value of £1,000 to the abbey for the maintenance of fifteen lepers and a chaplain to pray for his soul. See *Collection of Wills*, ed. Nichols, p. 194. Interestingly, acceptance of this testamentary bequest was the sole condition that Richard extracted from Bolingbroke at the time of his deposition in the Tower. See *Historia Vitae*, ed. Stow, p. 159; 'Manner of King Richard's Renunciation', in *Chrons. Rev.*, p. 164; Westminster Abbey Muniments 5257A, 5258 and 23986B.

[51] Saul, 'Richard II and Westminster Abbey', pp. 204–5.

spaces at the eastern end of the abbey church.[52] Significantly, however, this literal royal presence was amplified by Richard's proxy presence within the abbey by virtue of a proliferation of Ricardian imagery throughout the body of the monastic church. Many of the numerous objects, vestments and other embroidered materials given to the abbey by Richard II incorporated royal heraldry into their design.[53] Representations of Richard's personal badge of the white hart were the subject of wall-paintings in at least two different parts of the church interior. Meanwhile, the actual likeness of Richard II was displayed within the abbey not only in the guise of the king's gilt-copper tomb effigy, but also in the form of the surviving monumental panel painting of Richard, which possibly hung above the royal seat on the south side of the sanctuary.[54]

The likenesses of Richard II displayed at Westminster Abbey constituted an aesthetic challenge to the political rhetoric of Henry IV. Both the tomb effigy and the panel painting manifested the recognizable physical features of Richard II within a formal framework of imagery expressive of the institutional character of kingship. Although the images incorporated elements of 'likeness', they were not personal images so much as images of office that made prominent use of institutional iconography. An accentuated image of regality was suggested by the monumental scale of the likenesses, the representation of Richard in unnaturally frontal postures, and the prominent depiction of items of regalia on and around the king's image. Meanwhile, the use of gilt-copper in Richard's tomb effigy and the physical positioning of his tomb within St Edward's Chapel both served to emphasize themes of continuity in the representation of English kingship, and thereby locate the articulation of Richard II's retrospective identity within an established and recognized royal dynastic tradition.[55]

The regal connotations of the Ricardian imagery within Westminster Abbey were problematic for a new Lancastrian dynasty that desired to cast aspersions on the validity of Richard II's kingship. The Lancastrian regime had already proved itself sufficiently robust to deal with armed insurrection by supporters of Richard II. However, Henry IV felt no inclination to allow the moral authority of his regime to be sapped over time through the unfortunate juxtaposing of Richard II's corpse with a variety of semi-permanent and idealized representations of Richard as king. Though the Westminster panel painting could be removed from display with relative ease, the removal or alteration of Richard's tomb effigy image was consider-

[52] Saul, 'Richard II and Westminster Abbey', pp. 210–12.
[53] Saul, 'Richard II and Westminster Abbey', pp. 201–2.
[54] Binski, *Westminster Abbey*, p. 203, dates the portrait to the 1390s. See also J. J. G. Alexander, 'The Portrait of Richard II in Westminster Abbey', in *The Regal Image of Richard II and the Wilton Diptych*, ed. D. Gordon, L. Monas and C. Elam (London, 1997), pp. 197–206.
[55] Binski, *Westminster Abbey*, pp. 195–204.

ably more difficult to engineer; not least because this would have had implications for the memorialization of Anne of Bohemia.[56]

An added risk attached to burying Richard in his Westminster tomb was the danger that the tomb might become a magnet for the development of a cult of political opposition to the Lancastrian government. This had happened recently at the house of the Austin canons in London following the burial there of the executed Richard Fitzalan, earl of Arundel, in 1397. It would happen again later in Henry's own reign at the tomb of the executed Richard Scrope, archbishop of York, in York Minster.[57] The mid-fourteenth-century popular cult of Edward II at Gloucester indicated that even the most unprepossessing of kings might serve as a focus for devotion. Furthermore, the involvement of Abbot Colchester of Westminster Abbey in the conspiratorial discussions that served as a prelude to the Epiphany Rising underlined to Henry that the abbey could not be relied upon to police any popular veneration that occurred or was orchestrated at Richard's tomb.[58] In these circumstances, Henry IV chose to preserve the integrity of Richard's intended tomb at Westminster Abbey, but to divert any popular interest in the king's posthumous memory towards the politically neutral, less publicly accessible and aesthetically unprovocative environment of the Dominican friary at King's Langley.

It has already been noted that Richard II attempted to shape the character of his own memorialization through his lifetime commission of a double tomb for himself and his first queen. Interestingly, in the king's last will of April 1399, Richard II also laid down detailed specifications prescribing the nature of his funeral. An enormous sum of six thousand marks of gold was set aside by the terms of the will to cover the costs involved in carrying the king's corpse to Westminster, together with the more general costs of the funeral itself. According to the testamentary prescriptions, the king was to have a total of four funerary hearses, two of them located in the two principal churches on the route taken by his cortège, one at St Paul's Cathedral in London, and the last at the king's intended final resting place of Westminster Abbey. The first three hearses were each to contain five lights, while the final hearse at Westminster was to be '. . . greater, more principal and honourable . . . copiously supplied with splendid lights and befitting the royal eminence,

---

[56] Henry IV was willing in principle to move tombs within Westminster Abbey since the remains of Thomas, duke of Gloucester (d. 1397) were moved to the shrine chapel of St Edward shortly after the king's accession. See *Chronicle of Adam Usk*, pp. 84–5.

[57] On Arundel, see J. M. Theilmann, 'Political Canonization and Political Symbolism in Medieval England', *Journal of British Studies* 29 (1990), 261–3; S. K. Walker, 'Political Saints in Later Medieval England', in *The McFarlane Legacy: Studies in Late Medieval Politics and Society*, ed. R. H. Britnell and A. J. Pollard (Stroud, 1995), pp. 77–106 (p. 81). On Scrope, see Walker 'Political Saints', pp. 84–5; J. W. McKenna, 'Popular Canonization as Political Propaganda: The Cult of Archbishop Scrope', *Speculum* 45 (1970), 608–23.

[58] Crook, 'Revolt of the Earls', p. 402.

and magnificently adorned'.[59] Richard's will specifies that the cortège was to move a distance of between fourteen and sixteen miles per day, accompanied by torch-bearers carrying twenty-four torches kept continually burning. On reaching each place of nightly rest, the office of the dead was to be sung in the evening and a mass celebrated in the morning; in each case with 'twenty-four torches always and continually burning about the body'.[60] At London, an extra one hundred burning torches were to be added to the procession as it made its way through the city to St Paul's. The testamentary injunction prescribing the appearance of Richard's corpse in readiness for burial is worth quoting in full:

> Also we will and ordain that our body shall be clothed and also interred in white velvet or satin in a royal manner, with royal crown and sceptre gilded but without any stones, and that upon our finger in kingly wise a ring shall be placed with a precious stone of the value of twenty marks of our money of England.[61]

Clearly, the actual performed character of Richard II's funeral as recorded in contemporary narrative accounts differed significantly from the type of funeral envisaged in Richard's own recent will. Overall, the impression is that Henry IV accorded Richard a semi-royal funeral, which partially responded to the deposed king's testamentary prescriptions, but which also pointedly failed to do so in certain key respects. Richard's corpse was taken to London for the public performance of exequies, but it was not interred in Richard's completed tomb in Westminster Abbey. There is no indication that the corpse was displayed within a series of four royal hearses, but at least one source reports that Richard's body was attended by more than a hundred torchbearers in London, and several of the sources remark upon the honourable attendance at the exequies celebrated at St Paul's. Finally, while there is much evidence to suggest that the public display of Richard's corpse was a key element of the funeral celebrations, there is also strong evidence to suggest that it was not adorned with regalia in accordance with the aesthetic prescriptions outlined in Richard's will.

Richard II's concern to dictate the character of his own funeral might appear to serve as further evidence of the king's somewhat megalomaniac tendencies. In reality, however, this type of testamentary concern was not unprecedented within English royal circles in the later fourteenth century. Edward III's will of 1376 expressed a more limited interest in his funeral,

---

[59] *Collection of Wills*, ed. Nichols, pp. 192–3 (Harvey, *Plantagenets*, p. 224).

[60] *Collection of Wills*, ed. Nichols, pp. 192–3 (Harvey, *Plantagenets*, p. 224).

[61] *Collection of Wills*, ed. Nichols, p. 194: 'Item volumus et ordinamus quod corpus nostrum in velveto vel sathino blanco, more regio, vestiator, et eciam interretur, una cum corona et sceptro regiis deauratis absque tamen quibuscunque lapidibus, quodque super digitum nostrum, more regio, anulus cum lapide precioso valoris viginti marcarum monete nostre Anglie ponatur.' Translated in Harvey, *Plantagenets*, p. 224.

while the contemporaneous will of Richard II's father, the Black Prince, incorporated quite detailed specifications regarding the scale and aesthetic character of the prince's funerary celebrations.[62] Moreover, just weeks prior to the drawing up of Richard II's will on 16 April 1399, the king's uncle, John of Gaunt, was interred at St Paul's in London in full accordance with the very detailed funerary instructions contained in his will of 3 February 1399.[63]

What is unusual about the will of Richard II is not its concern to predetermine the character of the king's funeral, but rather the *tone* in which its prescriptive injunctions are expressed.[64] First, the will manifests an over-awareness of the need to formulate contingency arrangements for all manner of unpredictable eventualities. Two alternative sets of arrangements are prescribed in case the king should die either within the palace of Westminster or at a distance less than sixteen miles from the palace. More bizarrely, the will also specifies that Richard should enjoy the full solemnities of a royal funeral even if the king's body was lost at sea or could not be recovered from abroad.[65] Secondly, the phrasing of the will betrays an unusually paranoid concern to make Richard's testamentary injunctions binding on his unnamed successor. In two passages in particular, the bequest of Richard's disposable assets to a successor king is made conditional on the latter's full adherence to the terms of the will. In the first instance, it is specified that the successor will only be allowed inheritance of the residue of the king's household possessions if '. . . the same successor shall permit our executors wholly and freely to execute this our will in its every part'.[66] Later, in an astonishingly audacious passage, Richard's executors are charged to withhold 'the residue of our gold' from the king's successor unless he 'shall approve, ratify and confirm, keep and cause to be kept and to be firmly observed' all of the legislation passed in the period following the 'Revenge Parliament' of 1397–8.[67] Richard's confidence in his executors was perhaps not as high as he might have hoped, since he found it necessary to remind them of their duty to defend the provisions contained in the will '. . . according to their ability even to the death if need be'.[68] All in all, the tone of Richard II's will is illustrative of the acute insecurity of a king who lacked a proper heir who could be relied upon to honour his posthumous wishes.

[62] *Collection of Wills*, ed. Nichols, pp. 60, 66–9.

[63] *Testamenta Eboracensia*, ed. J. Raine, 6 vols., Surtees Society 4 (1836–1902), I, 223–39; J. B. Post, 'The Obsequies of John of Gaunt', *Guildhall Studies in London History* 5 (1981), 1–12.

[64] Here I dispute Davies's characterization of the will as predictable and conventional. See Davies, 'Richard II and the Church', pp. 103–4.

[65] A reference to the fact that the will was drawn up shortly prior to Richard's second military expedition to Ireland.

[66] *Collection of Wills*, ed. Nichols, pp. 194–5 (Harvey, *Plantagenets*, p. 224).

[67] *Collection of Wills*, ed. Nichols, pp. 197–8 (Harvey, *Plantagenets*, p. 225). On the tyranny of Richard II, see 'Annales', pp. 199–239 (*Chrons. Rev.*, pp. 71–7); Bennett, *Richard II*, pp. 82–147.

[68] *Collection of Wills*, ed. Nichols, p. 198 (Harvey, *Plantagenets*, p. 225).

Furthermore, it is suggestive of the political isolation experienced by Richard as a result of his decision to centre his government on a narrow clique of court-based nobles, thereby engendering a strong sense of political alienation among powerful sections of the wider political community.

Seen from a Lancastrian perspective the will of Richard II was a problematic document. On the one hand, the more extreme prescriptions contained in the will exemplified the accusation of tyranny that the Lancastrian regime had chosen to level at Richard. To this end, an extensive tract of the will was included within the accusatory text of the official 'Record and Process' of the deposition.[69] On the other hand, Richard's will remained a public and legally binding document, the greater circulation of which placed a certain degree of pressure on Henry IV to pay due respect to his predecessor's known wishes. The picture was complicated further by the fact that Henry IV had been forced to limit his claim to the throne to an overlapping set of secondary claims that did not in themselves seek to deny Richard's royal status or basic hereditary right to rule. Yet, if Henry felt politically obliged to provide his predecessor with a fitting funeral, he also needed to take account of the fact that in the absence of any clearly stated official line on Richard II's status in death, his funeral would itself inevitably become a powerful public indicator of the evolving perspective of the new regime on the deposed king.

Clearly, Henry IV did not feel obliged to adhere to Richard's testamentary injunctions in a slavish manner: indeed, he pointedly ignored the deposed king's wishes in a number of key respects. Nevertheless, Henry IV's arrangements for the funeral of Richard II went beyond what might have been regarded as strictly necessary for the funeral of a deposed and discredited predecessor. This seems particularly striking when the first Lancastrian funeral of Richard II is compared with the Yorkist funeral of Henry VI in 1471, or the Tudor funeral of Richard III in 1485, which were both designed with the clear intention of denying the royal status of the deceased.[70] Ultimately, Richard II's testamentary determination to safeguard his temporal legacy and to provide for his own posthumous commemoration proved to be too powerful a public statement of intent for the still insecure Henry IV entirely to ignore.

Any attempt to interpret the funeral of Richard II needs to give careful consideration to the strategic priorities of the Lancastrian regime. The most obvious political aim of the funeral was to establish as publicly as possible the fact of Richard's death. The desirability of articulating this news in the public domain was mentioned quite explicitly in council minutes dated 8 February 1400.[71] Furthermore, the author of the *Traïson* text also voiced the opinion that

[69] *Rot. Parl.*, III, 421 (*Chrons. Rev.*, pp. 181–2).
[70] On Henry VI, see B. P. Wolffe, *Henry VI* (London, 1981), p. 347. On Richard III, see C. Ross, *Richard III* (London, 1981), p. 225.
[71] *POPC*, I, 111–12.

Richard's body was shown in London so that people 'might believe for certain that he was dead'.[72] The desire to prove that Richard was dead explains two otherwise surprising aspects of the funeral arrangements. Firstly, it makes sense of the decision to locate the celebration of exequies for the deposed king in London, despite his death taking place well away from the capital in Yorkshire. Secondly, it explains the particular emphasis the narrative sources place on the showing of Richard's actual corpse with its face uncovered, in stark contravention of the recent royal tradition of displaying a funeral effigy in place of the royal corpse.

The public advertisement of Richard II's death through the display of his corpse was clearly a desirable course of action from the perspective of Henry IV. The living Richard was always liable to act as a magnet and focus for insurrection, so naturally it was to be assumed that the maximum public exposure of Richard's death could only serve to increase the political security of the new royal regime. In the short term, this viewpoint was vindicated by the response it engendered. All contemporary chroniclers, with the sole exception of Creton, accepted the truth of Richard's death without question.[73] Furthermore, at least two sources for the Percy rising of 1403 indicate that open acknowledgement of the reality of Richard's death was the position that was publicly espoused by the rebel leaders.[74] However, a number of scholars have shown that the early Lancastrian period nevertheless witnessed the development of a virulent rumour culture centred on the notion of Richard II's survival.[75] Analysis of the political agitation fuelled by this rumour culture suggests that a belief in Richard's survival tended to infect the lowest strata of political society, that is individuals who possessed some degree of political consciousness but who did not enjoy access to political representation. In this context, it can be said that Richard II's funeral exercised importance as a repository of memory primarily from the perspective of the Lancastrian royal authorities. In 1413, for example, a judgment at the King's Bench recorded incredulity that a king who had been buried so publicly could still be considered alive.[76] However, as Paul Strohm has

[72] *Traïson*, p. 261.
[73] 'Metrical History', pp. 220–1 (*Chrons. Rev.*, p. 244). Creton subsequently revised his opinion on this matter. See J. J. N. Palmer, 'The Authorship, Date and Historical Value of the French Chronicles on the Lancastrian Deposition', *BJRL* 61 (1978–9), 151–4.
[74] *Hardyng*, pp. 352–3 (*Chrons. Rev.*, pp. 194–5), has the Percies accuse Henry IV of Richard's murder in the manifesto they addressed to the Lancastrian king at Shrewsbury. Meanwhile, *Eulogium Historiarum*, III, 396, has the Percies correcting the opinions of credulous Welsh recruits to their army who persisted in the belief that Richard II still lived.
[75] Strohm, *England's Empty Throne*, pp. 106–11; P. McNiven, 'Rebellion, Sedition and the Legend of Richard II's Survival in the Reigns of Henry IV and Henry V', *BJRL* 76 (1994), 93–117; P. Morgan, 'Henry IV and the Shadow of Richard II', in *Crown, Government and People in the Fifteenth Century*, ed. R. E. Archer (Stroud, 1995), pp. 1–31.
[76] *Select Cases in the Court of King's Bench under Richard II, Henry IV and Henry V*, ed. G. O. Sayles, Selden Society 88 (London, 1971), pp. 212–13. See also Strohm, *England's Empty Throne*, p. 106.

argued, the vitality of a rumour is not wholly dependent upon the logical weighing and evaluating of available evidence.[77] If Richard II's funeral was devised as a strategy for defusing underlying dissent, then the government remained blind to the limitations of ritual as a mechanism for controlling beliefs and behaviour. Ultimately, the funeral of March 1400 probably did convince enough important people that Richard II was dead to ensure that any contrary opinion might easily be discredited. Nevertheless, the authorities remained unable to do more than marginalize the effects of Ricardian rumours, thereby ensuring that pro-Ricardian plots would remain a potential threat to the Lancastrian regime until at least the middle of the second decade of the fifteenth century.

However, the political usefulness of Richard II's funeral was not restricted to a basic official desire to prove that the deposed king was dead. While this certainly explains why a public funeral was staged for the king in London, it does not provide adequate explanation for the peculiar aesthetic character of the funerary rituals. A careful reading of the visual dimensions of Richard II's funeral suggests that it was utilized as an occasion to express symbolically and in retrospect the delegitimation of Richard's kingship. In essence, the imagery of the funeral sought to construct Richard's identity in terms that were literally true at the time of his death, so Richard was buried not as a dead king like Edward II in 1327, but as a dead *former* king.[78]

The symbolic separation of Richard II's dynastic and institutional identities was achieved by denying Richard's corpse access to the formal imagery of kingship. Richard was accorded recognition of his royal status through the arrangement of exequies that were appropriate for a prince of the royal blood; thus he was honoured, for example, with a requiem service at St Paul's that was attended by Henry IV. Nevertheless, it is clear from contemporary sources that Richard's corpse was presented visually in death stripped of the standard iconographical emblems of kingship, the royal robes and regalia. A policy of depriving the dead king of the visible manifestations of royal office also informed the decision to deny Richard burial in his completed tomb at Westminster Abbey. In this case, the regal connotations that emanated from the aesthetic representation of Richard in the imagery on his tomb clashed with the emphasis placed upon Richard's deprived royal status within the funeral celebrations. Clearly, it would have been difficult for Henry IV to control the political memory of his predecessor had he chosen to bury him within a visual environment that stood as bold testament to Richard's own very personal vision of regality. In these circumstances, the decision to bury Richard at King's Langley can be interpreted as a slightly unsatisfactory Lancastrian attempt to defuse the symbolic power of the errant Ricardian imagery at Westminster.

[77] Strohm, *England's Empty Throne*, p. 245 (n. 35).
[78] Burden, 'Rituals of Royalty', pp. 116–36.

CONCLUSION

As suggested at the beginning of this discussion, the Lancastrian approach to burying Richard II was informed by, and responded to, the underlying issue of the basis of Henry IV's own accepted claim to the throne in September 1399. Although the strength of Henry IV's claim had depended in great part upon the quality of his own royal pedigree, he had nevertheless retreated from making any formal declaration concerning the comparative quality of Richard II's royal pedigree. Indeed, Henry even resisted the usual usurper's temptation to justify a seizure of the throne by casting aspersions on his predecessor's true paternity.[79]

Henry IV's failure to challenge the legitimate basis of Richard II's kingship placed constraints on the Lancastrian king's subsequent freedom to manipulate the political memory of his predecessor. In essence, Henry's mandate for authority was a notion that Richard II had forfeited his right to rule by abusing the exercise of power. Henry's justification for his usurpation was dominated by a negative conception of his predecessor's actions, rather than a more positive conception of Henry's own qualities as a king. By binding the Lancastrian claim to the throne to allegations of Richard II's 'evil government', it became an inevitable aspect of Henry's claim that no doubts could be cast over the initial legitimacy of Richard II's rule. Paradoxically, since Henry was committed to the acceptance of a notion of Richard's rightful kingship as the necessary premise for his rightful deposition, it became all the more difficult for the new king to ignore the consequent pressure to provide Richard with a proper royal funeral. That Henry did resist this pressure in part, reflected his determination to shape the political agenda at the outset of his reign, and indeed it seems undeniable that Richard's funeral needs to be thought of as a Lancastrian occasion in its design as well as its execution. Yet, as with other aspects of his rule, the basic weakness of Henry's position as king hedged his ability to act as a truly free agent and take decisions that were not determined by his 'usurper's inheritance'. If Richard's funeral was Lancastrian in design and execution, it was also Ricardian in at least some of its essential flavour – indeed, it was a classic fudged affair. In the end, the rather confused messages that emanated from the symbolism of Richard II's funeral were not the product of any clear-cut ideological perspective, but instead reflected a not entirely successful attempt to communicate a sense of the peculiar transition that was still taking place in Richard's remembered identity as a king.

---

[79] Although allegations of Richard II's illegitimacy clearly did have some currency within society at large. See C 258/24/9, printed in A. J. Prescott, 'The Accusations Against Thomas Austin', in Strohm, *Hochon's Arrow*, pp. 161–77 (p. 175); *Chronicle of Adam Usk*, pp. 62–3.

4

Henry IV and Chivalry

Anthony Tuck

In the popular mind there is a great contrast between the personality of Henry IV and that of Henry V. Like much else in the Englishman's traditional view of his history, this contrast derives essentially from Shakespeare, and particularly from *Henry IV Part II*. In this play, Shakespeare portrays Henry IV as an ailing monarch, wearied by his experience of kingship: 'Health, alack, with youthful wings is flown/ From this bare wither'd trunk.'[1] His son, by contrast, is only too eager to assume the mantle of kingship, and in a famous scene he removes the crown from the king's chamber, believing that his father is on his deathbed.[2] Once his father is dead, the young Henry V immediately assumes all the characteristics of majesty, repudiating the friends of his youth, and in *Henry V* Shakespeare portrays the king as a heroic figure leading the English to their most famous victory over the French. Modern scholarship has done little to change this contrast between the two kings: although Professor Allmand has sounded some warning notes, virtually all work on Henry V over the past half-century has stressed his heroic and statesmanlike qualities. K. B. McFarlane, for example, went so far as to suggest that he was 'the greatest man that ever ruled England'. Henry IV, on the other hand, has generally been portrayed as something of a failure as king, a ruler of whom the best that can be said is that he survived to hand his throne on to his son.[3]

Henry V died at the age of thirty-six, whereas his father had lived for ten years longer. Neither was long-lived even by the standards of the fifteenth century, but Henry V achieved his greatest military successes – the victory at Agincourt and the conquest of Normandy – at an age when his father had not yet made himself king. Thus a comparison between father and son at the same age might well suggest a much greater similarity of character and ability than the traditional view of the two kings has allowed. It is the purpose of this discussion to examine how, before his seizure of the throne in 1399, Henry IV as earl of Derby acquired a European-wide reputation as a

---

[1] W. Shakespeare, *Henry IV Part II*, Act IV, Scene V, ll. 226–7.

[2] Shakespeare, *Henry IV Part II*, Act IV.

[3] C. Allmand, *Henry V* (London, 1992), pp. 435–43; *LKLK*, pp. 104, 133; Kirby, *Henry IV*, pp. 256–7, though Kirby discusses the promise of his youth.

chivalric warrior, and to suggest that his career in the 1390s was perhaps as full of military promise as that of his son twenty years later.

The generations to which Henry's father John of Gaunt and grandfather Henry, duke of Lancaster belonged had acquired their military reputations as Edward III's companions-in-arms in campaigns against the French, and to a lesser extent in Scotland and the Iberian peninsula. Froissart tells us in the prologue to his *Chronicles* that he sought the company of various nobles and great lords in France, England, Scotland, Brittany and other countries, and from them learnt of the 'grans merveilles et li biau fait d'armes' that took place during the wars between England and France.[4] Yet as Henry grew to manhood the opportunities for a young nobleman to acquire fame in battle against the French had much diminished. He had been too young (he was almost certainly born in 1366) to take part in the expedition his uncle Thomas of Woodstock led to Brittany in 1380, and he was perhaps well-advised not even to consider going on the bishop of Norwich's ill-fated 'crusade' to Flanders in 1383. His first experience on campaign was with his father in Scotland in 1384: the expedition was unsuccessful in discouraging Scottish nobles from launching raids into England, and neither Gaunt nor his son saw any serious military action.[5]

For reasons that remain unknown, Henry did not take part in the king's expedition to Scotland in 1385, when his father and Richard fell out over the strategy to be pursued once the army reached Edinburgh.[6] Nor did he accompany his father to Castile in 1386: as heir to the duchy of Lancaster, he was expected to remain at home and take responsibility for the inheritance. His first experience of battle came in December 1387, when he and his fellow-Appellants routed an army raised by Robert de Vere, duke of Ireland.[7] The battle was the culmination of the Appellants' campaign to force Richard to allow his favourites and courtiers to face their accusers in parliament, and according to the contemporary narratives Henry acquitted himself with distinction in the battle. Henry's advance to hold the bridge over the Thames at Radcot Bridge forced de Vere into a trap, and his army was easily dispersed: Knighton ascribes a prominent part in the battle to Henry, but this may reflect the information he or a member of his retinue gave to St Mary's Abbey, Leicester, where Knighton wrote. Adam of Usk recounts how after the battle he saw the victorious Appellants marching

[4] *Chroniques de J. Froissart*, ed. S. Luce *et al.*, 15 vols. (Paris, 1869–1975), I(2), 1.
[5] A. Goodman, *John of Gaunt: The Exercise of Princely Power in Fourteenth-Century Europe* (London, 1992), p. 99; Kirby, *Henry IV*, p. 22.
[6] *Westminster Chron.*, pp. 128–30.
[7] For the Radcot Bridge campaign see J. N. L. Myres, 'The Campaign of Radcot Bridge in December 1387', *EHR* 42 (1927), 20–33; R. G. Davies, 'Some Notes from the Register of Henry de Wakefield, Bishop of Worcester, on the Political Crisis of 1386–88', *EHR* 86 (1971), 547–58.

through Oxford on their way to London with Henry and the earl of Warwick in the vanguard.[8]

Both the short-lived Appellant regime and the restored government of Richard II after May 1389 sought peace with France and Scotland: Henry's father John of Gaunt was the principal English representative to the peace talks that were held at Leulinghem near Calais from 1389 onwards, and there is no evidence to suggest any rift between father and son over the policy of *rapprochement* with France, even though his uncle Thomas of Woodstock, duke of Gloucester and the earl of Arundel seem to have had reservations about it.[9] During the years of peace, however, Henry sought to establish a military reputation for himself by taking part in important tournaments and by campaigning in other parts of Europe. But there were also expeditions in which Henry did not participate, and these too can provide us with an important insight into the chivalric values of the western European nobility at the end of the fourteenth century. Henry first attracted international attention as a jouster when he accepted an invitation to attend a tournament at St Ingelvert, near Calais, in March 1390. The choice of the site, so close to English-held Calais, might have been intended as a challenge to the English. According to Froissart, English knights and esquires thought they would lose face if they did not attend a tournament only a few miles from Calais, and he goes on to say that over a hundred English knights and esquires responded to the call.[10]

Froissart gives a lengthy description of the tournament and the deeds of arms performed by several of the English knights, but he does not mention the presence of the earl of Derby. However, we know that Gaunt wrote to Jean de Boucicaut, one of the organizers of the tournament, asking him to joust with his son, and the anonymous poem 'The Jousts of St Ingelvert' records that Henry jousted towards the end of the tournament, on Wednesday, 16 April. The Monk of St Denis describes how Henry and his knights engaged in a perilous joust with the three knights who were hosting the tournament, and he goes on to say that Henry and his men were judged worthy of praise above all other foreigners at the tournament.[11]

It is quite possible that one of the matters discussed at the tournament was the proposal that the Genoese had put to Charles VI in the previous winter for a crusade to take the port of Al-Mahdiya, on the north African coast some one hundred miles east of Tunis. Anxious to cultivate closer relations with

[8] *Westminster Chron.*, pp. 220–4; *Knighton's Chron.*, pp. lxix–lxx, 420–4; *Chronicle of Adam Usk*, p. 12.
[9] Goodman, *John of Gaunt*, pp. 152–4; Kirby, *Henry IV*, pp. 41–2.
[10] *Oeuvres de Froissart*, ed. K. de Lettenhove, 25 vols. (Brussels, 1867–77), XIV, 55–8.
[11] *Chronique du Religieux de St Denys*, ed. M. L. Bellaguet, with introduction by B. Guenée, 6 vols. (Paris, 1994), I, 678–80; D. Lalande, *Jean II Le Meingre, dit Boucicaut, 1366–1421* (Geneva, 1988), pp. 31–6; Goodman, *John of Gaunt*, pp. 146, 170 n.8. The anonymous poem 'The Jousts of St Ingelvert' is printed in Froissart, *Oeuvres*, XIV, 407–19.

Genoa, Charles encouraged his uncle the duke of Bourbon to lead the expedition, dignified as a crusade.[12] After the conclusion of the St Inglevert tournament, Henry seems to have intended to join the crusade. On 6 May 1390 he appointed Richard Kingston as his treasurer of war for the expedition, which he had decided to undertake 'en les parties de Barbarye et de Pruz'.[13] Three days later he was back in Calais, mustering his retinue, and around 18 May 1390 he sent two esquires to Paris to obtain a safe-conduct from Charles VI of France that would allow him to travel through France to Genoa, where the crusaders intended to embark.[14] However, on 5 June Henry and his retinue returned to England. He had evidently called off his plan to join the crusade, but it is not clear why he did so. The Westminster annalist stated that Henry had failed to obtain a safe-conduct from Charles VI 'in the form asked for', and thus returned to England. This may be true, though since Henry's half-brother John Beaufort (who had also been at the St Inglevert tournament) joined the crusade with a retinue of twenty-four knights and one hundred archers and presumably travelled to Genoa through France, this explanation is not wholly convincing. Indeed, Froissart suggests that the foreign knights and esquires who enlisted were happy with the arrangements for the expedition.[15]

It may be that Henry was reluctant, when it came to the point, to place himself under the command of so prominent a member of the French royal family, especially on an expedition that might prove risky; but it is equally possible that he considered the crusade in Prussia a better alternative. Froissart makes the point that now there was a truce between England and France, the Genoese believed that their knights would have nothing to do and would be glad to join expeditions elsewhere,[16] but they were not the only power to see advantages for themselves in the cessation of Anglo-French warfare. The Teutonic Knights evidently held the same view, and encouraged western knights to join their crusades.[17]

Prussia was held in high esteem by western knights as a place where honour and fame might be won by participating in the crusade, or *Reise*, against the pagan peoples of Lithuania. Both Chaucer and Gower wrote that knights went to Prussia to win renown, and Chaucer's knight had 'reysed' in

[12] Lalande, *Boucicaut*, p. 36; *La Chronique du bon duc Loys de Bourbon*, ed. A. M. Chazaud (Paris, 1876), pp. 218–52; L. Mirot, 'Une expédition française en Tunisie au xive siècle', *Revue des Etudes Historiques* 98 (1931), 357–406.
[13] *Expeditions to Prussia and the Holy Land made by Henry Earl of Derby (Afterwards King Henry IV) in the Years 1390–91 and 1392–93*, ed. L. Toulmin-Smith, Camden Society n.s. 52 (London, 1894), pp. 1–2.
[14] Goodman, *John of Gaunt*, p. 147; Froissart, *Oeuvres*, XIV, 156.
[15] *Westminster Chron.*, pp. 432–4; Froissart, *Oeuvres*, XIV, 155; Goodman, *John of Gaunt*, p. 170 n.9; Kirby, *Henry IV*, pp. 29–30.
[16] Froissart, *Oeuvres*, XIV, 153.
[17] N. Housley, *The Later Crusades, 1274–1580* (Oxford, 1992), pp. 399–402.

Lithuania and Russia.[18] Chaucer also drew attention to a particular feature of the *Reise* that may have been attractive to Henry. The knight, Chaucer said, 'Full ofte tyme . . . hadde the bord bigonne/ Aboven alle nacions in Pruce.'[19] The 'bord' was the table of honour, or *eretisch*: a banquet given, usually at Königsberg (Kaliningrad), before going into battle or at the end of a Reise. Those who sat at the table were foreign knights chosen by heralds for their prowess in arms, and the knight who headed the table, or 'began the board', enjoyed the greatest honour. The establishment of a table of honour was generally proclaimed abroad in advance of a *Reise* in the expectation that it would act as an incentive for foreign knights to join the crusade, and the chivalric ambience that surrounded the *Reise* did much to raise the prestige and popularity of campaigns in a region that was unpromising in terms of booty that might be won, and against peoples who had nominally accepted Christianity in 1386.[20]

Henry's grandfather Henry of Grosmont, duke of Lancaster, had gone to Prussia on crusade in 1351–2,[21] and Chaucer may have acquired his knowledge of the table of honour from him. Henry would probably have known about it at least in general terms; but it is also possible that a table of honour was proclaimed in the west in advance of the planned *Reise* to Vilnius in the summer of 1390. The St Inglevert tournament attracted knights from Germany and Bohemia as well as England, and would have been the obvious place for the Teutonic Knights to make known details of the forthcoming campaign. If this is so, it would explain Henry's abrupt change of plan; the reputation he had won at the tournament, if the Monk of St Denis is to be believed, might well precede him to the north, and ensure his seating at the table of honour.

Henry and his retinue landed in Prussia in early August 1390, and caught up with the main body of the Teutonic Knights' forces near the river Memel nearly a fortnight later.[22] They then advanced into Lithuanian territory,

[18] 'Prologue to the Canterbury Tales', ll. 43–78, in *The Complete Works of Geoffrey Chaucer*, ed. W. W. Skeat (Oxford, 1912); *The English Works of John Gower*, ed. G. C. Macaulay, 2 vols., EETS ES 81 and 82 (London, 1900–1), I, 345 (ll. 1620–44); *Chronique du bon duc Loys*, pp. 65–6; E. Christiansen, *The Northern Crusades: The Baltic and the Catholic Frontier 1100–1525* (London, 1980), pp. 145–70; M. Keen, *Chivalry* (London, 1984), pp. 171–4.

[19] 'Prologue to the Canterbury Tales', ll. 52–3.

[20] A. S. Cook, 'Beginning the Board in Prussia', *Journal of English and Germanic Philology* 14 (1915), 375–88.

[21] K. Fowler, *The King's Lieutenant: Henry of Grosmont, First Duke of Lancaster 1310–1361* (London, 1969), pp. 105–6.

[22] For what follows, the principal source is *Expeditions to Prussia*, ed. Toulmin-Smith. For the size and composition of his retinue on his first expedition, see *Expeditions to Prussia*, ed. Toulmin-Smith, pp. xliii–xlv. Henry's expeditions to Prussia have been discussed by F. R. H. Du Boulay, 'Henry of Derby's Expeditions to Prussia 1390–1 and 1392', in *The Reign of Richard II: Essays in Honour of May McKisack*, ed. F. R. H. Du Boulay and C. M. Barron (London, 1971), pp. 153–72. There is also some comment in Housley, *Later Crusades*, pp. 355, 400–1.

attacked Vilnius, and succeeded in taking the outer, less well-fortified part of the town. The inner citadel, however, proved a much tougher proposition: after a siege of nearly five weeks the army, weakened by disease and shortage of gunpowder, withdrew. Both the English and the German chroniclers attribute an important part in the battle to Henry's forces. The monk of Westminster said that 'The capture of the city was due to the earl, who, together with his men, indeed behaved in this attack with great distinction and was the very first to plant his standard on the city walls.' Walsingham's account is very similar, as is that of the German chronicler John of Posilge, who comments that Henry had many good archers in his retinue. All three accounts may well be based on a common source, perhaps a newsletter written by a member of the retinue of the marshal of the army of the Teutonic Knights. On the other hand, an account of the storming of Vilnius in a letter from the Grand Master of the Teutonic Knights to Wenceslas king of the Romans makes no mention of the part played by Henry and his men.[23]

Henry returned to Königsberg on 20 October, and spent the next three months at the court of the Grand Master, no doubt participating in the seasonal festivities. For although the *Reise* took the form of a crusade, it was largely secular in character. Henry contributed a total of 37s 4d in offerings at four churches in Danzig for the indulgence granted him by Pope Boniface IX, and for 13s 4d he bought two boys from 'a certain man of Lettowe'. As Professor Du Boulay has commented, Henry probably intended to have them brought up as Christians, and the 'Henry Lettowe' recorded in the accounts for the expedition may have been one of them, to whom Henry gave his name. Nonetheless, Henry's expenditure on gambling, gifts and feasting greatly exceeded his expenditure on works of piety, though both forms of expenditure no doubt enhanced his reputation as a generous lord.[24] He left Königsberg on 9 February 1391, and arrived back in England at the beginning of May, 'in excellent health and spirits' according to the Monk of Westminster.[25] Little more than a year after returning home, Henry was planning another expedition overseas. On 15 July 1392 Kingston was again appointed Henry's treasurer for war, but the terms of his appointment suggest that Henry now had much more extensive travel in mind, for the expedition was to go 'versus partes Prucie et Sancti Sepulcri': not just to Prussia, but also to Jerusalem.[26] As far as Prussia was concerned, Henry's purpose was much the same as it had been in 1390, to join the Teutonic Knights on their summer *Reise* into Lithuania. He intended to go to Jerusalem, however, as a pilgrim

---

[23] *Westminster Chron.*, pp. 444–8; *Historia Anglicana*, II, 198; *Scriptores Rerum Prussicarum*, ed. T. Hirsch, M. Toppen, and E. Strehlke, 5 vols. (Leipzig, 1861–74), III, 167; *Codex Diplomaticus Prussicus*, ed. J. Voigt, 6 vols. (Königsberg, 1836–61), IV, 114–15.

[24] *Expeditions to Prussia*, ed. Toulmin-Smith, pp. 52, 90–1, 117; Du Boulay, 'Expeditions', pp. 170–2.

[25] *Westminster Chron.*, pp. 458–9.

[26] *Expeditions to Prussia*, ed. Toulmin-Smith, p. 148.

rather than as a crusader with an armed retinue, for no crusade to the Holy Land was either planned or undertaken in the 1390s.

Henry set off on 24 July 1392, but when he reached Prussia he abruptly changed his plans. The English chroniclers pay little attention to this second expedition, and do not satisfactorily explain its abandonment. John Capgrave, writing during the reign of Henry VI, suggested that Henry did not feel welcome when he arrived at Königsberg. The German chroniclers reported that there was tension between Henry and the Teutonic Knights caused by the killing of a local man by one of the members of Henry's retinue and by a dispute between Henry and his hosts over the banner of St George, which both sides claimed the right to carry. Almost certainly the real reason for Henry's change of plan, however, was that his presence was no longer needed: the political situation in Lithuania had changed suddenly in the summer of 1392, and the Teutonic Knights abandoned their proposed campaign. They paid Henry the generous sum of £400 to cover his expenses, and he evidently left Königsberg early in September with honour.[27]

Henry then travelled via Prague and Vienna to Venice, where he stayed in a house on the Isle of St George while waiting for a galley to be made ready for him. Venice was the usual point of departure for pilgrims to the Holy Land. Earlier in 1392, for instance, Thomas Swinburne, keeper of the castle of Guines, sailed from Venice to Alexandria and then travelled overland through Sinai to Gaza and on to Bethlehem and Jerusalem. Henry, however, intended to make the journey by sea direct to the Holy Land, as two fifteenth-century pilgrims who have left narratives of their expeditions were to do. Shortly before Christmas, probably on 23 December, he took ship for the Holy Land, arriving at Jaffa around 27 January 1393. From Jaffa he set out for Jerusalem, with a small entourage, probably all mounted on donkeys. They probably hired local guides, as Swinburne had done, though he and his companions made the journey through the Sinai desert on camels. Felix Fabri observed in the 1480s that the local guides objected to pilgrims making the journey on foot, because it was more difficult to keep a party together and increased the likelihood of pilgrims suffering from heat exhaustion and dehydration. About the end of January he arrived in Jerusalem, but little is known of what must have been the climax of his expedition. He spent only a short time in the city, but Capgrave says he visited the holy places, showing great devotion.[28] By Easter he was back in Venice, and from there returned to

[27] *Johannis Capgrave Liber de Illustribus Henricis*, ed. F. C. Hingeston (London, 1858), p. 99; *Scriptores Rerum Prussicarum*, III, 182; *Expeditions to Prussia*, ed. Toulmin-Smith, p. 149.

[28] *Expeditions to Prussia*, ed. Toulmin-Smith, pp. lxxvi–vii, 211; 'Voyage en Terre Sainte d'un maire de Bordeaux au XIVe siècle', ed. Comte Riant, in *Archives de l'Orient Latin II* (Paris, 1884), pp. 378–88; *The Wanderings of Felix Fabri (circa 1480–1483 A. D.)*, trans. A. Stewart, 2 vols. (London, 1892–3), I, 10, 17–26, 243; *The Itineraries of William Wey, Fellow of Eton College, to Jerusalem, A. D. 1458 and A. D. 1462; and to Saint James of Compostella, A. D. 1456*

England by way of Milan. The pilgrimage to Jerusalem was sufficient in itself to bring Henry some renown, and must have been a significant spiritual experience; but this second expedition was also important for the range of political and diplomatic contacts he made. In Prague he was entertained by Richard II's brother-in-law Wenceslas, king of the Romans and Bohemia; in Vienna he stayed with Duke Albert III of Austria, who himself had gained fame as a crusader with the Teutonic Knights, and he also paid a courtesy call on Sigismund, king of Hungary, Wenceslas's half-brother, at his Viennese residence. In Venice he was received by the Doge, and the Senate voted 360 gold ducats to pay for a public reception for him; at Rhodes he was received by the Grand Master of the Knights of the Hospital, and on his way back he was welcomed at Famagusta by King James I of Cyprus, who presented him with a leopard, which was shipped home, no doubt with some difficulty, and probably placed in the royal menagerie in the Tower of London.[29]

Of all the contacts he made on this expedition, however, perhaps the most important was that with the ruler of Milan, Gian Galeazzo Visconti.[30] Gian Galeazzo's sister had been married to Henry's uncle Lionel, duke of Clarence, who had died in Italy in 1368 and had been buried at Pavia before his remains were removed to the house of Austin Friars at Clare in Suffolk.[31] Gian Galeazzo took Henry to see his uncle's tomb, and, as befitted a tourist, Henry also visited the tombs of St Augustine and Boethius.[32] Gian Galeazzo appears to have established a cordial relationship with Henry. In 1394 he sent Henry a present of velvet cloth,[33] and in 1399, after he had been widowed, Gian Galeazzo's daughter declared that she would gladly marry him if and when he was restored to the king of England's favour.[34] While Henry was in Milan the Italian esquire Francis Court may have been attracted into his service. Court was described in 1394 as an esquire 'de partibus Ytalie', and Henry showed him particular honour. He received a special livery in 1395, and in 1396 Henry gave him a new year's gift of a gold clasp, an unusual honour for one of his station in Henry's household.[35] Court repaid Henry's generosity with loyalty and service. In 1398, when facing the prospect of

(Edinburgh, 1857), pp. x–xi, xiii–xiv, 56–9, 92–6 (I owe these two references to the kindness of Professor Anthony Goodman); *Liber de Illustribus Henricis*, ed. Hingeston, pp. 99–100.

[29] *Expeditions to Prussia*, ed. Toulmin-Smith, pp. lviii, lxv, 150, 191, 194–5, 229, 256, 285; *Calendar of State Papers: Venice, 1202–1509*, pp. 33–4; *Liber de Illustribus Henricis*, ed. Hingeston, p. 100; for the Lusignan dynasty in Cyprus, see P. Edbury, *The Kingdom of Cyprus and the Crusades 1191–1374* (Cambridge, 1991).
[30] D. Muir, *A History of Milan under the Visconti* (London, 1924), pp. 222–48; G. Mathew, *The Court of Richard II* (London, 1968), pp. 6, 8 and 29.
[31] *Liber de Illustribus Henricis*, ed. Hingeston, p. 100; *Historia Anglicana*, I, 306.
[32] *Liber de Illustribus Henricis*, ed. Hingeston, p. 100.
[33] DL 28/1/5, fol. 9r.
[34] *Calendar of State Papers: Milan, 1359–1618*, p. 1.
[35] DL 28/1/5, fols. 3r, 10v and 25r; *Expeditions to Prussia*, ed. Toulmin-Smith, p. 291.

single combat at Coventry against the duke of Norfolk, Henry sent him back
to Milan with a request that Gian Galeazzo should provide him with a suit of
armour. Gian Galeazzo ordered four of his armourers to accompany Court
back to England, and the armour which Henry wore for the aborted joust was
no doubt of their workmanship.[36] Later, after Henry became king, Court
played an important part in the campaign against the Welsh rebels, and was
made a life grant of the lordship of Pembroke.[37]

Henry's two expeditions had made him a more widely travelled man than
either his father or his king. They had brought him honour and fame, they
had demonstrated that service with him was attractive to at least one
ambitious esquire, and they had brought him a range of important political
contacts. If his later wish to unite western Christendom in a crusade to
recover the Holy Land was little more than a conventional aspiration shared
by many late medieval rulers, he at least had the advantage over most of
them in that he had actually been there. After his return home, Henry found
enjoyment in participating in various tournaments, though none were on the
scale of the St Ingelvert jousts of 1391. He took part in a tournament at
Hertford, a duchy of Lancaster Castle, on Christmas Eve 1394, and in the
following year he employed the famous painter Gilbert Prince to produce
four banners, which were to be taken to another tournament.[38]

Small-scale tournaments at home might satisfy Henry's appetite for
jousting, but by 1396 his mind began to turn once again to taking part in
an expedition overseas. It is on the face of it surprising that Henry did not
accompany Richard II on his expedition to Ireland in 1394–5. He had recently
been widowed, but grief for the loss of his wife is unlikely to have been the
main reason why he did not go to Ireland with the king. He was not the only
noble to find the prospect of service in Ireland unalluring: his father did not
go with Richard, nor did the warlike earl of Arundel, while the duke of
Gloucester went over in the king's company but returned early to England.[39]

Froissart tells us that Gloucester had a poor opinion of Ireland as a country
in which to campaign. He apparently unburdened himself to Sir John
Lakenheath, one of the members of his council, sometime after his return
from Ireland. Ireland, he said, was not a land of conquest or of profit; the Irish
were a poor and wretched people, and had a very poor and uninhabitable
country. All that was gained there in one year would be lost the next.[40] To an
English nobleman whose experience of campaigning had been acquired in
the comparatively familiar terrain of northern France or southern Scotland,

[36] Froissart, *Oeuvres*, XVI, 96–101.
[37] *A Calendar of the Public Records Relating to Pembrokeshire III*, Cymmrodorion Record Series 7
(London, 1918), p. 45.
[38] DL 28/1/4, fol. 8v; DL 28/1/5, fol. 24r.
[39] For Richard II's Irish expedition, see N. Saul, *Richard II* (London, 1997), ch. 12.
[40] Froissart, *Oeuvres*, XVI, 5; A. Goodman, *The Loyal Conspiracy: The Lords Appellant under
Richard II* (London, 1971), pp. 101–2.

the society of Ireland and the Irish approach to warfare might well have seemed alien and offering little opportunity for profit. Richard II created no table of honour for those who joined him in campaign against Art McMurrough,[41] and McMurrough's stronghold in the Wicklow mountains contained no city such as Vilnius where English knights could win fame by being the first to place their banner on the walls of the city. Ireland was not a country where a chivalric knight was likely to enhance his reputation.

Froissart tells us that when he came to England in 1395 he heard a lengthy account from one Henry Cristede about the expedition to Ireland from which he, and Richard, had recently returned. Froissart was particularly impressed by Cristede's account of how Richard had rapidly compelled four kings in Ireland to submit to his rule, when his grandfather Edward III, 'who was such a valiant man', had not been able to do so.[42] In a significant passage, which has not received the attention it deserves in England, Froissart went on to say that when he returned to Hainault he expected to be closely questioned by Albert of Bavaria, count of Hainault and Holland and by his son William, count of Ostrevant about Richard's expedition to Ireland. The reason for this, Froissart tells us, is that the count of Holland was also lord of Friesland, 'qui est ung grant royaulme et puissant', but the Frisians refused to submit to the authority of the count.[43] The implication of this is that Froissart drew a parallel between Richard II's difficulties in enforcing his authority in Ireland and the count of Holland's problems in Friesland. The parallel between the two places is implicitly taken further by words that Froissart puts into the mouth of the duke of Guelders when the latter visited England in 1396. In an attempt to persuade Henry not to campaign in Friesland, the duke said that the Frisians were a people without honour or reputation. They showed no pity or mercy, and they acknowledged no lord. They lived in a strongly defended country surrounded by the sea and formed of isles, hollows and marshes: no one apart from the Frisians themselves had ever been able to govern it.[44] The duke's description of Friesland echoes that of Adam of Bremen, writing in the twelfth century. He wrote of the Frisians that their country was a maritime region of impenetrable marshes, and that its inhabitants were always ready to risk their lives for freedom.[45]

Both the duke of Guelders and Adam of Bremen were correct in their description of the geography of the country. Much of it had been won from the sea and marshland in twelfth and thirteenth centuries, but the major inundations of the late thirteenth and early fourteenth centuries had made

---

[41] Richard's main concern was to redefine his own relationship with his Irish, particularly his Gaelic, subjects: Saul, *Richard II*, pp. 282–3.

[42] Froissart, *Oeuvres*, XV, 170–1, 179.

[43] Froissart, *Oeuvres*, XV, 179.

[44] Froissart, *Oeuvres*, XV, 226–9.

[45] Adam of Bremen, *History of the Archbishops of Hamburg-Bremen*, trans. F. J. Tschau (New York, 1955), pp. 17, 149.

the country more isolated and inaccessible. In particular, the breaking of the barrier between the North Sea and the Zuyder Zee after *c.*1280 made the approach to Friesland from Holland more difficult. Friesland had never been feudalized, and the native nobility retained *de facto* political control, while engaging in numerous feuds among themselves. They recognized the shadowy overlordship of the counts of Holland, but resisted any attempt to make that overlordship a reality: in 1345, for instance, Albert of Bavaria's father William IV, count of Holland had been killed in battle with the Frisians at Warns in southwest Friesland while on a campaign to enforce his authority there.[46]

Although the parallels between Friesland and Ireland should not be pressed too far, they were both lordships where geographical isolation, difficult terrain and a social structure different from much of feudal Europe created problems for the rulers who claimed authority there. Both lordships enjoyed much autonomy in practice while acknowledging the nominal authority of a distant ruler. Campaigning in both countries was likely to be unrewarding in terms both of profit and prestige: the duke of Guelders' remarks about Friesland seem to echo those of the duke of Gloucester about Ireland. In 1395 Albert of Bavaria began to plan an expedition to enforce his authority over Friesland.[47] Whether he was influenced in his decision to do so by what he had heard of Richard II's apparently successful attempt to assert his overlordship in Ireland is debatable, but Froissart's account suggests that it is at least a possibility. No doubt the wish to avenge his father's death and to make effective the lordship he claimed over Friesland were uppermost in his mind: Richard's Irish expedition had perhaps done no more than demonstrate that the assertion of effective lordship over a remote and rebellious region was possible.

In raising an army for the expedition, Albert faced some competition. Since 1394 the grand project of a western crusade against the Turks had been under consideration, and both John of Gaunt and Philip, duke of Burgundy had agreed to take part.[48] Sigismund of Hungary, whom Henry had met in 1393, welcomed the proposed crusade, and it seemed likely to involve the participation of many of the leading nobles and knights of England, France and the Low Countries. Many leading European nobles had joined the Order of the Passion, sponsored by Philippe de Mézières, with the intention of participating in the crusade against the Turks. Henry, however, did not do so; nor, unlike his father, did he agree to put his name

---

[46] J. J. Kalma, J. J. Spahr van der Hoek and K. de Vries, *Geschiedenis van Friesland* (Leeuwarden, 1973), p. 157.

[47] E. Verwijs, *De Oorlogen van Hertog Albrecht van Beieren met de Friezen in de Laatste Jaren der XIV Eeuw*, Werken uitgeven door het Historisch Genootschap gevestigd te Utrecht 8 (Utrecht, 1869), pp. xiii–xxv.

[48] Goodman, *John of Gaunt*, pp. 200–3; J. J. N. Palmer, *England, France and Christendom 1377–99* (London, 1972), ch. 11; R. Vaughan, *Philip the Bold* (London, 1962), pp. 61–3.

Anthony Tuck

forward as willing to assist the new order.[49] The projected crusade was delayed all through 1395 and the early months of 1396; Gaunt and Burgundy withdrew, and the leadership of the crusade was eventually entrusted to Burgundy's impetuous son and heir, John of Nevers.[50] According to Froissart, John of Nevers wanted Albert's son William, count of Ostrevant to join the crusade, but Albert counselled against it, saying that there was no reason for him to go 'except for the vainglory of this world', and that he would do better to go to Friesland and 'conquer our inheritance, which the Frisians by their pride and uncouthness are withholding from us'.[51] As Professor Ainsworth has pointed out, Froissart is concerned in this passage to make the point that a wise father will seek to warn his son against the excesses of youthful chivalric enthusiasm, but this need not detract from the essential truth of the story.[52] The count of Ostrevant would be much more use to his father if he joined him on the campaign in Friesland than if he went crusading in the Balkans.

The count of Ostrevant took advice from one of his close companions-in-arms, a Hainault esquire named Fier-à-Bras, or the Bastard of Vertaing. He encouraged the count to accede to his father's wishes and abandon any thought of going on crusade. He also suggested that the count should go to England and seek permission from Richard II to recruit knights, esquires and archers to go with him on the Frisian campaign. He added that if the count could recruit the earl of Derby, the expedition would be more distinguished and of greater renown: such, evidently, was Henry's reputation in Europe at this time. In the event, the count sent Fier-à-Bras to England; he approached Henry of Derby, whose initial reaction was favourable.[53] At the same time, however, the duke of Guelders was in England, and Gaunt asked him what the proposed expedition to Friesland was all about. The duke replied that it was likely to be dangerous and that Friesland was not a 'terre de conquest' – the same phrase that Froissart has Gloucester use about Ireland. The duke went on to enlarge on the point with his description of Friesland that has already been discussed.[54] The duke may have had his own reasons for seeking to dissuade Henry from participating in the expedition – the successful imposition of the authority of the count of Holland north of the Zuyder Zee was not necessarily in his interests – but Gaunt took what he said seriously, and together with the king persuaded Henry not to join the expedition. Again, Froissart uses the episode to point the moral that the wise father counsels his son against participation in a rash enterprise, but Froissart's moral purpose is not inconsistent with the truth of

---

[49] *Archives de l'Orient Latin II* (Paris, 1881), pp. 362–3.
[50] Vaughan, *Philip the Bold*, p. 63.
[51] Froissart, *Oeuvres*, XV, 226–8.
[52] P. F. Ainsworth, *Jean Froissart and the Fabric of History* (Oxford, 1990), pp. 209–15.
[53] Froissart, *Oeuvres*, XV, 228–9.
[54] Froissart, *Oeuvres*, XV, 270.

66

his account.[55] Although Fier-à-Bras failed to recruit Henry, he managed to persuade other Englishmen to join the campaign. Froissart says that eight knights and 200 archers agreed to serve; the accounts for the expedition record payment to at least thirty English archers, but there is no record of any Englishman of knightly rank taking part.[56] Thus Henry took no part in either of the expeditions in which the nobility of France and the Low Countries were engaged in 1396. We do not know whether he considered joining the crusade to the Balkans: after Gaunt himself withdrew, he entrusted the leadership of the Lancastrian contingent to his eldest illegitimate son, John Beaufort, rather than to Henry, and there is no evidence that John of Nevers made any approach to Henry. In retrospect Henry no doubt thought he had been lucky: the crusaders were massacred by the Turks at Nicopolis on the Danube and, although nothing is known about Beaufort's part in the battle (if indeed he was there), John of Nevers was captured and ransomed and Ralph Percy, the younger son of the earl of Northumberland, was killed.[57] Gaunt's role in Henry's plans in 1396 is probably crucial. Henry was his only son and heir; his grandson, the future Henry V, was only nine or ten years of age, and Gaunt probably believed that as he himself approached old age the risks to the Lancastrian inheritance if Henry were to be killed on campaign overseas were unacceptably high.

Henry was no doubt disappointed that his father had discouraged him from going to Friesland, though Froissart's hostile portrait of the duke of Guelders may owe more to the fact that the count of Hainault and Holland was his patron and he presented the Frisian expedition in a rather more favourable light than was probably justified. The outcome of the expedition, and of those that followed it in 1398, 1399, 1400 and 1401, suggests that the duke of Guelders' reservations about campaigning there were justified. Albert and his son enjoyed some immediate success, partly by exploiting the rivalry among the Frisian nobility, but the count's power in northeast Friesland was extinguished by 1399, and in the following year he lost control of all the land to the east of the Lauwers. Eventually only Stavoren, on the Zuyder Zee, remained in the hands of men loyal to the count, and that too fell to the Frisians in 1414.[58] Although Albert was prepared to campaign more regularly and to devote more resources to imposing his authority in Friesland than Richard II in Ireland, the parallel between the two is evident. In the end, the duke of Guelders' opinion that Friesland was not a land of conquest proved correct, as did Gloucester's similar remark about Ireland. The outcome of the various campaigns in Friesland suggests that Henry would have won little fame by taking part in them, and it is significant that as far as we

---

[55] Froissart, *Oeuvres*, XV, 270–2.

[56] Verwijs, *Oorlogen*, pp. 12–16.

[57] Palmer, *England, France and Christendom*, pp. 204–6; Goodman, *John of Gaunt*, pp. 202–3; A. S. Atiya, *The Crusade of Nicopolis* (London, 1934), pp. 155–6.

[58] Verwijs, *Oorlogen*, pp. xiii–cxlviii.

know he never, after he became king, contemplated taking a royal expedition to Ireland.[59]

By taking no part in campaigns that were likely to bring him little profit or renown, Henry ensured that his chivalric reputation remained high; at the time of his banishment in 1398 some of the nobles at Richard II's court believed he would have little trouble finding campaigns in Europe that he could join. They pointed out that he had already travelled to Prussia and the Holy Land, and that his sisters were the queens of Castile and Portugal, whose nobility might welcome him and encourage him to join a crusade against the Moslem kingdom of Granada. They also thought he might revive his plan to join the count of Ostrevant in a campaign against the rebels in Friesland. 'He cannot fail of doing well, wherever he goes,' the nobles supposedly concluded.[60]

As it turned out, however, Henry spent his exile in Paris, under the surveillance of the French court, though he evidently felt restless there. He responded eagerly to Jean de Boucicaut's invitation to join an expedition he was planning against the Turks on the Hungarian border. He sent one his knights (probably Sir Thomas Dymmock) to England to seek Gaunt's consent for his participation in the expedition, but Froissart suggests that Gaunt advised him not to go and commented instead that he should visit his sisters in Castile and Portugal. Dymmock also brought word back to Henry that his father's physicians believed he had not long to live, and this news was perhaps decisive in Henry's decision not to join Boucicaut's expedition.[61]

Thus when Henry took the throne in 1399, he already had an established reputation in both England and western Europe as a chivalric warrior, and his reputation probably made his acceptance as king, both in England and by the courts of western Europe, easier than if he had been an unknown nobleman of no fame. He had been fortunate to enjoy, in his years of greatest vigour, the freedom to acquire fame in theatres of war overseas. As long as his father lived, he had no responsibility for a great inheritance, and he played only a marginal part in affairs of state in England. His father may have exercised some paternal caution in advising him against joining expeditions that looked unprofitable or unduly risky, but Gaunt also showed some paternal generosity in helping to finance Henry's two major expeditions in 1390 and 1392–3. Henry himself had to find little more than one-fifth of the cost of both his expeditions, with much of his father's contribution probably coming from the payment he had received in 1389

[59] A. Cosgrove, 'England and Ireland, 1399–1447', in *A New History of Ireland II: Medieval Ireland 1169–1534*, ed. A. Cosgrove (Oxford, 1993), pp. 525–7; B. Blacker, 'A Lancastrian Prince in Ireland', *History Ireland* 6 (1998), 22–6.

[60] Froissart, *Oeuvres*, XVI, 107–8.

[61] Froissart, *Oeuvres*, XVI, 132–3; Lalande, *Boucicaut*, pp. 82–4.

from the king of Castile in return for Gaunt's renouncing his claim to the Castilian throne.[62]

Henry's career before 1399 allows us to draw some conclusions about why young men of noble rank both participated in and abstained from the campaigns that took place in the 1390s and for which the leaders recruited throughout western Europe. The crusade remained an attractive ideal, and the trappings of chivalry with which the Teutonic Knights surrounded their campaigns in the difficult and unprofitable terrain of northeast Europe attracted young nobles to a theatre of war that otherwise offered little. Henry V was to demonstrate in 1415 that warfare against the French could still attract the enthusiastic participation of English nobles and knights, and the account Froissart gives of the battle of Otterburn in 1388 suggests that the northern border was still regarded as a theatre where nobles might win renown through their chivalric deeds.[63] Yet if France, Scotland and the crusade were attractive venues for the chivalric warrior, it is equally clear from the debates at the English court in the mid-1390s recounted by Froissart that there were venues that were regarded as unattractive. They were unattractive partly because of their danger, but mainly, if the dukes of Gloucester and Guelders are to be believed, because the kind of warfare a young noble might expect to encounter was not the kind that would bring him profit and renown. Fame might be found in France or Scotland, Prussia or Barbary, but not in the hills and bogs of Ireland or the marshes and secret places of Friesland. Neither the ideology of the crusade nor the trappings of chivalry were pressed into service to make campaigning in these lands popular with the young martial nobility of western Europe.

After Henry's accession to the throne, however, the cares of kingship, and the breakdown of his health that became increasingly apparent after 1409, gradually tarnished his chivalric image, to his own evident frustration and, perhaps, to that sense of disappointment with Henry as king that some contemporaries evidently felt. At the outset of his reign, his vigour and presence of mind were well demonstrated in his prompt and effective reaction to the rebellion of the earls in January 1400.[64] His expedition to Scotland, later the same year, began with the kind of rhetoric his subjects perhaps expected from him: he came before parliament in November 1399 and, having declared that God of his grace had sent him into the realm and placed him in his present estate for the safeguarding of the realm, he announced his intention to lead an expedition to Scotland. He assembled a large army at York on Midsummer Day 1400: it consisted for the most part of the king's retainers, many of whom were duchy of Lancaster servants

---

[62] Goodman, *John of Gaunt*, p. 147; *Expeditions to Prussia*, ed. Toulmin-Smith, pp. xlvii, lxxxvi–lxxxvii.

[63] *Chroniques de J. Froissart*, ed. Luce *et al.*, XV, 119–74.

[64] A. Rogers, 'Henry IV and the Revolt of the Earls, 1400', *History Today* 18 (1968), 277–83.

and retainers, and some had served with Henry on his expedition in the 1390s. The expedition, however, ran up against problems of money and supplies: it did not reach Edinburgh until 18 August, and with the town well defended Henry decided not to risk a siege that might drag on over the winter, and he returned to Newcastle.[65] The campaign demonstrated all too clearly the constraints under which Henry now had to conduct his military operations. He depended for finance on parliamentary grants, and for military service not just upon his loyal Lancastrian servants but upon a wider body of men, many of whom were ready to desert when they found the going difficult.

Henry never campaigned again in Scotland; nor, despite declarations of intent and preparations to do so from time to time, did he ever lead an expedition to France or Gascony. His spirit remained willing and warlike, but after 1405 his health so weakened that he was not physically up to campaigning either in the British Isles or in France.[66] He still retained affectionate memories of his time in Prussia, and this helped to oil the wheels of diplomacy with the Hanse towns. In August 1409 he apparently told envoys from Thorn, Elbing and Danzig that he felt more at ease with the Grand Master of the Teutonic Knights and in his lands than anywhere else, while in the following year, interviewing an envoy from Prussia at Eltham, he was reported to have said that he would favour the Grand Master above all, for he was 'a child of Prussia' ('ich bin eyn kint der von Preusen').[67] To an extent, this is merely the politeness and flattery of diplomacy, but it also suggests a certain regretful nostalgia for what he had achieved in his youth. After he came to the throne he was never able to live up to the chivalric reputation he had gained as a young man with few responsibilities. In another sense, however, his expeditions in the 1390s were to prove of enduring value, in that the ties of service he formed then provided him with a nucleus of loyal supporters who served him well for much of his reign and who helped to underpin the Lancastrian regime.

Foremost among these men were Sir Thomas Erpingham, Sir Thomas Rempston, Sir Thomas Haseldene, John Norbury, the Waterton brothers Hugh, John, and Robert, and, of course, Francis Court. Erpingham, who was appointed Henry's chamberlain and Warden of the Cinque Ports at the beginning of the reign, was the man Henry chiefly relied upon to maintain Lancastrian influence in East Anglia, where both the Mowbray and Mortimer families had substantial estates. Sir Thomas Rempston, appointed constable

---

[65] A. L. Brown, 'The English Campaign in Scotland, 1400', in *British Government and Administration: Studies Presented to S. B. Chrimes*, ed. H. Hearder and H. R. Loyn (Cardiff, 1974), pp. 40–54.

[66] The best recent discussion of this subject is P. McNiven, 'The Problem of Henry IV's Health', *EHR* 100 (1985), 747–72 (pp. 761–72). See also Biggs in this volume.

[67] *Die Recesse und Andere Akten der Hansetage von 1256–1430* 5 (Leipzig, 1880), pp. 479, 493; see also Wylie, *Henry IV*, IV, 8–9, cited by Du Boulay, 'Expeditions', p. 153.

of the Tower of London after Henry's accession, performed a similar role in Nottinghamshire, and Sir Thomas Haseldene in Cambridgeshire, while the Waterton family were a key bastion of Lancastrian support in Yorkshire. John Norbury, whom Henry appointed Treasurer at the beginning of the reign, had few obvious qualifications for the post: almost certainly, his close relationship with Henry was the main reason for his appointment. He and Henry had fought together before Vilnius, and Henry was godfather to one of his children.[68] The ties of loyalty and service that Henry formed during his expeditions as a young man proved enduring, despite his illness and in face of some disappointed expectations of him after he became king. These bonds of loyalty proved their value during Henry's exile in 1398–9, and, perhaps more significantly, when he was faced during his reign with disaffection and rebellion. For some members of his affinity, the fame and reputation he had acquired as a young man endured through the very different experiences of his reign.

---

[68] See, e.g., T. John, 'Sir Thomas Erpingham, East Anglian Society and the Dynastic Revolution of 1399', *Norfolk Archaeology* 35 (1970), 96–108; S. J. Payling, *Political Society in Lancastrian England: The Greater Gentry of Nottinghamshire* (Oxford, 1991); M. Barber, 'John Norbury (c.1350–1414): An Esquire of Henry IV', *EHR* 68 (1953), 66–76.

5

Scotland, the Percies and the Law in 1400

Cynthia J. Neville

In the summer of 1400, less than a year after his accession to the English throne, King Henry IV embarked on a hugely expensive invasion of Scotland at the head of an army that has been described as 'one of the largest ever assembled in medieval England'.[1] The expedition was in many respects a model of military expertise, involving careful planning and the deployment of some 15,000 fighting men, several convoys of ships out of ports of the South, the East, London, the North and even Ireland, and several hundred administrative personnel.[2] Rather surprisingly, the invasion attracted little comment from chroniclers: a reflection, no doubt, of its utter lack of success in accomplishing anything of moment. Thomas Walsingham, normally a voluble and well-informed commentator,[3] dismissed the expedition in a single sentence.[4] Even Adam Usk, who was well disposed to Henry IV in the opening years of the reign,[5] could muster little more than a few desultory comments about the king's great undertaking, though he did take the trouble to chastise the Scots for refusing to fight fairly.[6] The chroniclers' muted response to the expedition of 1400 is all the more notable in that it stands in marked contrast to the lengthy descriptions made of the great campaign to Scotland led by Henry's predecessor, Richard II, in 1385.[7]

Devoid of military glory the expedition certainly was; and like their medieval predecessors, historians of later medieval England have given it

---

[1] A. L. Brown, 'The English Campaign in Scotland, 1400', in *British Government and Administration: Studies Presented to S. B. Chrimes*, ed. H. Hearder and H. R. Loyn (Cardiff, 1974), pp. 40–54 (p. 44). I wish to acknowledge the financial support of the Social Sciences and Humanities Research Council of Canada in the preparation of this article, and to thank the participants in the Henry IV Symposium for their comments and suggestions for improving this paper.

[2] Wylie, *Henry IV*, I, 131–5.

[3] A. Gransden, *Historical Writing in England II: c. 1307 to the Early Sixteenth Century* (London, 1982), pp. 123–9; *Chrons. Rev.*, pp. 4–6.

[4] 'Annales', p. 333; *Historia Anglicana*, II, 246.

[5] Gransden, *Historical Writing in England II*, pp. 177, 183–4; *Chrons. Rev.*, p. 6.

[6] *Chronicle of Adam Usk*, pp. 98–101. See also 'A Northern Chronicle', in C. L. Kingsford, *English Historical Literature in the Fifteenth Century* (New York, 1913), p. 280.

[7] *Historia Anglicana*, II, 131–2; *Knighton's Chron.*, pp. 334–7; *Polychronicon Ranulphi Higden monachi Cestrensis*, ed. J. R. Lumby, 9 vols. (London, 1865–6), IX, 62–5; *Westminster Chron.*, pp. 124–31.

short shrift. King Henry IV's indefatigable biographer, James Wylie, could not find anything positive to say about it, noting merely that Henry IV succeeded in 'bringing nothing from his Scottish raid but confusion and discredit'.[8] The only detailed study of the campaign, that of A. L. Brown, describes the expedition more harshly still as 'utterly futile', a 'disastrous failure', and 'unnecessary'.[9]

Studies of the early years of Henry IV's reign have focused variously on the king's attempts to justify his claim to the throne, the establishment of the new dynasty and the unsettling rebellion of 1403 led by members of the Percy family.[10] Indeed, many scholars suggest that it is almost impossible to portray accurately the early years of the reign without taking into consideration Henry's relations with the Percies, and the arguments of two of the other authors in this collection reflect this view.[11] The chronicler John Hardyng's shrewd (if retrospective) observation that the Percies 'have the hertes of the people by north and ever had'[12] is an entirely appropriate paradigm by which to problematize the challenge to his authority that Henry IV encountered in the Percy family in the opening months of his rule. This essay argues, however, that the king perceived Percy power in the North to be a potentially more dangerous threat than mere mistrust of a very powerful magnatial family might have warranted. One of the aims of this essay is to suggest that while the king was aware of the debt of gratitude he owed the Percy family for supporting his seizure of the throne, there were specific aspects of Percy strength in the border region that were of immediate and pressing concern to him. It seeks further to establish a link between Henry's perceptions of magnate power in the northernmost regions of the kingdom and the motives that informed his decision to mount an invasion of Scotland. Such a link may be found in contemporary understandings of the role of the king in the

[8] Wylie, *Henry IV*, I, 140.

[9] Brown, 'The English Campaign in Scotland', pp. 40, 54. Similarly bland opinions of the invasion from the perspective of Scottish historians are expressed in R. Nicholson, *Scotland: The Later Middle Ages* (Edinburgh, 1978), p. 219, and A. J. Macdonald, *Border Bloodshed: Scotland, England and France at War, 1369–1403* (East Linton, 2000), pp. 139–40.

[10] The literature here is considerable, but see esp. P. McNiven, 'Legitimacy and Consent: Henry IV and the Lancastrian Title, 1399–1406', *Mediaeval Studies* 44 (1982), 470–88, together with the many sources cited therein; Wylie, *Henry IV*, I, 47–9; J. H. Ramsay, *Lancaster and York*, 2 vols. (Oxford, 1892), I, 1–68; A. L. Brown, 'The Reign of Henry IV', in *Fifteenth-Century England 1399–1509: Studies in Politics and Society*, ed. S. B. Chrimes, C. D. Ross and R. A. Griffiths (Manchester, 1972), pp. 1–28; D. Biggs, 'The Reign of Henry IV: The Revolution of 1399 and the Establishment of the Lancastrian Regime', in *Fourteenth Century England I*, ed. N. Saul (Woodbridge, 2000), pp. 195–210. For the rebellion of 1403, see esp. J. M. W. Bean, 'Henry IV and the Percies', *History* 44 (1959), 212–27, with the sources cited therein. For an interesting revisionist perspective on the early Lancastrian years see P. Strohm, *England's Empty Throne: Usurpation and the Language of Legitimation, 1399–1422* (London, 1998), esp. pp. 1–31 and 173–95.

[11] See the essays by Mark Arvanigian and Andy King below.

[12] *Hardyng*, p. 378.

proper governance of his realm and more particularly of the king's exclusive authority to make, change and execute the law. Especially pertinent in this context was the existence of a system of law peculiar to the border counties that flourished in Henry's time. By the year 1400 the customs and practices that collectively made up border law constituted a highly sophisticated as well as a crucial feature of English domestic and foreign policy. And more closely than with anyone else, the operation of border law around the year 1400 was identified with the Percy men in their capacities as Wardens of the Northern Marches.

The rise of the Percy family to political and social predominance in the North during the later fourteenth century has been amply illustrated and need not be rehearsed afresh here.[13] Equally compellingly argued has been the importance of the role of the first earl of Northumberland in the defence of the North. As far back as 1917 Rachel Reid commented on the crown's utter dependence on 'over-mighty subjects' to keep the marches secure.[14] Forty years later Robin Storey echoed Reid's arguments when he set out to document the military authority in the border lands of Henry, earl of Northumberland and his son Hotspur,[15] and he and others have remarked in a variety of subsequent works on the ability of northern magnate families such as the Percies and Nevilles to control the course of the Anglo-Scottish conflict that was so prominent a feature of fourteenth-century politics.[16]

Less well explored, however, is the legal authority that the magnate families, including, and perhaps especially, the Percies exercised both in the northern counties generally as well as within the territories designated as the Anglo-Scottish marches in particular.[17] The latter half of the fourteenth

---

[13] See J. M. W. Bean, *The Estates of the Percy Family 1416–1537* (Oxford, 1958), pp. 2–22; R. Lomas, *A Power in the Land: The Percys* (East Linton, 1999), pp. 39–79; J. A. Tuck, 'Richard II and the Border Magnates', *Northern History* 3 (1968), 27–52; A. Tuck, *Richard II and the English Nobility* (London, 1973), pp. 201–2; R. L. Storey, 'The North of England', in *Fifteenth-Century England*, ed. Chrimes, Ross and Griffiths, pp. 129–44 (pp. 130–2).

[14] R. R. Reid, 'The Office of Warden of the Marches: Its Origin and Early History', *EHR* 32 (1917), 479–96 (p. 488).

[15] R. L. Storey, 'The Wardens of the Marches of England towards Scotland, 1377–1489', *EHR* 72 (1957), 593–615 (p. 602).

[16] P. McNiven, 'The Scottish Policy of the Percies and the Rebellion of 1403', *BJRL* 62 (1979), 498–530; Bean, 'Henry IV and the Percies', pp. 212–14; Storey, 'The North of England', p. 133; R. L. Storey, *The End of the House of Lancaster* (Gloucester, 1986), pp. 108–9; Tuck, 'Richard II and the Border Magnates', p. 30; Lomas, *A Power in the Land*, pp. 71–9; A. Tuck, 'The Percies and the Community of Northumberland in the Later Fourteenth Century', in *War and Border Societies in the Middle Ages*, ed. A. Tuck and A. Goodman (London, 1992), pp. 178–95 (pp. 182–91).

[17] The medieval marches of England included the coastal lands situated between Newcastle and Berwick, as well as Coquetdale, North and South Tynedale, most of the county of Cumberland and parts of Westmorland. See T. Hodgkin, *The Wardens of the Northern Marches* (London, 1908), pp. 4–11.

century witnessed the rapid development of the system of rules, regulations and procedures that governed the operation of the northern tribunals which, from the time of Edward I, dealt with cross-border crime as well as a host of offences arising out of the interminable war with Scotland. In tandem with the increasing military authority that they exercised in the wardenial commissions by which the crown engaged their services, Henry Percy and his son came to play a leading role in the shaping of border legal procedures. And it was the flexing of the powerful Northumberland family's muscles in the realm of law-making and law-keeping, just as much as it was their extraordinary military might, that troubled Henry IV in the opening years of his reign.

When the crown first appointed Wardens of the Marches of England towards Scotland following the outbreak of war in 1296, the authority and responsibilities assigned to these officials were exclusively military. They were charged with overseeing the provisioning of the garrisons established at key border fortresses, with defending these strongholds against Scottish incursions, and with organizing regular arrays of fighting men. The renewal of hostilities with the Scots in the 1330s after the so-called 'peace' of 1328[18] ensured that the office would become permanent, and by the middle years of the fourteenth century the wardens had come to play an indispensable role not only in the defence of the North but increasingly, too, in the maintenance of law and order there.[19] The reign of Edward III in particular was a period of rapid development of the warden's office. The treaty of Berwick of 1357, which marked the release of the Scottish king David II from captivity in England, was accompanied by the issue of wholly new commissions to the Wardens of the East and West Marches, Henry Percy and Ralph Neville. Here, they were directed to seize, imprison and punish anyone who violated the newly restored peace throughout the marches,[20] and from the late 1350s on the wardens presided over a regularly summoned series of tribunals known as days of march or days of truce. Just a decade later, in 1367, the English warden together with his Scottish counterpart drafted the first of a continuous series of indentures, which set out in increasingly elaborate fashion the procedures that wardens and conservators of the truce would employ in the settlement of cross-border disputes.[21] By the closing decades of the fourteenth century the wardens had established themselves as the

---

[18] The treaty of Edinburgh–Northampton, sealed in 1328, marked the end of the first phase of the Scottish Wars of Independence. The 'peace' that it established was of brief duration. See Nicholson, *Scotland: The Later Middle Ages*, pp. 120–2.

[19] Reid, 'The Office of Warden of the Marches', pp. 481–2. For much in the following paragraphs, see C. J. Neville, *Violence, Custom and Law: The Anglo-Scottish Border Lands in the Later Middle Ages* (Edinburgh, 1998), pp. 15–95; C. J. Neville, 'Keeping the Peace on the Northern Marches in the Later Middle Ages', *EHR* 109 (1994), 1–25.

[20] *Rot. Scot.*, I, 808, 811.

[21] *Foedera*, 10 vols. (The Hague, 1739–45), III(ii), 137–8.

unrivalled leaders of northern political and military society, and had become the 'over-mighty subjects' that so alarmed nineteenth- and early twentieth-century historians.

The growth of the military and political authority of the wardenial office was paralleled by similar developments in the legal powers they exercised within the territories of the English marches proper. For most of the four-teenth century the English crown proved successful in limiting the authority and powers of these officials both in geographical as well as jurisdictional terms in matters that did not involve the war with Scotland. Thus, the wardens operated only within the marches proper (although contemporaries often understood these to be coterminous with the counties of Northumber-land, Cumberland and Westmorland). As Rachel Reid cautiously noted many years ago, the wardens' commissions granted them 'all the powers necessary to the military governor of a frontier district', but little more.[22] In the early years of the office, moreover, the judicial authority exercised by these royal officials was carefully circumscribed and only jealously delegated: thus, in 1323 Andrew Harcla was publicly humiliated and put to death as a traitor when he presumed to effect a truce with the Scots without first securing the express consent of his king.[23]

The ongoing war with the Scots, however, made of the northern border lands a particularly troublesome region of the kingdom. By the middle of the fourteenth century the wardens were regularly convening courts within the English marches themselves for the trial and punishment of English subjects who committed breach of the many truces that maintained a fragile peace in the North. Almost inevitably, the wardens became closely involved in the maintenance of law and order more generally in the border lands. Certainly, their commissions continued to emphasize the specific limitation of their authority to matters involving the Scots and their power to punish offences done against the truce,[24] and procedurally their courts remained distinct from those of the common law. Juries of presentment in the later fourteenth century, for example, still consisted of mixed panels of English and Scots in accordance with ancient border custom.[25] But little by little the wardens' courts began to encroach on the business of the common law courts, at least in the three northernmost counties of the realm. The trend was aggravated by the crown's failure to draw a clear line between the jurisdiction of the wardens' authority and that of the justices of assize, particularly in the

---

[22] Reid, 'The Office of Wardens of the Marches', p. 483.

[23] M. H. Keen, 'Treason Trials under the Law of Arms', *TRHS* 5th s. 12 (1962), 85–103 (pp. 88–91); J. G. Bellamy, *The Law of Treason in England in the Later Middle Ages* (London, 1970), pp. 52–3; J. Mason, 'Sir Andrew de Harcla, Earl of Carlisle', *Transactions of the Cumberland and Westmorland Antiquarian and Archaeological Society* n.s. 29 (1929), 121–35.

[24] See the wardenial courts held at Carlisle in the 1350s: *CPR, 1348–50*, p. 588; *CPR, 1350–4*, p. 202.

[25] See E 13/71, mm. 41, 41d.

matter of felonious and other serious offences.[26] In the closing decades of the fourteenth century the disruptions caused by Scottish raids became so intense that royal justices sometimes refused to travel beyond Yorkshire, and in their absence the wardens of the marches assumed increasing responsibility for the trial and punishment of a wide variety of offences occurring within the marches. Conflicts between jurisdictions arose, for example when the sheriff of York refused to deliver to another official a man indicted in Henry Percy's wardenial court,[27] or when a plaintiff purchased a writ of *certiorari* to remove to the King's Bench a case that had originated in a wardenial court.[28] The lines between the jurisdictions were further blurred when a single man operated in a dual capacity as justice of the peace and warden. Henry Percy was such a man: Richard II repeatedly appointed him to the peace sessions of Northumberland, Cumberland and Westmorland while he held the king's commission as warden.[29] The period of intense rivalry between the wardens of the marches on the one hand and the justices of the peace and of assize on the other belonged to the fifteenth century rather than to the fourteenth, but already in the reign of Richard II contest between the jurisdictions had begun.

Under the rule of a strong king jurisdictional competition between the common-law and other courts was not in and of itself problematic. Edward III in particular had been well aware of the benefit to his own coffers of the flexibility of civil process in the area of merchant law,[30] and both the king and his legal counsellors viewed the growth alongside the common law of the principles and procedures of the prerogative or conciliar courts of equity (notably the Court of Chancery) as complementary to contemporary notions of regal authority.[31] Edward III had nevertheless proved extraordinarily cautious in meting out to all his justices, common and conciliar, the power to make or to alter the law, or to exercise the power of life and limb over his subjects. The most striking example of the crown's reluctance to delegate full authority to hear and determine the most serious of offences (that is, those involving the penalty of death) was the series of experiments undertaken with the office of keeper of the peace, which Bertha Putnam and, more recently, Anthony Musson and Mark Ormrod have described in some

---

[26] Neville, *Violence, Custom and Law*, pp. 57–60, 84–8.

[27] C 54/235, m. 5.

[28] C 47/22/7 (67).

[29] *CPR, 1381–5*, pp. 85, 248, 253; *CPR, 1385–9*, p. 81; *CPR, 1388–92*, pp. 345, 346; *CPR, 1391–6*, pp. 292, 437, 727; *CPR, 1396–9*, pp. 98, 237.

[30] For general discussions of the relations between merchant law and common law in the medieval period see J. H. Baker, *The Legal Profession and the Common Law* (London, 1986), pp. 341–68; T. F. T. Plucknett, *A Concise History of the Common Law*, 5th edn (London, 1956), pp. 657–65.

[31] J. H. Baker, *An Introduction to English Legal History* (London, 1971), pp. 38–44, 54–6; A. Harding, *The Law Courts of Medieval England* (London, 1973), pp. 99–100; T. Haskett, 'The Medieval English Court of Chancery', *Law and History Review* 14 (1996), 246–80.

detail.[32] Edward III was a jealous guardian of royal prerogatives of all kinds, and the keen interest he displayed in the exercise of royal authority in the persons of his justices was but one manifestation of the deep respect for the dignity of the royal image that he simultaneously safeguarded and celebrated throughout his reign.[33] The steady growth of the office of warden and the increasing role of the men who held this office in the administration of the law in the North were challenges that King Edward III, however, proved more than competent to balance.

Richard II, troubled almost from the outset of his reign with a variety of problems, proved much less adept at defending the royal prerogative from those who would encroach upon it. As noted above, the 1380s and 1390s saw clashes of jurisdiction between common-law officials and the wardens of the marches; when such conflicts occurred it was frequently the latter who asserted their authority over the former. From the mid-1380s, moreover, real and effective governance of the northern border lands was in practice almost exclusively the preserve of the Percy family, whose prominence in the region was ultimately acknowledged when, in 1377, Henry Percy was created earl of Northumberland. Other families, it is true, were active in the borders on behalf of the crown, chief among them the Nevilles and members of their following, the Dacres, Cliffords and Greystokes. But even during the brief period in the early 1380s, when Richard II's uncle, John of Gaunt, governed the North in the king's name as lieutenant,[34] Percy supremacy was only temporarily eclipsed. Royal efforts to 'play one border family against another'[35] by awarding the office of warden to a bewildering variety of men who knew little about the complex ways in which the Anglo-Scottish conflict shaped the politics of the region were eventually abandoned as unworkable.

Despite the crown's appointment of Gaunt, Henry Percy maintained a firm hand in the resolution of cross-border disputes, even if his actions were played out behind the scenes. The duke of Lancaster presided on behalf of his king at elaborately staged days of march with representatives of the Scottish

[32] B. H. Putnam, 'The Transformation of the Keepers of the Peace into the Justices of the Peace, 1327–1380', *TRHS* 4th s. 12 (1929), 19–48; B. H. Putnam, 'Shire Officials: Keepers of the Peace and Justices of the Peace', in *The English Government at Work, 1327–1336*, ed. J. F. Willard, W. A. Morris, J. R. Strayer and W. H. Dunham, 3 vols. (Cambridge, 1950), III, 185–217; A. Musson and W. M. Ormrod, *The Evolution of English Justice: Law, Politics and Society in the Fourteenth Century* (London, 1999), pp. 50–4.
[33] W. M. Ormrod, *The Reign of Edward III: Crown and Political Society in England 1327–1377* (London, 1990), pp. 46–50, 54–6.
[34] Gaunt was appointed lieutenant in 1379. He left the North to go on campaign in 1384. *Rot. Scot.*, II, 5; Neville, *Violence, Custom and Law*, pp. 67–8; Tuck, 'Richard II and the Border Magnates', pp. 39–42; *Westminster Chron.*, pp. 28–9, 50–1.
[35] Tuck, 'Richard II and the Border Magnates', p. 27. The careers of some of the Percy followers in this period are discussed in Andy King's essay, below, and in Tuck, 'The Percies and the Community of Northumberland', pp. 184–7.

crown at Berwick in 1380 and again a year later at Ebchester,[36] where indentures of truce were sealed and subsequently proclaimed as far away as Ireland.[37] Yet there can be little doubt that in the day-to-day administration of border-related business it was the wardens and the conservators of the truce who were above all responsible for the shaping of legal practice. Thus, Gaunt's rare and elaborately ceremonial days of march were far outnumbered by smaller, more frequent, if less grandiose, meetings in which the earl of Northumberland played a leading role in the settlement of outstanding grievances. It was Henry Percy, for example, who assumed responsibility for the payment of damages awarded to the Scottish warden when one of Gaunt's retainers allowed his men to commit an assault on the town of Roxburgh; and it was Percy who oversaw the mundane tasks of summoning plaintiffs and defendants and organizing panels of jurors for sessions of the border tribunals.[38]

Despite concerted royal efforts to offset Percy dominance by appointing outsiders to key wardenial positions, for most of the 1380s the earl of Northumberland remained instrumental in the elaboration of the procedures employed at border law, at times assuming a level of authority that Richard II's grandfather would have considered quite unacceptable. In 1385, for example, acting under no authority save his own experience Percy arranged a meeting with Archibald Douglas, lord of Galloway, not within his own East March (to which he had been appointed as warden in August 1384),[39] but at the River Esk on the West March, now governed by his rival John, Lord Neville.[40] Here, both men sealed an indenture of 'special Trewe and Assurance' for the West March, which was, as Anthony Tuck noted, as much a private agreement between border magnates as it was a formal truce.[41] The contents of the agreement make it clear that Percy had no qualms about deploying to the fullest extent his newly recovered authority in the border lands, and even about exercising quasi-royal powers. Thus, he undertook to release into Douglas's hand Scottish prisoners then in his custody (as well as their pledges) and, further, to declare that in future the death penalty would be imposed on all persons who committed cross-border theft in breach of the truce.[42] In the later years of

---

[36] *Rot. Scot.*, II, 29–31, 38–9.

[37] *Rot. Scot.*, II, 41.

[38] E 101/620/18; E 364/17, mm. 1d, 3; E 101/39/30; *Rot. Scot.*, II, 52, 53; Neville, *Violence, Custom and Law*, p. 75. See also Henry Percy's strict injunctions to his man, Sir William Swynburn, to be sure to attend forthcoming march tribunals, discussed in Neville, *Violence, Custom and Law*, pp. 86–7.

[39] *Rot. Scot.*, II, 65–6.

[40] *Rot. Scot.*, II, 66, 70.

[41] Tuck, 'Richard II and the Border Magnates', p. 33. The text of the truce is found at *Foedera*, III(iii), 182; *Rot. Scot.*, II, 73. See also C 71/67, m. 4.

[42] *Foedera*, III(iii), 182; *Rot. Scot.*, II, 73. See also C 71/67, m. 4; Carlisle, Cumbria Record Office DRC, 1/ 2, fol. 133 (Register of Bishop Thomas Appleby of Carlisle).

the fourteenth century, moreover, the earl of Northumberland was still pursuing what might be termed a private war with the Douglas family in the Jedburgh area, seeking to preserve the revenues generated by the castle, constabulary and rich forest lands that had been granted to his grandfather by Edward III in 1334,[43] and had single-handedly launched raids into Scotland in defence of those lands.[44] It is difficult to imagine bolder statements of Percy's right to define the substance of border legal procedure and to control its practice. Even Richard II thought it advisable to limit the extent of his warden's actions in the regulation of legal matters in the North. Commissions issued after 1385 explicitly denied him the authority to release prisoners without royal warrant.

Percy involvement in the regulation of border-related legal matters continued into the 1390s. Days of march were convened at least annually between 1391 and 1396 while the earl of Northumberland was Warden of the East March, and his experienced hand in the settlement of disputes relating to a host of truce-time violations is evident in a variety of extant record materials. In 1392, for example, Percy ordered the seizure of the goods of a group of Scottish merchants in distant Yarmouth in retaliation for the robbery of English merchants in Edinburgh;[45] on two occasions he ordered the construction of lists in Berwick and Rulehaugh in preparation for judicial combats between English and Scottish litigants.[46] By contrast, the earl's exclusion from the wardenial office in the closing years of Richard II's reign also left an indelible mark on the effective resolution of border problems. In 1398 royal agents negotiated with the Scots two indentures of great importance for the future, in that each set out in more detailed fashion than ever before the procedures that would govern acts of cross-border lawlessness in the years to come.[47] The provisions included in the indentures were those that had been developed by Northumberland during his tenure of the warden's office. Moreover, the second document included in its preamble a highly critical assessment of the recent performance of Richard II's officials (none of whom hailed from the North) and urged that henceforth the king ensure that wardens and conservators of the truce be men well versed in the complexities of border legal practice and custom. Just a few months later one of Richard's own nominees to the Wardenship of the East March, the duke of Albemarle, criticized the king for expecting him to govern the region without Percy's assistance and experience, noting that Scottish grievances, too long unresolved, were threatening the peace and

---

[43] *The Percy Cartulary*, ed. M. T. Martin, Surtees Society 117 (Durham, 1911), no. 1070; Bean, *Estates of the Percy Family*, p. 7.

[44] Neville, *Violence, Custom and Law*, p. 66; Macdonald, *Border Bloodshed*, pp. 14, 33, 34, 36–7, 78 and 104.

[45] SC 1/43/45.

[46] E 30/1631; 'Annales', pp. 166–7.

[47] E 39/95/2; *Foedera*, III(iv), 150–1; E 39/95/3; *Foedera*, III(iv), 152–3.

security of the borders.[48] The duke's dire warnings were not mere posturing: the marked decline in extant source materials attesting the smooth operation of border tribunals, so prominent a feature of Henry Percy's period as warden and conservator in the 1380s and earlier 1390s, suggests that the complex business of dispute settlement was all but suspended between 1396 and 1399.[49]

Richard II realized too late that his experimentation with the office of the warden of the marches and his determination to exclude the earl of Northumberland amounted to a grave error both on the diplomatic front and in the maintenance of a semblance of law and order in a dangerously unstable frontier region. His supplanter, Henry of Bolingbroke, was in some senses much wiser. Within five years of his accession Henry IV may well have come to rue his dependence on the support of the earl of Northumberland, but in the earliest weeks of his rule, with the Scots threatening the northernmost reaches of his newly acquired kingdom, he knew that he had little choice but to trust Henry Percy's unrivalled experience in handling a wide variety of border-related matters.

Percy himself can hardly have welcomed the events of the summer and early autumn of 1399 with less enthusiasm than Bolingbroke. There is abundant evidence to suggest that the earl set out with alacrity to reverse the challenge to his power in the North that had been the hallmark of the last years of Richard II's reign. Not least among the many rewards that fell to Percy was his immediate restoration to a pre-eminent position in the regulation of the military and legal affairs of the border lands. As early as 2 August Bolingbroke had appointed him Warden of the West March by means of a ducal commission. Soon after the coronation he was retained for a period of ten years, and the commission was confirmed by royal mandate.[50] The grant of the West March brought with it not only command of the royal fortress of Carlisle, but, equally important, authority once again to exercise extensive legal powers within the march. It was quickly followed by a renewal of the peace commission outwith the march lands of Northumberland, Cumberland and Westmorland and with the earl's appointment to the office of sheriff.[51] With Percy's son Hotspur already in control of the East

---

[48] C 47/22/11(10). This letter should be redated to 11 July 1399: see *Calendar of Documents relating to Scotland, V (Supplementary), A. D. 1108–1516*, ed. G. G. Simpson and J. D. Galbraith (Edinburgh, n.d.), p. 111. Albemarle had been appointed to the Wardenship of the East March in February 1398 and as conservator of the truce in July. *Rot. Scot.*, II, 140, 142. See also Tuck, *Richard II and the English Nobility*, pp. 201–2.

[49] See Neville, *Violence, Custom and Law*, p. 79, and the record evidence discussed there.

[50] E 404/13/46, 108; E 404/15/52; *Rot. Scot.*, II, 151–2. Other grants to Percy are reviewed in Lomas, *A Power in the Land*, pp. 74–5, and McNiven, 'The Scottish Policy of the Percies', p. 499.

[51] *CPR, 1399–1401*, pp. 557, 562, 565 (28 November 1399); *List of Sheriffs for England and Wales*, PRO List and Index Society 9 (repr. London, 1963), p. 98.

March,[52] the way was clear for a resumption of a leading role in law-making that Richard II's policies had threatened to extinguish, and Percy did not hesitate to exercise his legal powers some months later when he oversaw the execution of several border traitors.[53] Indeed, Percy's already imposing authority was further enhanced when he was granted a lifetime appointment as constable of England.[54] The new office added significant dimension to his influence in the border lands, for the constable was not only the highest military official in the realm but also a judicial officer of considerable importance. By the later fourteenth century the constable enjoyed 'permanent authority from the prince to try matters arising out of war by law of arms',[55] and in combining the offices of sheriff, justice of the peace, warden and constable the earl of Northumberland now enjoyed comprehensive jurisdiction over a wide variety of legal business in the border lands. Historians have debated at length the question of whether or not Richard II transformed the Court of Chivalry (over which the constable presided with the marshal) as a political tool,[56] but there can be little doubt that in combination with his other appointments the tremendous authority inherent in the office added considerable *gravitas* to the earl of Northumberland's stature in the border lands.

In the weeks following Bolingbroke's coup the new king had good reason to appreciate Percy's experience in the North, for not surprisingly the Scots sought to turn the unsettled political situation in England to their advantage. The late summer months witnessed an intensification of cross-border reiving, followed in early autumn by a full-scale attack on Wark Castle. The keeper of the castle, Sir Thomas Grey, complained that the fortress had been burned, goods and chattels worth some £2,000 had been destroyed, and members of his family and tenantry compelled to pay a collective ransom of a further £1,000 for their lives. More disturbing still to Bolingbroke was the Scots' refusal to acknowledge him as the new ruler of the English realm. A letter sent on behalf of King Robert III in November 1399 addressed Henry merely as 'duke of Lancaster, earl of Derby and steward of England', and provided only vague reassurances that the current truce would be respected.[57]

[52] Hotspur had been appointed Warden in the East by Richard II in 1396: E 101/73/41, 42; *Rot. Scot.*, II, 119, 130, 131. He was confirmed in the office for a period of ten years in October 1399: E 404/15/37; *Rot. Scot.*, II, 151.
[53] E 404/16/695.
[54] *CPR, 1399–1401*, p. 12. For other grants to the earl in the early months of the new reign see Bean, 'Henry IV and the Percies', p. 220; Wylie, *Henry IV*, IV, 23–6.
[55] M. H. Keen, *The Laws of War in the Late Middle Ages* (London, 1965), p. 27.
[56] Tuck, *Richard II and the English Nobility*, pp. 150–2; G. D. Squibb, *The High Court of Chivalry: A Study of the Civil Law in England* (Oxford, 1959), pp. 17–20; M. Keen, 'The Jurisdiction and Origins of the Constable's Court', in *War and Government in the Middle Ages: Essays in Honour of J. O. Prestwich*, ed. J. Gillingham amd J. C. Holt (Woodbridge, 1984), pp. 159–69 (pp. 159–61).
[57] BL MS Cotton Vespasian F VII, fol. 70, printed in *A Collection of Royal and Historical Letters during the Reign of Henry IV*, ed. F. C. Hingeston, 2 vols. (London, 1860), I, 8–10. The letter

Scholars have traditionally regarded the attack on Wark Castle and Robert III's affront to the new king's dignity as the motives for Henry IV's decision to go to war against the Scots,[58] and subsequent events certainly suggest that Scottish insults were a powerful incentive for the king to abandon détente with the enemy kingdom in favour of open conflict. Yet the same body of evidence is open to more than a single interpretation, as are the king's actions in the months leading up to the campaign. Surviving source materials, in fact, suggest that the expedition to Scotland in the summer of 1400 was the response to a complex state of affairs, and that it represented as much a strike against Percy dominance within the marches of England as it was an assertion to the Scots of the legitimacy of the new Lancastrian dynasty. It is, admittedly, difficult to separate the strands that characterized the various motives that led to war, but it would appear that in Henry IV's estimation most of these were of equal importance.

An expedition against Scotland was first mooted in the new king's first parliament on 10 November 1399, less than a week after Henry had received King Robert III's insulting reply to his request for observance of the current truce. The entry in the parliamentary record is worth citing here at length:

> At the command of the king the earl of Northumberland, constable of England, showed the Lords temporal that, as had been revealed to them earlier, the king intended to march against his Scottish enemies; and some had then said that such a course of action should only be taken with the advice and under the leadership of the said earl, together with the earl of Westmorland, the Marshal of England. The earls nevertheless pleaded that the king make known his will on this matter. Whereupon the lord king himself spoke in full parliament about how God had of his grace sent him into the realm and had raised him to his present estate for the salvation of the said realm, and said that he intended to undertake the expedition in person. Afterwards he ordered the earl of Northumberland to enquire of all the Lords about their will in this matter, all of whom declared themselves willing to consent to the royal will, that is, that the king lead the expedition in the name of God against the great malice and rebellion that the Scots had demonstrated towards him without any deceit or offence on his part. Whereupon the king graciously thanked the Lords in his own words, telling them that despite the risk of expending his own life or blood and for the salvation of his realm he would not desist from undertaking the expedition.[59]

Henry Percy and the king were both clearly in favour of going to war, yet each had his own reasons for ensuring that the expedition receive the

and its consequences are discussed in Brown, 'The English Campaign in Scotland', p. 40; Wylie, *Henry IV*, I, 81.
[58] Brown, 'The English Campaign in Scotland', p. 40; Wylie, *Henry IV*, I, 81–2; Kirby, *Henry IV*, pp. 99–100; Neville, *Violence, Custom and Law*, p. 99.
[59] *Rot. Parl.*, III, 427–8.

sanction of parliament. The earl of Northumberland supported a royal campaign because he had an enormous amount to gain from it. For several years his chief rival on the Scottish side of the border had been Archibald 'the Grim', earl of Douglas, whose reputation as a magnate of unparalleled authority in the marches was recognized throughout both realms. In addition to the many hundreds of men he could call to his service Douglas was the most powerful landowner in southwestern Scotland, and he exercised a virtual monopoly over the Scottish wardenship of the marches.[60] Douglas's authority in the legal sphere, moreover, was subject to fewer limitations than was Percy's: in addition to the border tribunals over which he presided as warden, Douglas exercised broad jurisdiction over the people of south-western Scotland in his own baronial courts.[61]

The scope of Douglas's judicial powers alone was sufficient to arouse Percy jealousy, but there were also more concrete reasons for Northumberland to promote an expedition against Scotland. Percy's possession of the castle, constabulary and forest of Jedburgh, all located firmly within Scottish territory, set him apart from other English magnates and provided him with a justifiable claim to be the sole representative of the English crown within that realm. Already in his own estimation defender of the *res publica* in the North, he also believed that he had an obligation to advance royal interests beyond the border as strenuously as possible. War with Scotland represented a challenge to his landed interest north of the border, but also offered significant opportunities to expand these in the name of the king. A Scottish expedition further promised to offset Percy's concerns about the promotion to positions of prominence and influence of his family's rivals in northern England, the Nevilles. Elsewhere in this volume Mark Arvanigian and Andy King present convincing arguments for seeing in many of Henry IV's northern policies an attempt to counter Percy authority in the border lands by extending royal favour to Ralph Neville, earl of Westmorland, and his adherents. Other evidence demonstrating the king's intentions in this respect is reviewed below. A variety of source materials, therefore, suggests that Henry Percy's motives for supporting the Scottish were both public and private. This combination of interests goes some way towards explaining his actions in the first months of Henry IV's reign.

The king's reasons for mounting a punitive expedition against Scotland were both more numerous and more complex. In the parliament of November 1399 the constable and the marshal were careful to recognize that the decision to go to war belonged ultimately to the king himself. Henry IV must nevertheless have been aware that in practice no campaign could take place

---

[60] M. Brown, *The Black Douglases* (East Linton, 1998), pp. 53–156.

[61] For the authority of baronial courts in late medieval Scotland, see *The Court Book of the Barony of Carnwath 1527–1542*, ed. W. Croft Dickinson, Scottish History Society 3rd s. 29 (Edinburgh, 1937), pp. lxxiv–cxii.

without the support of his most influential northern earls. Insecurity about the nature of his own prerogative, characteristic of so much of the early period of his reign according to some historians, stood in marked contrast with the rule of even his less capable predecessors. The authority of the earl of Northumberland in Anglo-Scottish affairs threatened the very essence of his royal prerogative powers, for contemporary theory held that only a sovereign prince might declare a 'just' war on his enemies.[62] War, moreover, and especially war against the Auld Enemy of Scotland, had a long history in England as a proving ground, a rite of passage, for newly crowned monarchs, and a significance comparable to that which underlay the transformation of a mere man into a crowned and anointed king. Richard II's expedition to Scotland in 1385 had been mounted just a short time after his assumption of personal rule and, as Anthony Tuck has noted, marked 'the attainment, in military terms, of the king's independence'.[63] Edward III had similarly signalled his transition, not only to manhood but more important, to the royal dignity with a military campaign against the Scots. By contrast, Edward II's weakness against the national foe and his failure to engage them in open battle after the English defeat at Bannockburn in 1314 had contributed in no small measure to the perception of his rule as miserable and inglorious. The English royal tradition alone, then, demanded that Henry IV recall the great expeditions of his predecessors.

In related fashion, fourteenth-century English jurisprudence had long upheld the notion that the authority to make and to change the law was the prerogative only of a sovereign prince, especially when such alterations involved the death penalty.[64] Henry IV's predecessor, Richard II, had been especially vocal in his exaltation of the king's position as supreme lawgiver, drawing heavily on the writings of Giles of Rome and other civilian lawyers to support his contentions.[65] In the autumn of 1399, conscious of the uncertainty of his claim to the English throne, Henry IV came to appreciate fully that the judicial, military and diplomatic powers he had bestowed on the earl of Northumberland in his capacity as sheriff, justice of the peace,

---

[62] Keen, *Laws of War*, pp. 63–81; F. H. Russell, *The Just War in the Middle Ages* (Cambridge, 1975), passim.

[63] Tuck, *Richard II and the English Nobility*, p. 97.

[64] H. Cam, *Law-Finders and Law-Makers in Medieval England* (London, 1962), pp. 11–19; T. F. T. Plucknett, *Statutes and their Interpretation in the First Half of the Fourteenth Century* (Cambridge, 1922), pp. vi–xxi; R. C. Van Caenegem, *The Birth of the English Common Law*, 2nd edn (Cambridge, 1988), pp. 1–28; F. Pollock and F. W. Maitland, *The History of English Law before the Time of Edward I*, 2nd edn, 2 vols. (Cambridge, 1968), I, 174–86, 511–18; II, 449–68.

[65] N. Saul, 'The Kingship of Richard II', in *Richard II: The Art of Kingship*, ed. A. Goodman and J. L. Gillespie (Oxford, 1999), pp. 37–57 (pp. 44–6). For the influence of Giles of Rome's treatise, *De regimine principum*, on Richard II see R. H. Jones, *The Royal Policy of Richard II: Absolutism in the Later Middle Ages* (Oxford, 1968), pp. 155–7; S. B. Chrimes, 'Richard II's Questions to the Judges, 1387', *Law Quarterly Review* 72 (1956), 363–90.

warden, constable and chief supporter posed a grave challenge to his own royal authority. It is small wonder, then, that he should have been adamant about leading a Scottish expedition in person.

Henry's uneasiness at the extraordinary position enjoyed by the earl is revealed in the record of events leading up to the expedition; collectively these sources speak to the king's determination to give real and meaningful expression to his newly acquired title. More important, the king's actions point to a clearly articulated intent to assert within the border lands the kind of regal authority that had hitherto been the near-exclusive preserve of Henry Percy. As other historians have argued, the chief beneficiary of Henry IV's designs to minimize Percy influence was Ralph Neville, earl of Westmorland. There were good reasons for this choice. The king's predecessor, Richard II, had already taken preliminary steps to advance Neville interests in the border region generally when he created him earl of Westmorland in 1397, when he began to show favour to Neville litigants in disputes about property, and when he assigned Nevilles to key administrative posts in the northern counties.[66] The family's connections by blood and marriage to the royal family made them natural candidates for advancement, but in 1400 Henry IV also knew that they had no landed interests beyond the Anglo-Scottish border line, and so were not in a position to entertain territorial ambitions there to the same extent as was Henry Percy. In like fashion, extensive though it might be, Ralph Neville's legal authority in the North was exercised exclusively by royal commission. There was little danger – as yet – that the earl of Westmorland would build the kind of legal, military and political base that Henry Percy had built and enjoyed for more than twenty-five years.

On 26 November 1400, therefore, it was Ralph, earl of Westmorland, rather than Henry Percy who was dispatched northwards to treat for a truce 'in the event that our enemies the Scots are willing to treat and come to an agreement with us'.[67] Similarly, a new commission to hold a day of march was directed not to Percy, but to the keeper of Wark Castle, Thomas Grey, the Gascon esquire Jean D'Artois and, significantly, to Master Alan Newark, Bachelor of Civil Laws.[68] The following month the king wrote again to Robert III, noting in a carefully worded text that while he lamented the 'great and horrible' offences that his unfortunate English subjects had suffered of late, he and his council were nevertheless willing to discuss the pacification of the border lands.[69] These were the actions of a king determined to make a

---

[66] See Mark Arvanigian's essay below; also Tuck, 'Richard II and the Border Magnates', pp. 41–2, 50. Ralph Neville was appointed to many of the same peace commissions as Henry Percy (*CPR, 1385–9*, pp. 81, 82, 172), as well as to commissions to enforce the truce in the marches: *Foedera*, III(iv), 78, 99–100, 145; *Rot. Scot.*, II, 118 and 125.

[67] *Rot. Scot.*, II, 152.

[68] *Rot. Scot.*, II, 152–3.

[69] BL MS Cotton Vespasian F VII, fol. 96, printed in *Royal and Historical Letters*, ed. Hingeston, I, 11–14.

public showing of his sovereign powers to enforce the truce, to effect the reparation of laws that had been violated, and to direct the course of diplomatic affairs. Throughout the autumn of 1399, moreover, Henry kept the earl of Northumberland (as well as the latter's son, Hotspur) close to hand at Westminster.[70]

Henry IV took other measures designed to distance himself from the overweening authority of Percy and his family, and it is in this light that his decision to welcome at court the Scottish nobleman, George Dunbar, earl of March, should be viewed. The earl's breach with the king of Scots occurred in February 1400;[71] just a month later he had entered into secret negotiations with Henry IV, eventually promising to come into the English allegiance and to bring with him title to several border fortresses and some 2,000 men.[72] Henry must have regarded this turn of events as very promising indeed: in the powerful earl of March, a Scottish border lord of considerable import- ance, he saw the opportunity simultaneously to strike at Scottish insults and at Percy pretensions. The arrangements for the Dunbar defection he entrusted to Ralph Neville, earl of Westmorland.[73]

Meanwhile, Henry himself exerted a firm control over ongoing negotia- tions with the Scots. In May he sent three minor northern noblemen of his own choosing to demand that Robert III observe the peace that had been negotiated in 1396 between England on the one hand and France and its Scottish allies on the other, and to demand reparation for a number of offences committed in violation of that agreement.[74] Henry was aware that the welcome he had extended to the earl of March had made open war with the Scots inevitable, but he was fast learning and now deliberately employing the skills required of a king in the diplomatic sphere. Several further overtures for peace were made, even after the English army had begun to muster in the North,[75] but not once in the course of the events that transpired in the spring or summer of 1400 was the earl of Northumberland assigned a leading role in the conduct of Anglo-Scottish affairs.

Henry IV's troops began to assemble at York in late June 1400; from there

---

[70] Kirby, *Henry IV*, pp. 81–5; A. L. Brown, 'The Commons and the Council in the Reign of Henry IV', *EHR* 79 (1964), 1–30 (p. 30); J. L. Kirby, 'Councils and Councillors of Henry IV, 1399–1413', *TRHS* 5th s. 14 (1964), 35–65 (pp. 41, 45–6).

[71] The circumstances of Dunbar's defection from the allegiance of Robert III are discussed in Brown, *The Black Douglases*, pp. 99–101; Wylie, *Henry IV*, I, 127–9; Nicholson, *Scotland: The Later Middle Ages*, pp. 218–19. See also *Scotichronicon by Walter Bower, Vol. VIII: Books XV and XVI*, ed. D. E. R. Watt (Aberdeen, 1987), pp. 30–3.

[72] *Facsimiles of National Manuscripts of Scotland*, ed. C. Innes, 3 vols. (Southampton, 1867–72), II, no. 53, printed in *Royal and Historical Letters*, ed. Hingeston, I, 23–5; *Rot. Scot.*, II, 153.

[73] *POPC*, I, 114–15; BL MS Cotton Vespasian F VII, fol. 68, printed in *Royal and Historical Letters*, ed. Hingeston, I, 28–30.

[74] *Foedera*, III(iv), 184.

[75] *CPR, 1399–1401*, pp. 352–3; Wylie, *Henry IV*, I, 133; *POPC*, II, 41; Brown. 'The English Campaign in Scotland', p. 42.

the army moved through county Durham and on to Newcastle upon Tyne.[76] Deeply entrenched in Percy territory, the king kept the earl himself occupied with orders to raise a contingent, though he pointedly required Percy to contribute a mere seven men-at-arms and 160 archers to the royal forces.[77] The Scots' offer to treat for peace with England solely according to the terms of the agreement that had been made in 1328 provided an unexpected opportunity for the king to give further expression to his legitimacy as ruler of England and to link his actions in real and meaningful fashion to those of his Plantagenet predecessors. Even as he was crossing the border at the head of an army Henry made it known that he intended to raise afresh the matter of English sovereignty over Scotland, a claim that had lain dormant since the time of Edward III. Just as his predecessors Richard II, Edward III and Edward I had all done, Henry issued instructions to several religious houses to search their records for evidence of English lordship over the northern realm.[78] The call for historical records was soon followed by a demand that the Scottish king and his chief noblemen prepare themselves to render him homage at Edinburgh. Lest there be any chance that his demands be misunderstood Henry further ordered that proclamations requiring the presence of Scotland's nobles be made at Kelso, Dryburgh, Jedburgh, Melrose and Edinburgh, 'as well as in other public places within the realm'.[79]

Henry's abrupt revival of the claim to overlordship has struck most English and Scottish historians as bizarre and inexplicable.[80] Yet for Henry a tangible link with the Plantagenet past was of crucial importance. The acts of going to war and of demanding Scottish homage were key features of a conscious appeal to history. So, too, was the systematic searching of relevant records generated by his ancestors. In much the same spirit as Richard II had dealt with the Scots, Henry IV intended that his actions portray him as 'self consciously playing a role in history',[81] and that they serve to connect his ambitions to those of his royal predecessors.

The king's pretensions to legitimacy as the representative of a new dynasty of English rulers, together with his determination to exert firm control over the most powerful of his northern magnates would undoubtedly have benefited from a resounding victory over the Scots. But Henry did not really need a military triumph to give meaning to his intentions. Although

---

[76] Wylie, *Henry IV*, I, 135.

[77] Brown, 'The English Campaign in Scotland', p. 45.

[78] E. L. G. Stones, 'The Appeal to History in Anglo-Scottish Relations between 1291 and 1401: Part II', *Archives* 9 (1969–70), 80–3 (pp. 80–1); *POPC*, I, 122–3.

[79] *Foedera*, III(iv), 188–9.

[80] Brown, 'The English Campaign in Scotland', p. 42; Wylie, *Henry IV*, I, 13. For a similar Scottish view, see Stones, 'The Appeal to History', pp. 80–1; Macdonald, *Border Bloodshed*, pp. 138–9; Nicholson, *Scotland: The Later Middle Ages*, p. 219.

[81] P. J. Eberle, 'Richard II and the Literary Arts', in *Richard II: The Art of Kingship*, ed. Goodman and Gillespie, pp. 231–53 (p. 239).

the English chroniclers were not much interested in the expedition, Scottish observers noted with approval that the king returned home on 29 August (after only fifteen days) 'doing only a little damage to the country', and stressed the king's clemency in sparing not merely religious houses but also castles, peel towers, 'certain villages and lesser places'.[82] Henry knew that the one of the marks of a sovereign prince was the authority to bestow mercy, just as it was to declare open war. Indeed, the king's grandiose displays of clemency while on Scottish soil stood in marked contrast to the destruction that recent English border raids, many of them led by members of the Percy family, had regularly wrought in the last hundred years. In juxtaposing Percy ferocity within the frontier region with acts of royal mercy, generosity and protection Henry IV cast the earl of Northumberland in a less than exemplary light. The message was not lost on contemporary observers, nor can it have escaped Henry Percy.

The Scots' refusal to perform homage to the English king at Edinburgh meant that the matter of sovereignty remained unresolved; the issue was eventually raised at a great day of truce held at Kirk Yetholm in October 1401,[83] only to be abandoned once again. The Scottish war, however, had proven something of a public relations success for Henry IV, and in the months following the disbanding of the army he redoubled his efforts to make good his assault on the second of the challenges he had come to regard as most dangerous in respect of the North, the power of the earl of Northumberland (and, increasingly now, his son Hotspur). There was no overt criticism of, or move against, the family: Henry could not yet afford an open breach with the Percies. Instead, he effected in more subtle ways the assertion of his unique royal authority to direct the course of Anglo-Scottish affairs and to curb Northumberland's overweening authority in the border lands. A request by the Percies, *père et fils*, for payment of a sum of 1,000 marks 'to make a raid into Scotland' does not appear to have been favourably answered.[84] More pointedly, the earl's demand for the reimbursement of expenses incurred in operating the border courts were carefully scrutinized.[85] Equally telling, Percy received bad tallies worth £700 in the spring of 1401 while his rival Ralph, earl of Westmorland, was granted the same sum in cash without difficulty.[86] Hotspur, too, began to experience some trouble in securing payment for his service in the border lands.[87]

[82] *Scotichronicon VIII*, ed. Watt, p. 35.
[83] *Anglo-Scottish Relations 1174–1328: Some Selected Documents*, ed. E. L. G. Stones (Oxford, 1965), pp. 346–65.
[84] E 28/27, calendared in *Cal. Docs. Scot. V*, ed. Simpson and Galbraith, no. 908.
[85] E 404/16/695.
[86] A. Steel, *The Receipt of the Exchequer 1377–1485* (Cambridge, 1954), p. 84.
[87] In the spring preceding the expedition to Scotland Percy and Hotspur were the 'principal sufferers' in a series of bad loans issued by the Exchequer: Steel, *Receipt of the Exchequer*, p. 84.

There can be little doubt that the crown's refusal to live up to its financial obligations by rewarding the Percies for their efforts in the marches in tangible fashion was one of the leading causes of the revolt they led in 1403. Many years ago Anthony Steel's painstaking examination of Exchequer records revealed the extent to which the border service of the first earl of Northumberland and his son between the years 1399 and 1402 was undertaken 'very largely at their expense'.[88] The issue of bad tallies began in earnest as early as the spring of 1400; these were, moreover, significantly higher in number and value than those with which the earl of Westmorland had to contend.[89] Steel was only the first among modern scholars to link the Percies' dissatisfaction with their troubles in Exchequer to their break with Henry IV in 1403; several others have since explored this connection in much greater detail.[90] The earl's financial woes were, however, only one of many grievances. Chief among these was the perception that the crown was unfairly favouring the earl of Westmorland and indeed promoting his intrusion into a regional sphere of influence that Percy had worked for more than a quarter of a century to make his own. Robin Storey has argued that in the year 1403 'as at other times, north-country politics can be seen as a king-Percy-Neville triangle'.[91] The same metaphor might be applied in respect of the exercise of judicial authority in the border counties generally, as well as in the more specific territories of the English marches. Ralph Neville's new position as a major landholder assured him a prominent place not merely in English domestic affairs and in the negotiations that were carried out with the Scots between 1399 and 1403, but also in the administration of both common law and border law in the North. If Percy had enjoyed a near monopoly of legal authority as warden, conservator of the truce and justice of the peace until Bolingbroke's coup in 1399, this was no longer the case thereafter, when Neville joined him in all these offices, adding even more to his stature when he was appointed marshal of England on the same day as Percy became constable.[92] In this capacity he became, overnight, as important a military official in the North as Percy. From 1399 the earl of Westmorland was also a more regular fixture on ambassadorial missions to Scotland, and in October 1401, when Percy travelled to Kirk Yetholm as one of the royal representatives sent to discuss with the Scots the homage that Henry IV was still demanding, Neville accompanied him as a fellow ambassador.[93] Perhaps the most irritating demonstration of Neville's rapid rise to a position of Percy-like proportions was revealed in the extent to which he was granted wide

---

[88] Steel, *Receipt of the Exchequer*, p. 139; see also p. 115.

[89] Steel, *Receipt of the Exchequer*, p. 89.

[90] Bean, 'Henry IV and the Percies', pp. 212–27; Kirby, *Henry IV*, pp. 153–5; Neville, *Violence, Custom and Law*, p. 101.

[91] Storey, 'The North of England', p. 135.

[92] *CPR, 1399–1401*, p. 9.

[93] *Anglo-Scottish Relations*, ed. Stones, p. 347.

judicial powers comparable to those of his rival. From 1399 to 1401 Neville joined Percy on the peace commissions for the counties of Northumberland, Cumberland and Westmorland,[94] and while he does not appear to have presided over any sessions of the border courts during this period, his appointment to an unlimited term in the warden's office (a privilege never granted to Percy) swiftly followed the earl of Northumberland's disgrace in 1403.[95]

By 1403 Percy's position and influence as a border magnate of unparalleled stature had suffered a series of serious blows. In sharp contrast, Henry IV had gone some way towards making real and effective the Lancastrian hold on the throne of England. In 1400, when he declared open war on the Scots and marched his army northwards through Percy territory,[96] Henry made a masterful and unmistakable statement as a sovereign; during the expedition, moreover, he made a deliberate show of displaying the merciful qualities of a true Christian prince. The declaration of war and the granting of mercy bore witness to the kind of authority that a prince alone was authorized to exercise. The promotion of Ralph Neville to a military office of first rank, the advancement of the latter to key positions in the political business of the Anglo-Scottish frontier and, finally, the bestowal of judicial powers alienable only by a king were of equally momentous significance, for just as contemporary political theory stressed the prince's lone right to declare open war, so too did it reserve to him the last word in delegating his sovereign authority.

In the end, of course, Henry's bold assertions of his status as the sovereign ruler of all the regions of his kingdom proved fruitless: his throne was threatened more than once with rebellion from Wales and the North, as well as from elsewhere within the realm. Lancastrian mistrust of the Percy family's pretensions, moreover, was quickly translated into an equally profound fear of Neville dominance after 1403, when the wardenship of the West March (and, for long periods, the East March as well) became the nearly exclusive preserve of the Neville family.[97] But the king did not enjoy the gift of seeing into the future. When he came to the throne in 1399 Henry Bolingbroke knew only that his predecessor had alienated to the wardens of the Northern Marches, and the earl of Northumberland in particular, a degree of political, military and judicial autonomy that earlier English kings had been far too cautious to permit. In the course of trying to effect a dynastic revolution Henry IV confronted many difficult tasks. The establishment of a legitimate title for the Lancastrian dynasty was by far the greatest of

---

[94] *CPR, 1399–1401*, pp. 557, 562 and 565.

[95] *CPR, 1401–5*, pp. 258–9.

[96] Henry actually stayed at Felton, near Alnwick, in early August on his way into Scotland. Wylie, *Henry IV*, I, 138.

[97] Storey, 'The Wardens of the Marches', p. 603; Storey, *End of the House of Lancaster*, p. 109.

these challenges, and one that Henry knew would take several years to effect. The promotion of the royal dignity and image, however, was a more immediately manageable goal, and in his early years Henry succeeded admirably in achieving this modest but important aim.

6

Henry IV's Council, 1399–1405

Gwilym Dodd

For those wishing to investigate the workings of the council under Henry IV there is an extremely rich body of records on which to draw. These records can be divided into three main categories. First is Sir Robert Cotton's collection of conciliar memoranda, taken for the most part from the Privy Seal Office in the late sixteenth century and printed (with other records) by Sir Nicholas H. Nicolas in the mid-nineteenth century in his *Proceedings and Ordinances of the Privy Council*. This collection comprises a mixture of minutes of meetings, letters, ordinances, lists of council members, and so on. The second source comprises the many hundreds of petitions that were sent to the council for adjudication. These survive in the Public Record Office in various classes, but principally in the Treasury of the Receipt: Council and Privy Seal Records (E 28).[1] The great value that these petitions have for the modern historian is the light they shed on the personnel of council, since it was customary at this time for the clerk of the council to endorse petitions with the date and names of the council members who were present. The third source is the parliament rolls because the composition and conduct of the council became a matter of great concern for the parliamentary Commons during the reign of Henry IV.

In 1964, J. L. Kirby and A. L. Brown both published articles that made very effective use of these records and which have come to form the mainstay of historical writing on the council under Henry IV. Kirby focused his attention on the councillors themselves.[2] Dividing the reign into the terms of office of the different chancellors, he demonstrated how the membership of the council fluctuated and changed as a result of parliamentary agitation and concluded that across the reign as a whole there was a general shift away from the large and rather unwieldy collection of men who attended the council in the early years to a smaller, more compact group of councillors at the end of the reign. Brown, on the other hand, looked at the parliamentary

---

[1] Besides the class E 28, lists of councillors' names can be found on documents in the PRO classes PSO 1, C 49 and SC 8. The research for this article was made possible by the award of a British Academy Post-Doctoral Research Fellowship. I am grateful to John Watts and Douglas Biggs for commenting on earlier drafts of this paper.

[2] J. L. Kirby, 'Councils and Councillors of Henry IV, 1399–1413', *TRHS*, 5th s. 19 (1964), 35–65.

agitation itself and addressed the key issue of how far the Commons claimed or exercised control over the council.[3] He argued that although the Commons were intent on knowing who the king's councillors were, to the extent that they demanded their formal appointment in parliament in 1401, January 1404 and 1406, they did not attempt to dictate to the king who his advisers should be. The Commons' overriding concern, Brown asserted, was for 'better government in the formal, public appointment and swearing of the council'.[4]

Conscious of the fact that some aspects of the council under Henry IV have already been addressed in great detail, the present essay seeks to cover rather different ground by paying special attention to the petitions that were submitted to the council and which survive in large numbers for the first half of Henry's reign (over 150 petitions have been identified for the period 1399–1406). These 'council petitions' have not been neglected: as noted, Kirby utilized them for the lists of councillors' names that they provide, and in a separate and seminal study on secretarial practice within the Chancery, Brown included a detailed consideration of those petitions that were handled by the council.[5] But many questions remain unanswered, both about the petitions themselves and about the wider implications this particular source has for our understanding of the nature and function of the council under Henry IV. There is a need to clarify, synthesize and in some places revise our perception of the council under the first Lancastrian king, and to set this new perception against some more recent work on the council done by historians working in other periods.

Before turning to these issues, however, the term 'council' needs some clarification. In the past, historians have characterized several types of council: the continual council (set up during a king's minority or illness), the great council (*ad hoc* meetings of the broader community of the realm), the 'political' council (attended by selected magnates, prelates and others to advise the king on domestic and foreign policy) and the ordinary or 'administrative' council (usually fixed at Westminster and made up of the key ministers of state and a few others to attend to more routine legal and financial matters).[6] A decade ago John Watts questioned the whole concept of the existence of a 'council', with its connotations of institutional permanence, and advanced a new model in which *counsel*, as an abstract phenomenon, was seen to be the key to understanding how kings were guided and advised in

---

[3] A. L. Brown, 'The Commons and the Council in the Reign of Henry IV', *EHR* 79 (1964), 1–30, repr. in *Historical Studies of the English Parliament*, ed. E. B. Fryde and E. Miller, 2 vols. (Cambridge, 1970), II, 31–60. Subsequent references are from the reprint of this article.

[4] Brown, 'Commons and the Council', p. 58.

[5] A. L. Brown, 'The Authorization of Letters under the Great Seal', *BIHR* 37 (1964), 125–56.

[6] W. M. Ormrod, *The Reign of Edward III: Crown and Political Society in England, 1327–1377* (London, 1990), pp. 74–5.

their decisions.[7] The present discussion has been written with this revised perspective in mind; but for reasons that will become clear it sticks with the older interpretations and the older terminology. The focus, for the most part, will be on the political/administrative council, since it is the regular work-ings of medieval government during active and effective kingship that carries the main focus of interest. The discussion is also limited chronologically to the period between 1399 and 1406 because the majority of 'council petitions' of the reign date to these years, and because after 1406 new factors, such as Henry IV's illness and the rise to political prominence of the prince of Wales, fundamentally changed the nature of the council and its relationship to the king.

In the light of the Commons' repeated requests in the first half of Henry IV's reign to be informed of the identity of council members, it is tempting to see the practice of endorsing petitions with councillors' names as a sign that the crown was pandering to the wishes of the political community. Indeed, if it were not for the fact that there are a handful of endorsed petitions that predate 1399, it would also be tempting to see such practice as indicative of Henry Bolingbroke's wish to preside over a more open and accountable government machinery. Such sentiments were expressed in 1399 when the king stated his willingness to be 'advised by the wise men of his council on matters touching his estate and that of his realm'.[8] But while Bolingbroke undoubtedly had many lessons to learn from the mistakes of his predecessor, and particularly from the way that Richard acquired a reputation for shunning the advice of his advisers (hence his epitaph, 'Richard the Redeless' – or 'uncounselled'),[9] the practice of endorsing petitions with councillors' names was neither a sop to popular opinion nor a bureaucratic innovation of the new Lancastrian regime. The earliest such example appears to date to 1397, to a time when the sensibilities of the political community would not have been at the top of the crown's political agenda.[10] Changes in record-keeping conventions often coincided with the turnover of the officials responsible for the records, so it is possible that the appearance of councillors' names on petitions was the initiative of Robert Frye who became clerk of the council some time in the late 1390s, and very possibly in 1397 itself.[11] In the early 1390s Frye had acted as a clerk for his predecessor, John Prophet, who had been responsible for some far-reaching changes in record-keeping pro-cedure for the council. It may therefore have been this period of service as

[7] J. Watts, 'The Counsels of King Henry VI, c. 1435–1445', *EHR* 106 (1991), 279–98.

[8] *Rot. Parl.*, III, 433.

[9] For a useful discussion on this subject see B. Millar, '*Richard the Redeless* and the Concept of Advice', *Reading Medieval Studies* 24 (1998), 53–77.

[10] SC 8/269/13406.

[11] For this and what follows see A. L. Brown, *The Early History of the Clerkship of the Council* (Glasgow, 1969), pp. 8–19. I hope to explore the career of Robert Frye in greater detail in a separate study.

subordinate to the innovative Prophet that spurred Frye towards further reform once he had become clerk of the council himself in the second half of the 1390s.[12]

Whatever the precise circumstances, it is almost certain that the purpose of providing the councillors' names was to serve internal bureaucratic needs, for the crucial characteristic of these petitions (and one that has been inadequately recognized) was that they were handled by the council in the absence of the king. Providing a list of councillors' names was not only a way of ensuring accountability within the royal bureaucracy for decisions that had been taken without the direct input of the king; it also provided extra weight to the petition's endorsement so that it might act as a warrant to move the privy and great seals. Although there are no explicit statements to this effect at the start of the fifteenth century, in the minority of Henry VI the provision of names to decisions taken by the council was clearly intended for this purpose. In the ordinances of 1422, for example, it was declared that the clerk of the council should be charged to record the names of the lords present in the council 'to see what, howe, and by whom eny thing passeth',[13] and in 1424, it was further stipulated that in dispatching bills, 'att alle tyme the names of thassenteurs to be writen of their owen hand in the same bille'.[14]

The usual explanation for the existence of these petitions is that they concerned cases that had initially been presented to the king, but were then passed on to the council because the king was either unable or unwilling to dispatch them by himself. Such petitions account for a good proportion of the examples that survive. They can be identified by the presence of the name of the chamberlain on the right-hand side of the lower margin. As one of the household officers who was in constant attendance on the king, the chamberlain probably fulfilled a role similar to that of the receivers in parliament, acting as a first point of contact for petitioners arriving at the royal court, weeding out those petitions considered unsuitable for considera-tion and passing on the remainder, with his signature affixed, to the king. In the vast majority of cases such petitions, and especially those requiring the king's grace, were dispatched without reference to the council, with the note 'le Roy ad grante' inserted in the top right-hand margin; but some (and those which concern us presently) were annotated 'le Roy ad grante par avys de son conseil' and were endorsed with lists of councillors' names. It was probably common practice for such petitions to be forwarded to the council with a covering letter issued under the signet seal briefly outlining the content of the petition and asking the council to give its attention to the matter and ensure that adequate justice was provided.[15]

[12] It is not certain whether Frye took over from Prophet immediately after the latter's retirement in 1395.

[13] *POPC*, III, 18. See also Watts, 'Counsels of Henry VI', p. 286.

[14] *POPC*, III, 150, 216.

[15] A number of these letters survive and have been printed in *Signet Letters*, passim.

The principal reason why the king deferred petitions to his council lay in its crucial role as provider of remedies for difficult legal cases. From the late thirteenth century the king's council had enjoyed wide jurisdictional powers, which enabled it to resolve private disputes or grievances that could not be brought to justice through ordinary common-law procedure.[16] While the council met regularly in the king's presence, as it did at this time, its enhanced legal role raised few concerns; but the increasing tendency for the council to meet separately from the king under Edward III created anxiety in parliament about the increased opportunity this gave councillors to abuse their power.[17] The jurisdiction of the council was a particularly sensitive issue at the beginning of Henry IV's reign when the Commons complained that under Richard II litigants had used maintenance and bribery to secure favourable outcomes to cases brought before the council.[18] They asked that in future all kinds of personal actions should be tried by the common law. Henry was careful to concede nothing that affected his council's utility as a clearinghouse for difficult or problematic legal cases, and throughout his reign he regularly sent petitions to his councillors that he was unable to deal with himself.[19] For example, on 17 December 1401, the king sent his councillors a petition from John Shirlock and his wife Annabel ordering them to summon into their presence Richard de la Panetrie to answer the charges brought against him.[20] On 18 January 1402, the council was ordered to hear the charge brought against John Norton and others in a petition that the king had forwarded to the council while he was staying at his manor at Eltham,[21] and on 8 May 1403 the king, who was staying in his manor in Windsor Park, sent the petition of William Wymundeswold and his wife Katherine to the council, instructing the latter to summon the respective parties into its presence and ensure that justice was done.[22]

While some petitions ended up with the council only after they had first

---

[16] B. Wilkinson, *Studies in the Constitutional History of the Thirteenth and Fourteenth Centuries*, 2nd edn (Manchester, 1952), pp. 121–4.

[17] J. F. Baldwin, *The King's Council in England During the Middle Ages* (Oxford, 1913), pp. 278–80. The council's capacity for independent action was greatly enhanced from the second decade of the fourteenth century when the privy seal ceased to be a part of the household and began to write letters on the instructions of the council alone: A. L. Brown, *The Governance of Late-Medieval England 1272–1461* (London, 1989), p. 34.

[18] *Rot. Parl.*, III, 446. It may have been a measure of the sensitivity towards council 'sleaze' that Lord Lovell excused himself from council membership on 22 May 1406 on the grounds that he was currently involved in several actions in the king's courts; *Rot. Parl.*, III, 573.

[19] In the first months of Henry IV's reign, the council may have been more sensitive to the concerns voiced in parliament than the king: on 9 December 1399 the councillors responded to two petitions that had been forwarded to them by Henry by stating that the matters they raised would be better resolved at common law: E 28/7/34, 37.

[20] *Signet Letters*, no. 57

[21] *Signet Letters*, no. 63.

[22] *Signet Letters*, no. 131.

passed under the eye of the king, the vast majority appear to have been handed direct to the council and dispatched without ever receiving the king's attention or approval. We can discern this by the absence of the chamberlain's name on the petition – the tell-tale sign indicating that it had been in the presence of the king. In spite of parliamentary anxiety, this was a legitimate and well-established procedure. The Ordinances of the Council drawn up in March 1390 expressly stated that the job of the council was independently to dispatch as much business as possible by sending it directly to the justices, chancellor and exchequer, and only those matters that could not be decided without reference to the king were to be passed to him for his consideration.[23] The provision of two potential sources for redress was evidently the cause for some confusion because in 1399 the Commons complained that petitioners were not able to have replies to their petitions because they did not know to whom such requests should be made. The king replied that they had a choice: they could either sue to the chamberlain or to the council.[24] It was normal practice for petitioners to address their petitions to the king, but a small minority were addressed specifically and exclusively to the council. Interestingly, many of these latter petitions were from individuals connected to central government. They included Robert Fry (the clerk of the council), Thomas Hoccleve (a privy seal clerk), Sir Arnold Savage (a council member), John Cheyne (a council member), Robert Markele (a serjeant-at-arms), Robert Waterton (a serjeant-at-arms), John Chamberlain (clerk of the king's ships) and John Barel (a royal clerk and messenger).[25] It was probably their proximity to the centre of power, and the knowledge they possessed as to the whereabouts of the king, which explains why they could address the council with such confidence in their supplications.

Whichever way petitions ended up with the council, it is important that we do not overstate the council's role in handling petitionary business. The overall volume of petitions dealt with by the council was in no way comparable with the number of petitions the king himself had to consider on a day-to-day basis. A. L. Brown estimated that Henry IV received as many as 2,000 petitions each year, which was an average of five–six petitions a day.[26] In the period 1399–1406, the largest number of 'council' petitions that survive for any one month was just eighteen (in May 1405), which was an average of only one petition every two days. This figure accords with the journal of council

---

[23] See A. Goodman, 'Richard II's Councils', in *Richard II: The Art of Kingship*, ed. A. Goodman and J. L. Gillespie (Oxford, 1999), pp. 59–82 (pp. 72–3).

[24] *Rot. Parl.*, III, 444.

[25] E 28/18/2, 9/34, 16/6, 20/6, 21/29, 9/15; SC 8/335/15832.

[26] Brown, 'Authorization', p. 154. This figure is probably an exaggeration. However, Brown's underlying point, that at the start of the fifteenth century the king still spent much of his time discharging business of a fairly routine nature, remains substantially true.

proceedings kept by John Prophet between 1392 and 1393.[27] According to Prophet's record, the council's daily workload rarely consisted of more than three items of business, and it was unusual for more than one to have been initiated by a petition. Although the council served an important administrative, judicial and executive capacity, it did not bear the brunt of royal government, which was still overwhelmingly dependent on the personal input of the king himself.

These petitions provide a valuable insight into the workings of the king's council, but they are also a useful reminder of the peripatetic existence of a medieval king. This was particularly true of Henry IV who, between 1400 and 1405, spent little more than a few weeks every year in the capital, except for periods when parliament was in session.[28] Where it has been possible to work out the king's itinerary, it is evident that a great majority of 'council petitions' were handled when the king was away from London. For example, the eighteen petitions that date to May 1405 coincide with the period when Henry IV was staying in Worcester (3–10 May), Hereford (14–23 May) and Nottingham (30–31 May). The council, for its part, remained in or near London.[29] The reason why the council invariably stayed in the vicinity of the capital is very straightforward, for it was at Westminster that the main administrative departments of government – the chancery, exchequer and privy seal office – were located. In addition to their conciliar duties, the king relied on his council members to coordinate and direct the business of these departments in his absence; this is why the chancellor, treasurer and keeper of the privy seal almost always headed the lists of councillors' names recorded on the petitions: they formed the core element of the council.[30] It was their seniority in the king's government that made these officers so indispensable to the council; but their often lengthy periods in high office, with the attendance at council meetings this inevitably required, also meant that they were the most experienced and probably the most proficient of the council's members. Thomas Langley, for example, was keeper of the privy seal between November 1401 and March 1405, and then chancellor from this point until January 1407.[31] His presence at council meetings is recorded on

---

[27] Baldwin, *The King's Council*, Appendix II; Brown, *Governance of Late-Medieval England*, pp. 37–8.

[28] The king's itinerary can be worked out by using *Signet Letters* in conjunction with Wylie, *Henry IV*, Appendix Q.

[29] For the council's presence in London on 8 and 10 May 1405 see *Calendar of Signet Letters*, nos. 341, 347; for 9 May see *POPC*, I, p. 259. The council did not necessarily convene at Westminster, for its meetings were recorded on other occasions at the London Blackfriars and various private houses in the capital including, interestingly, the city house of the earl of Northumberland forfeited after his rebellion in 1405 (see SC 8/335/15833, dated to 28 September 1406).

[30] *LKLK*, p. 85; Brown, *Governance of Late-Medieval England*, ch. 3.

[31] See I. C. Sharman, *Thomas Langley: The First Spin-Doctor (c.1363–1437)* (Manchester, 1999), pp. 60–6.

virtually all the extant 'council petitions' dating to this period. Undoubtedly, he and other high-ranking government officers such as John Scarle, Edmund Stafford and Henry Beaufort, who each served as chancellor for approximately two years in the first half of Henry's reign, not only provided expertise but also a vital sense of continuity to council meetings. Henry would have been confident in the knowledge that when he left the capital his government was in capable hands, though he still evidently kept in close contact with his councillors and closely monitored their conduct.[32]

In view of the fact that 'council petitions' recorded the names of councillors who met in the king's absence, and that the petitions themselves were primarily routine in nature,[33] it is inevitable that we should characterize this body of men (for the most part)[34] as the 'administrative council' – as a compact body of hard-working and efficient administrators who saw to the day-to-day running of government. There were essentially two types of individual who served on the administrative council between 1399 and 1406: career churchmen and waged 'commoners' (of the latter, some belonged to the household; some were duchy of Lancaster officers; and others were simply close and trusted acquaintances of the king himself). Of the churchmen, the bishops of Durham (Walter Skirlaw), Hereford (John Trevenant), Bangor (Richard Young), Rochester (John Bottlesham), Exeter (Edmund Stafford) and Bath (Henry Bowet) were all frequent attenders of the council in (but not throughout) the period 1399–1406. Henry Beaufort, as chancellor, attended the council regularly, but not before his appointment to this office. Of the 'commoners', John Pelham, John Doreward, Arnold Savage, John Freningham, John Norbury, John Curson, John Cheyne, Thomas Erpingham and John Prophet most frequently attended the council.[35] The most frequent attenders of the council from among the nobility were the earl of Northumberland and the earl of Worcester. It is not the purpose of the

[32] On 15 May 1402, writing from Berkhamsted Castle, Henry informed the council of his 'great surprise' that the money assigned for the marriage of his daughter Blanche had been assigned elsewhere, which had resulted in an unwelcome delay to her voyage (to Germany): the council was ordered to pay up. (It is interesting to note that at the end of the letter Henry Beaufort, bishop of Lincoln, was especially singled out to be informed that the king was unable to pay himself: *Signet Letters*, no. 71; printed in *POPC*, I, 184–5.) On 8 May 1405, Henry sent a letter from Worcester asking the council to pressure the treasurers of war for payment of the wages of soldiers in Wales and 'to send news of what is happening with them from time to time, and more frequently than they have done since he left'; *Signet Letters*, no. 341. Finally, on 3 January 1406, from Eltham manor, the king expressed his great surprise that nothing had yet been done to assemble a great council despite the council's agreement to do so eight days previously; *Signet Letters*, no. 524.

[33] Brown, 'Commons and the Council', p. 37.

[34] See my discussion below.

[35] The careers of all these men, except for Erpingham and Prophet, are detailed in *House of Commons*, II–IV, passim. For Erpingham see T. John, 'Sir Thomas Erpingham, East Anglian Society and the Dynastic Revolution of 1399', *Norfolk Archaeology* 35 (1973), 96–108. For Prophet see Kirby, 'Council and Councillors', p. 43.

present study to examine the individual careers of these men, since these details have been elucidated elsewhere.[36] Insofar as it is possible to generalize, there were essentially two principal qualifications for council membership: loyalty to the regime; and a proven track record in legal and/or administrative matters. Such qualities were vital if the council was to function successfully and independently when the king was not present in person to oversee its affairs.

All these men served as councillors of Henry IV, but as members of a body that frequently functioned separately from the king, it is important to remember that they were not necessarily the only individuals who *counselled* the king. It is a common fallacy to think of the king's council as comprising the king's most important and influential advisers, but under Henry IV many of the king's closest confidants and friends rarely, if ever, attended council meetings. This is demonstrated by a comparison between the lists of councillors' names endorsed on the petitions, and the lists of individuals who were recorded as witnesses to royal charters.[37] These witness lists should be treated with caution, since they record people whom chancery clerks *thought* were present with the king when a charter was issued; they were not actual registers of attendance. However, the lists shed important light on the sort of people who were considered at the time to have been close intimates of the king, and for this reason they retain considerable value. In his work on the reigns of Edward III and Richard II, Chris Given-Wilson pointed out that royal charters were witnessed in chancery rather than in the royal household, and concluded that they 'probably reflect not so much the personnel of the court as the personnel of the council'.[38] Under Henry IV, however, there appears to have been a very clear divergence between those individuals witnessing charters and those attending the council: the vast majority of charter witnesses were *not* in fact council members. This was probably because for much of the first half of the reign, king and council operated as separate entities; it would therefore have been only natural for Henry's closest and most intimate advisers to gravitate towards the court rather than to his council. In fact, even on the occasions when the court and council were meeting at the same time in London the membership of the two bodies was quite distinct. This highlights the fact that most courtiers were probably little interested in the rather mundane administrative and legal business that formed a large part of the work to which the council attended. On 9 December

[36] Kirby, 'Councils and Councillors'; Brown, 'Commons and the Council'; L. Betcherman, 'The Making of Bishops in the Lancastrian Period', *Speculum* 41 (1966), 397–419.

[37] For a recent consideration of the witness lists see J. S. Hamilton, 'Charter Witness Lists for the Reign of Edward II', in *Fourteenth Century England I*, ed. N. Saul (Woodbridge, 2000), pp. 1–20.

[38] C. Given-Wilson, 'Royal Charter Witness Lists 1327–1399', *Medieval Prosopography* 12 (1991), 35–93, (pp. 44, 59). R. Virgoe reaches similar conclusions for the period 1437–61: 'The Composition of the King's Council, 1437–61', *BIHR* 43 (1970), 134–60 (pp. 139–40).

1399, for example, nineteen individuals attended a council meeting and on the following day, 10 December, a royal charter was recorded that included a list of sixteen names; only four names, however, can be found on both documents.[39] On 8 March 1401, the council comprised eleven people and on the following day a royal charter was recorded with fifteen witnesses: again, the overlap was just four individuals.[40] Finally, on 11 November 1404 – at the time of the Coventry parliament – seven people were recorded as councillors, of whom (again) just four were recorded as charter witnesses, leaving nine who had no recorded connection to the king's council.[41] The individuals who appeared as witnesses to these three charters, but who were not regularly listed on the dorse of the council petitions in the period 1399–1406, included: the king's half brother John, earl of Somerset (also the king's chamberlain); Henry Beaufort (until he became chancellor in February 1403); Edmund, duke of York; Edward, duke of York; Ralph, earl of Westmorland; Thomas Arundel, archbishop of Canterbury; Richard Scrope, archbishop of York; Lord Roos; Lords Grey of Ruthyn and Grey of Codnor; Lord Willoughby; Lord Cobham; and William Heron, Lord Say.[42]

If these men were not councillors, then most could be termed 'counsellors' in the sense that they were high in the king's confidence and enjoyed especially trusted positions in the Lancastrian regime. Not all of them necessarily attended the king on a permanent basis, or were at court regularly, but their presence as charter witnesses provides a glimpse of the sort of people who might have influenced the king's decisions and policies in a more informal (and unrecorded) way. Indeed, when we consider that our knowledge of the council's membership derives mostly from petitions that were handled by the council when the king was removed from it by some distance, it is a logical step to conclude that the true locus of power within the regime rested not with the councillors but with the charter witnesses and other courtiers of whom some, such as Somerset and Henry Beaufort, enjoyed direct access to the king and to the king's chamber. It could even be argued that membership of the council actually denoted a *lack* of influence within the regime. Addressing petitions and tackling other administrative tasks independently of the king undoubtedly indicated bureaucratic and legal profi-

---

[39] E 28/7/37; C 53/169, m.28. The dating of charters is problematic since it was the day when they were authorized by the privy seal that was normally recorded on the enrollment, rather than the day when they were witnessed. However, Given-Wilson states that this discrepancy would have been very small, and would probably have been no more than a few days; 'Royal Charter Witness Lists,' p. 44.

[40] E 28/8/65; C 53/171, m.1; and see C 53/172, m.3.

[41] E 28/15/63; C 53/175, m.14.

[42] See also Kirby, 'Councils and Councillors', pp. 45, 48; G. L. Harriss, *Cardinal Beaufort: A Study of Lancastrian Ascendency and Decline* (Oxford, 1988), p. 12. The careers of the barons have been detailed by A. L. Brown, 'The Reign of Henry IV', in *Fifteenth Century England 1399–1509*, ed. S. B. Chrimes, C. D. Ross, and R. A. Griffiths, 2nd edn (Stroud, 1995), pp. 1–28 (pp. 11–14).

ciency, but it did not denote political indispensability – a point which makes the earl of Worcester's absence from the charter witness lists so significant, in spite of his good record of council attendance.[43]

The hidden influence of courtiers on the king's decisions and policies also raises an important point from a procedural point of view. It is easy to assume that petitions handled by the council were the only supplications that went through a 'collective' decision-making process, and that those which were presented to the king, and which were answered by the king, were dealt with by him alone. On the contrary, it is unlikely that the king was ever alone when attending to the business of the realm, and even when physically separated from his 'council', he must still have drawn on the 'counsel' of his close and intimate advisers within the household who could assist and influence the decisions he made.[44] It was an awareness of this fact that probably explains the measures prescribed by the Commons in the third clause of their 'Thirty-one Articles' of 1406, which stated that 'if any persons in the entourage of the royal person of our lord the king . . . tries to sway the king's mind to meddle in any quarrels, [the king should] send the bills to his council . . . so that they can investigate this matter and submit to the common law those things that can be determined by it'.[45]

For the most part our impression that 'council petitions' shed light on the actions and personnel of the 'administrative council' is supported by the small size of the body of men who were usually recorded on the dorse of the petitions. It was fairly common for just half a dozen councillors to be noted, and sometimes as few as three or four names were provided. Frequently, the council would consist of the chancellor, treasurer, keeper of the privy seal and one or two 'commoners' such as John Doreward or Arnold Savage. On several occasions in early 1405 the council comprised the three great officers of state alone; on 3 May, the council's membership was reduced to just the chancellor and the guardian of the privy seal. On other occasions, however, the council was considerably larger and could number as many as nineteen individuals.[46] Moreover, large fluctuations in the council's size might occur over a matter of days, as happened in the spring of 1404 when there were fourteen councillors on 21 April and just four a week later.[47] To explain these great variations in the number of men attending council meetings, it is necessary to make an important qualification to the notion that petitions were endorsed only when the council was 'administrative' in nature and was operating independently of the king at Westminster. In a good many cases

---

[43] Kirby, 'Councils and Councillors', p. 45.

[44] Note, for example, that on 12 April 1405 a signet letter was sent to the keeper of the privy seal that was first 'shown to the king in his chamber at Windsor in the presence of the bishop of Winchester [Henry Beaufort]'; *Signet Letters*, no. 277.

[45] *Rot. Parl.*, III, 586.

[46] E 28/7/37, which is dated to 9 December 1399.

[47] E 28/12/29, 27.

this explanation holds true; but there were occasions when petitions were dealt with by the council when the council itself had acquired other functions and when its members were responsible for more than routine administrative, judicial or bureaucratic duties. Sometimes the council became more 'political' in nature, in the sense that its members were expected to advise the king *in the king's presence* on the formulation of government policy or on decisions that had major political implications. The obvious occasion when this happened was during parliament or when a great council was called, but king and council met up on a regular basis throughout the period under investigation. The 'council petitions' make it clear that there was a close correlation between the size of the council and the proximity of the king: when Henry was away from London the council was small and administrative in profile, whereas when he was in the capital (or if the council itself moved into the provinces to be with the king) it tended to expand and include a greater aristocratic presence. It is to be emphasized that this does not contradict our earlier supposition that petitions were endorsed with councillors' names only when the council dealt with supplications in the absence of the king, for even when the king and council were in close proximity there must have been occasions when the council was left to its own devices while the king attended to other matters. The so-called 'Advice' of the council of 1401, which will be discussed shortly, is a good example of precisely this situation, when king and council were both at Westminster but were acting independently of each other.[48]

These points are demonstrated by looking at the composition of the council in the first eighteen months of Henry's reign. In the autumn of 1399 the council was very large because the king and political community had gathered for a meeting of parliament at Westminster to lay down the foundations of the new Lancastrian regime. The council had other purposes besides simply seeing to routine government business, and its membership was therefore quantitatively and qualitatively substantial. This enlarged council of the first few months of the reign did not last, however, because for much of 1400 petitions recorded a membership of just half a dozen or so councillors. These petitions coincided with periods when the king was away from London (usually at Eltham), and it seems reasonable to assume that the council at Westminster was now primarily administrative in character, that it was now a compact professional group of men. To some extent, this is confirmed by the fact that in March 1400 Northumberland and others were described as belonging to the king's council *at Eltham*, as if to distinguish it

[48] The councillors were personally charged by the king to consider the matters they eventually articulated in the 'Advice'. They expected to report back to the king, while he was still in London, a day later. However, Henry left the capital before this report could be made, and the 'Advice' was therefore brought to him by John Doreward, with an accompanying letter from the council.

from the council assembled at the same time at Westminster. The council at Eltham was presumably 'political' and advisory in nature (that is, the king's 'counsel'); and the council at Westminster probably fulfilled a more administrative role.[49] On 11 November 1400 Henry was back at Westminster, and the council, in turn, had increased its size to ten individuals.[50] A month later, on 18 December, the council was still substantial although by this time the king was at Hertford Castle: the council was probably reinforced for the purpose of preparing for parliament in the new year, and the unusual presence of the two household chamberlains (Somerset and Erpingham), the steward of the household (Thomas Rempston) and John Curson, suggests that the king's wishes were very well represented there.[51] Petitions recording council attendance in the first half of March 1401, when parliament was in session, and when king and council were together, indicate that the council was still substantial and aristocratic (eleven members on 8 March and thirteen members on 11 March, the day after parliament).[52] But by 17 March, after the assembly had ended, and after the king had left for Eltham, the council's membership was reduced to just seven individuals. Once again the council had reverted to an executive body running the day-to-day affairs of government, and its membership reflected this fact (it comprised the three great officers of state, plus Prophet, Cheyne, Doreward and Curson).[53]

* * *

The link between business and personnel has important implications for the way in which we project Henry IV's council on to the broader political canvas of his first years in power. The council has traditionally been viewed as a source of great tension in Henry's parliaments, and if historians have been careful not to over-exaggerate the coercive powers the Commons in parliament could exercise over the king, nevertheless a strong case has been put

---

[49] *POPC*, I, 117. A letter from the king and his council 'at Eltham' was issued to the pope on 15 March 1400. A list of the members attending the council at Westminster survives for 16 March (these were the three great officers, plus Prophet, Bowet and Rounhale): E 28/7/31. A similar situation prevailed in May 1405 when a signet letter was written to the council (at Westminster) 'with the advice of those members of the council at present with the king [at Worcester]': *Signet Letters*, no. 348. Note also that article three of the 'Thirty-one Articles' of 1406 referred to bills being sent to the council by members of the council remaining about the king's person: *Rot. Parl.*, III, 586.

[50] *Signet Letters*, no. 21; E 28/8/13.

[51] E 28/8/26.

[52] 'Council' petitions also survive for the period when the parliament of October 1404 was in session. They show that Thomas Arundel, archbishop of Canterbury, and Edward, duke of York, both of whom were not normally recorded as council members, were now serving in this capacity. This was almost certainly because the council was meeting at the same time and place as parliament.

[53] E 28/11/16.

forward that depicts the Commons taking a prominent role in shaping the make-up and duties of the king's council.[54] Even this, however, may be overstating the case. Elsewhere in this volume Douglas Biggs has offered a convincing reassessment of the circumstances of the Long Parliament of 1406, and there seems little point in repeating in detail the points he has made. In brief, Biggs dismantles the old view that in 1406 Henry IV was shackled by a council imposed on him at the behest of the Commons, and argues that the real reason why the king submitted to conciliar government was the recurrence of his debilitating illness and his inability to continue his personal rule unaided. The council of 1406 was therefore set up primarily to support rather than undermine the king's authority. There is no evidence to suggest that it was imposed on the king against his wishes.

The other parliament of the reign in which the council was of particular concern to the Commons met in 1401. Here, the Commons' principal demands, so far as they were noted by the council in the 'Advice', were that the king should ordain as his great officers (and council) to be of honourable estate, that they should remain in office until the next parliament, and that the Commons should know their identity and duties before the end of parliament.[55] It was as a result of these demands that, according to A. L. Brown, the council became larger and attracted more men of higher status in the period following 1401. In other words, as a result of political pressure the king was obliged to concede important changes in the make-up and size of his council. Such a theory was supported by A. Rogers, who claimed that in consequence of the 'crisis' in the parliament of 1401, 'magnate representation on the Council was significantly increased'.[56] These interpretations raise a number of important problems. First, they assume that council membership was highly sought after by members of the aristocracy when we have seen already that the council was not necessarily the primary locus of political power and that a great deal of its business was taken up with mundane administrative duties that the aristocratic elite would not necessarily have sought. Secondly, they imply that Henry IV deliberately barred magnates from council membership, though there is no evidence to support this, and there are no clear reasons why such a policy should have been adopted. In fact, in the 'Advice' which the council sent to the king the lords – presumably the lay lords – expressed their *reluctance* to serve on the council for any great period of time because of the adverse effect this would have on the management of

---

[54] Brown, 'Commons and the Council', passim; Kirby, 'Councils and Councillors', p. 37; Watts, 'Counsels of Henry VI', pp. 281–3.

[55] The Advice is printed in *Select Documents of English Constitutional History, 1307–1485*, ed. S. B. Chrimes and A. L. Brown (London, 1961), no. 183. For discussion see Brown, 'Commons and the Council', pp. 33–9.

[56] A. Rogers, 'The Political Crisis of 1401', *Nottingham Medieval Studies* 7 (1968), 85–96 (pp. 90–1).

their estates and men.[57] Thirdly, one of the key figures who supposedly benefited from the 'New Council' set up after March 1401 was Thomas Percy, earl of Worcester, who is seen to have 'taken the lead' in its subsequent meetings.[58] Close scrutiny of the frequency with which he attended council sessions both before and after the parliament of 1401, however, suggests that if anything this assembly had the reverse effect on the pattern of his attendance. Worcester attended council meetings well before the parliament of 1401 (his name appears in each of the six lists preceding the assembly, dating to the period between 11 October and 18 December 1400) and in the three lists following the assembly (dating to 17 March, 7 May and 19 May 1401) his name is absent. Fourthly, if we are to believe that one result of the parliamentary agitation of 1401 was that the size of the council increased, then we must account for the fact that just a week after the assembly had ended (i.e. 17 March) the council comprised just seven members.[59] This was the smallest recorded attendance of the council since 11 October 1400.

There is an element of truth to the notion that the council's membership became more substantial in the longer term, in the *months* following the parliament of 1401; but the explanation has more to do with practicalities than it does with politics. If we view the council's membership in the summer of 1401 in the context of the king's movements and, where possible, in the light of other non-petitionary business the council attended to (as printed in the *Proceedings and Ordinances of the Privy Council*), it becomes clear that what affected the council's membership was not a crisis brought about by parliamentary opposition, but a crisis brought about by rebellion. In June and early July 1401 the council was indeed large and substantial; but this was in a period when Henry IV had left London for Worcester to deal with the revolt of Owain Glyn Dŵr.[60] It was, perhaps, natural for the king to leave behind in the capital a reinforced council capable of dealing with some key political issues that required attention (including the return of Richard II's queen, Isabella, to France and negotiations with Scotland).[61] The council meeting of 19 June 1401 was also a particularly large one; but this was almost certainly because it met within a few days of a meeting of a great council that convened at the end of the month to consider the desirability of war against France.[62] Towards the end of July, the size and composition of the council was less impressive, and by 1 August, it comprised just three members. The crisis had passed. The council was no longer needed to ensure political stability

---

[57] *Select Documents*, ed. Chrimes and Brown, no. 183.
[58] Rogers, 'Political Crisis', p. 91.
[59] See above, p. 107.
[60] Kirby, *Henry IV*, p. 119; R. R. Davies, *The Revolt of Owain Glyn Dŵr* (Oxford, 1997), pp. 104–6.
[61] *POPC*, I, 133–5.
[62] *POPC*, I, 143–6.

while Henry dealt with the urgent military situation. The king, for his part, had left the Welsh Marches and was spending time at Southampton and Bishop's Sutton.

To gain a more accurate picture of what occurred in the parliament of 1401 it seems advisable to return to the records themselves. The so-called 'Advice' of the council, and the letter that accompanied it,[63] are the only sources we have indicating that the council and king's officers were the subject of concern on the part of the Commons. A general consensus exists that places some significance on the fact that there is no hint in the parliament roll of the requests that were articulated in the 'Advice'. It has been assumed that this was because the crown deliberately 'suppressed' the official parliamentary record in an attempt to hide evidence that there had been dissension during the assembly.[64] This has fed into a more general belief that the parliament of 1401 witnessed a major constitutional crisis over the role and function of the council. In particular, the crown's apparent manipulation of the parliament roll has come to be regarded as an indication of the severity of the threat posed to the king by the Commons' demands. In fact, the absence of the council as an 'issue' on the parliament roll may have a more mundane explanation, for there is compelling evidence to suggest that the letter and 'Advice' sent by the council to the king were produced after parliament had ended. In the letter, the council is said to be meeting at the Friar Preachers' (if parliament was held at Westminster, then the council would have been at Westminster too); the king is said to have already departed London (he would not have done this when parliament was in session); and, in the 'Advice' reference is made to the oaths the newly appointed household officers took on 9 March (one day before parliament ended and surely too late for the Advice to have been produced during parliament itself).[65] Each of these points suggests that the letter and Advice were produced some time after parliament had been dissolved, possibly on or about 12 March,[66] and that in consequence the issues that these documents

---

[63] Printed by Brown, 'Commons and the Council', p. 59.

[64] *LKLK*, p. 88; Brown, 'Commons and the Council', p. 36; Rogers, 'Political Crisis', pp. 85–6.

[65] There is no basis for McFarlane's assertion that the king departed early in this parliament: *LKLK*, p. 88. The charges referred to in the Advice, which were taken by the steward, treasurer and controller of the household, were dated by Rogers to 9 March: 'Political Crisis', p. 87. This appears to disprove Brown's hypothesis that the Advice was written on 5 March: 'Commons and the Council', p. 33.

[66] Parliament ended on Thursday, 10 March 1401. The letter explains that the council had met on a Friday and had postponed making a report to the king until the following morning, only to learn that the king had already left London for the country. The earliest the king is recorded to have been outside the capital (at Leeds Castle) is 26 March, over two weeks (and three Fridays) after parliament finished. It seems doubtful, however, whether such weighty matters would have been left for so long after parliament had ended. In fact, the rather abrupt and unexpected nature of Henry's departure from London points to Saturday, 12 March – just two days after parliament had ended – as the most likely date when the council had intended to present their Advice to the king; by this

alluded to were not extensively discussed during parliament itself. There-fore, there was no need for the parliament roll to be doctored in the way historians have postulated.[67] Possibly what happened was that towards the end of the session the Commons made certain requests (*not* necessarily in the form of a formal common petition) and that those relating to the council could not be sufficiently considered in the time that was left and so were deferred until after parliament had ended. The particular request by the Commons that they should be informed of the identity and duties of the officers and councillors before leaving parliament would certainly imply that their concerns were aired at the very end of the assembly and that there was some uncertainty in their minds as to whether these would be addressed in time.

The new chronology that has been suggested for the letter and 'Advice' shows that the Commons' fears were realized. In some ways, however, the most surprising fact is that what the Commons asked for was considered at all. If we accept the traditional interpretation of the parliament of 1401, which sees the council as the source of great contention and political acrimony between the crown and the Commons, one would expect the postponement of these requests to have been part of a deliberate royal strategy enabling the king simply to brush them aside once parliament had ended. Henry IV would not have been the first king to delay consideration of a particular issue in parliament in order to be able to forget it once MPs had departed to their constituencies.[68] But in 1401 this did not happen. Apparently acting in good faith, Henry charged his council to address the Commons' concerns even when the latter were no longer present at Westminster to press for this in person. To explain the king's actions, one is inevitably drawn to the requests themselves and the possibility that the crown did not regard them as being quite so offensive or threatening to the royal dignity as historians have previously thought. These requests did not aim to dictate who the king should be counselled by or what his councillors should do. In asking for the names and duties of the councillors to be proclaimed in public and for the councillors to serve at least until the next parliament the Commons' aim was

point Henry had been in the capital to preside over parliament for at least two months and was probably keen to escape to a more healthy environment as soon as he could. Note that McFarlane dated the initial council meeting to Friday, 18 March: *LKLK*, p. 88.

[67] In support of the idea that the crown suppressed all evidence of a political crisis in 1401, historians often cite the request made by the Commons that 'business done and to be done in parliament be enacted and engrossed before the departure of the justices, so that they have it fresh in their memory'. In fact, this request could be explained by the suspicion, articulated later in the parliament of 1401, that the parliament roll of 1399 had incorrectly recorded the modification to the Statute of Provisors: *Rot. Parl.*, III, 457, 465.

[68] This was a particular feature of the 1370s when a number of common petitions were promised a hearing in the following parliament, only to be dropped once the current parliament had finished: G. Dodd, 'Crown, Magnates and Gentry: The English Parlia-ment, 1369–1421' (unpublished D. Phil. thesis, University of York, 1998), p. 44.

to establish a measure of accountability, not to secure control of royal government. Their aim was to exhort the councillors to provide better governance of the realm. Indeed, limited though these requests were, it is worth remembering that even these failed to make any headway when the council eventually came to consider them. As we have seen, there is no evidence that conciliar membership became more 'honourable' after March 1401; the Commons were not given notice of the duties and identity of the councillors; and there is no indication that the request that councillors stay in office until the next parliament was heeded. It is difficult to avoid the conclusion that in 1401 the demands made by the Commons regarding the king's council, far from demonstrating their assertiveness and strength, actually highlighted the inherent weakness of their political position, for they failed to make any impact whatsoever on what the council did and who the king's councillors were.[69]

In a sense, the underlying problem in 1401, at least for the Commons, was that they had overly high expectations of what the council could do. Either the Commons did not recognize, or else if they did they were unable to change, the fact that whatever requests they made in terms of the king's council, these could do very little to restrict or influence who *counselled* the king. The men whom the Commons wanted to be named as councillors in parliament could not possibly have included all the individuals who had access to the king and who could provide him with advice and recommendations about how money should be spent, what policies should be adopted, and so on. To this extent the Commons' efforts were misdirected. The only way they might have influenced the actions of the king *through his council* was if they pursued the policy adopted in 1386 of setting up a commission of reform in which all executive and prerogative powers were taken away from the king and vested solely in the council members.[70] But this would have been anathema to a political community that was fundamentally united behind the king, his authority and his regime.[71] The Commons' deep-seated allegiance to Henry IV effectively precluded the possibility that they might attempt, or

[69] In January 1404 the Commons achieved more success insofar as the names of the councillors were recorded on the parliament roll; but even here it is important to emphasize that Commons did not succeed in establishing a council with a 'fixed' membership, for the list of names pronounced in 1404 represented a *pool* of all the men whom the king considered to be council members. It is noticeable that the twenty-two individuals named in this list were described as being of the king's 'great' *and* 'continual' council, which was recognition, perhaps, of the distinction between the different political and administrative roles the council fulfilled, as well as the fact that only a minority of the men listed would actually attend the council on a continual basis: *Rot. Parl.*, III, 530.

[70] A. Tuck, *Richard II and the English Nobility* (London, 1973), pp. 104–17; W. M. Ormrod, 'Government by Commission: The Continual Council of 1386 and English Royal Administration', *Peritia* 10 (1996), 303–21 (pp. 317–20).

[71] G. Dodd, 'Conflict or Consensus: Henry IV and Parliament, 1399–1406', in *Social Attitudes and Political Structures in the Fifteenth Century*, ed. T. Thornton (Stroud, 2000), pp. 118–49.

even contemplate, making any serious imposition on his power and author-ity. In effect, it was their sense of loyalty to the king that constituted the Commons' principal weakness – and Henry's main source of political strength. The Commons could exhort Henry and his council to provide better governance, which meant above all the more effective management of royal finances, but they could not bring themselves to take any effective measures to ensure that the better governance they wished for would be forthcoming.

Such a conclusion is more difficult to sustain in terms of the king's great officers – the other aspect of royal government that featured in the Advice, and one that deserves brief consideration here. In the last few days of parliament the three senior officers of the household were changed, and the chancellor, John Scarle, was replaced by Edmund Stafford, bishop of Exeter.[72] Historians have seen these changes as a significant victory for the Commons who, acting against the king's wishes, managed to replace a group of incompetent ministers who enjoyed royal backing, with individuals who had a proven track record of administrative experience. The Commons are seen to have taken positive steps towards alleviating the financial difficulties that had beset Henry's administration, and particularly his household. This particular aspect of the parliament of 1401 deserves detailed consideration in its own right. For present purposes, however, it is worth briefly suggesting a different scenario in which the king was far less resistant to the changes in his government than historical tradition has been prepared to concede. In the 'Advice' it is noticeable that the Commons were reported to have asked the king to *ordain* his great officers, not to replace them. It is quite possible, therefore, that this request came after the old ministers had been dismissed and that what the Commons hoped to influence was merely the choice of the new ministers. The fact that the Commons asked to be informed of who these new ministers were would seem to support the idea that there was a period of uncertainty in parliament when the king was still contemplating the identity of the replacements. In any case, such a request underlines the fact that the choice of new ministers remained unequivocally with the king. This makes the view that the new ministers were imposed on Henry rather hard to sustain. Without further evidence it is difficult to establish whether Henry made these changes because of the difficult political circumstances or because of a personal realization that his government could only benefit by the appointment of men who had more experience in running his administration.[73] But whichever of these views is adopted, it

---

[72] Kirby, *Henry IV*, pp, 112–13; Rogers, 'Political Crisis', pp. 86–9.
[73] After all, further changes were made after parliament had ended: John Norbury, the treasurer, was replaced on 31 May 1401, and the keeper of the privy seal, Richard Clifford, was kept in office until 3 November when he was replaced by Thomas Langley: Rogers, 'Political Crisis', p. 88.

may be more appropriate to characterize these changes of government officers as the medieval equivalent of a cabinet reshuffle rather than a purge of government imposed on the king in complete disregard of his wishes.

* * *

The foregoing discussion has ranged widely in its consideration of the council in the first half of Henry IV's reign, and it is worth highlighting several key points by way of conclusion. First, attention has been given to the problematic nature of endorsed petitions as a source for councillors' names. Endorsed petitions were the products of business conducted by the council in the absence of the king, so the evidence they provide for membership of the council inevitably places undue emphasis on the council as an administrative body. This is why Brown's assertion that Henry had trouble maintaining an 'honourable council' is misconstrued.[74] Henry did not have any trouble attracting magnates to his council when the council met in his presence to discuss important matters of state. At other times, when the council attended to the day-to-day government of the realm, it did not require a strong magnate presence, and in this Henry's council was no different to the councils of his predecessors.[75] Nor was there a struggle over the role or composition of the council in the period 1399–1406, either between the king and the Commons or the king and his magnates. To depict the council in these years as anything but a body of men whose primary purpose was to serve Henry by helping him govern the kingdom in an advisory or administrative capacity is to misread the broader political circumstances of the period. The council, like parliament, was an institution of central government wholly devoted to securing and strengthening Henry IV's position as king. By the same token, there was nothing remarkable or unusual about Henry IV's council until the extraordinary circumstances of the king's illness in 1406 led to the formal setting-up of a permanent advisory body. This marked a significant departure from what had occurred since the beginning of the reign. Between 1399 and 1406 the council was indeed a permanent aspect of royal government, and to this extent it was most assuredly an 'institution'. But it did not provide institutionalized counsel: it was not a permanent advisory or *political* body. The council did not monopolize counsel. As we have seen, the essential characteristic of the council under Henry IV was its constantly changing nature. Sometimes it advised the king on matters that were of fundamental importance to the realm, and its membership reflected this fact; but on other occasions its political significance drained away, its membership contracted, and its duties

---

[74] Brown, 'The Reign of Henry IV', p. 11.
[75] Ormrod, *Reign of Edward III*, pp. 75–7.

were confined to more routine administrative matters. In the final analysis, changes in the size and composition of the council were not the result of pressure from the political community, but reflected the basic needs and demands of a very active and mobile king.

7

Henry IV, the Northern Nobility and the Consolidation of the Regime

Mark Arvanigian

Since the publication of his influential essay on the subject nearly thirty years ago, A. L. Brown's view of the kingship of Henry IV – namely that he was a weak usurper with few powerful friends among the realm's political elite – has been the one generally accepted by historians.[1] Following on from this view, Henry's modern biographer, J. L. Kirby, has painted a broadly similar picture of his reign.[2] Describing Henry's relationship with parliament as acrimonious and his relationship with money as ephemeral, Kirby practically marvels at Henry's good fortune at simply remaining in power. There are several reasons for the predominance of these views, among them simple neglect. Modern historians of the later Middle Ages have generally preferred the action of the later fifteenth century, while much recent scholarly attention has been focused on the life and times of Henry's predecessor and chief antagonist, Richard II. Partly for these reasons, Henry IV has not been the subject of much modern scholarly inquiry and so the conclusions reached by Kirby and Brown have endured. Brown's Henry had numerous problems as king, perhaps none greater than a shortage of political allies in the early part of his reign – a fact that Kirby relates to his severe shortage of funds. Both essentially conclude that these deficiencies led Henry to struggle both with the consolidation of power and with his subsequent attempts to form and operate an effective government in the years leading up to the battle of Shrewsbury in 1403.[3]

This essay will, in part, attempt to untangle the merits of this interpretation and consider Henry's support among a distinct political group, the northern baronage. Their support proved critical to Henry's usurpation, making them, with the duchy of Lancaster, one of the great pillars upon which the reign was constructed. A number of studies have already dealt with power politics and governance in Henry's early years, though with a few notable exceptions they have concentrated on purely formal elements of government. Chris

---

[1] A. L. Brown, 'The Reign of Henry IV', in *Fifteenth Century England, 1399–1509*, ed. S. B. Chrimes, C. D. Ross and R. A. Griffiths (Manchester, 1972), pp. 1–24.

[2] Kirby, *Henry IV*.

[3] Brown, 'The Reign of Henry IV', p. 7.

Given-Wilson's study of the royal household certainly looks at the very heart of government: those within the 'organisation' closest to the king's person, the household.[4] Yet while it was powered by informal personal relationships, the household was nonetheless an institution, replete with structures and procedures, not the least of which was the quest for title and office. After all, the chief motivations behind household service were the promise of prefer-ment and the exercise of influence. But this same set of motivations also applied to institutions of a less exalted stature. Simon Walker's study of the Lancastrian affinity addresses the numerous (mostly formal) relationships within the Lancastrian affinity and as such forms the real basis for a fuller understanding of Lancastrian politics.[5] His work points to the role of retaining as a key in the exercise of political power, and both J. M. W. Bean and Michael Hicks have helped elucidate more fully the structure and nature of retaining in the later Middle Ages, while also demonstrating its complex-ities.[6] Indeed, as Helen Castor has recently argued in her study of East Anglia, the king's use of the Lancastrian affinity after 1399 is an important part of the answer to the question 'How did Henry IV exercise his political will in the localities?'[7]

Thus, in spite of the prominence of institutions of government, a more rounded and complete answer to that question must also make room for the operation of other more *informal* elements within political society. Real insight into the political world in which the king and his great subjects operated requires that we move beyond office-holding, the acceptance of royal commissions and membership in established retinues. We should also address the possibility of a network of friends, allies, colleagues and relations – men often operating without portfolio or official charge – who nonetheless acted in the king's interest in the localities. These men might be described simply as 'supporters' or 'partisans' and were frequently called upon to bolster the power of the crown and insure effective royal control of the countryside. Separate studies of two of Henry's closest friends and allies – the household knights John Norbury and Thomas Erpingham – have contributed much to our understanding of the connection between private relationships and political power in Henry's reign, where old friends, comrades and personal retainers became instrumental in royal governance. In the North – a region that had famously troubled both his predecessor and his father – members of the king's household, old servants of the duchy and newly won allies comprised this coterie. This essay will show that this informal network is very much in evidence after 1399 and may help to address the lingering

---

[4] Given-Wilson, *Royal Household*.

[5] S. Walker, *The Lancastrian Affinity, 1361–1399* (Oxford, 1990).

[6] J. M. W. Bean, *From Lord to Patron: Lordship in Late-Medieval England* (Manchester, 1989); M. Hicks, *Bastard Feudalism* (London, 1995).

[7] H. Castor, *The King, the Crown and the Duchy of Lancaster: Public Authority and Private Power, 1399–1461* (Oxford, 2000).

question left by Professor Brown's conclusions about Henry's relative strength: 'How did a king so bereft of powerful allies secure and govern a kingdom?'

It has become clear, as has been recently established by Douglas Biggs, that the suppositions behind this question require some fundamental rethinking. Simply put, the argument that the new king lacked powerful established allies and as a consequence was forced to rely on the gentry and a confrontational parliament for political support, now appears tenuous. Henry was never in fact short of high-level political allies and was well supported from the first by an extensive network of friends, servants and kinsmen representing all sections of the political community.[8] Led in the North by the king's brother-in-law, Ralph Neville, earl of Westmorland, Henry could count among his supporters in the region a large contingent of barons and knights. This included men such as the Lords Roos, Greystoke and Willoughby, as well as Sir Ralph Eure of Durham (the leading adminis-trator in the North) and Sir Thomas Gray of Northumberland. While many of those managing the North from 1399 to 1403 were old duchy retainers, many others were not. Yet all of them had a common point of intersection: an association with the earl of Westmorland.

This essay will therefore argue that it was Westmorland and not the Percies that stood at the real heart of Henry's 'northern strategy', and that this strategy was in evidence from the very beginning of the reign. This relied primarily upon the new king's role as heir to his father's affinity. As king, Henry had at his disposal the enormous human and financial resources of the duchy of Lancaster, and made extensive use in government of a number of Lancastrian retainers.[9] The roles of Thomas Erpingham and John Norbury are well known, and Lancastrians such as John Scarle, Thomas Rempston and Thomas Tutbury also served in high office in these early years.[10] But the Lancastrian retinue also provided strong baronial support, particularly in the form of the northern earls and barons; some, like Westmorland, had close connections with the duchy and the Beauforts. Given this fact, and the origins of these associations, it is therefore the case that Simon Walker's treatment of the Lancastrian affinity represents the proper starting point for any study of Henry's early government.[11]

---

[8] A recent and welcome response to Brown has been made by D. L. Biggs, 'The Reign of Henry IV: The Revolution of 1399 and the Establishment of the Lancastrian Regime', in *Fourteenth Century England I*, ed. N. Saul (Woodbridge, 2000), pp. 195–210.

[9] Helen Castor's recent work on the duchy during the reign of the Lancastrian kings plainly shows Henry's tendency to use its assets to meet royal commitments, and vice versa: Castor, *Duchy of Lancaster*, pp. 22–31, 59–72 and 202–24.

[10] T. E. John, 'Sir Thomas Erpingham', *Norfolk Archaeology* 35 (1973), pp. 96–109; H. E. Castor, 'The Duchy of Lancaster and the Rule of East Anglia, 1399–1440: A Prelude to the Pastons', in *Crown, Government and People in the Fifteenth Century*, ed. R. E. Archer (Stroud, 1995), pp. 53–78.

[11] Walker, *Lancastrian Affinity*.

The very question of the nature and formation of that first government is an interesting one. Michael Bennett's characterization of the Doncaster gathering as a 'coalition' is apt, in that it implies the creation there of something like a loose confederacy.[12] Yet a closer look also reveals that the Doncaster gathering was a convocation of Henry's initial government. Those who took leadership roles in his army would soon find themselves similarly employed in royal government. Yet in spite of his unusually extensive private assets, and in spite of the real goodwill implied by Henry's bloodless coup, few historians have gone so far as to suppose that – far from scrambling for money and friends – he was actually endowed with an extensive array of resources after 1399.

These wellsprings of support were also interrelated. By 1399, instability in the far North had become a clear threat to the realm's unity and security. Always critical in its capacity as a buffer zone with Scotland, the northern border was now arrayed with standing military garrisons. Its generals, the two wardens of the marches, were by the late fourteenth century powers unto themselves; for that reason, the region, from a royal perspective, was virtually ungovernable.[13] Yet coinciding with John of Gaunt's return to England in 1389, the North itself became an important source of Lancastrian political support. The evidence from Gaunt's retaining certainly points to this in his pattern of recruitment. In a deliberative manner, the duke solicited the services of families such as Neville, Roos and Willoughby as counterweights to Percy influence in the borders.[14] The apparent size and composition of the Doncaster contingent (one chronicler placed the number well above 30,000, drawn mostly from the North) is certainly testimony to the policy's success, and to Richard II's failure to gain the support of the region's important figures.[15] This failure to come to terms with the northern gentry and nobility, and Henry's ability and willingness to use his hereditary power base and regional connections to capitalize on that failure, were decisive factors in the dynastic changeover of 1399. Further, his skill in managing and enhancing the core elements of that support were critical in carrying him through the precarious early years of his reign.

One critical region that Henry needed to bring under closer control was the palatinate of Durham, with its wealthy and powerful prince bishop and concentrated landed wealth. By the time of Henry's accession, Durham had long been strategically important to the English crown. The creation of the Norman kings, the palatinate functioned as a royal stronghold in the North and an outpost against potential enemies. Over time, it had proven itself to be

---

[12] Bennett, *Richard II*, pp. 154–6.

[13] Storey, 'North of England', pp. 134–5 and 137.

[14] A. Goodman, *John of Gaunt: The Exercise of Princely Power in Fourteenth-Century Europe* (New York, 1992), pp. 286–91; Walker, *Lancastrian Affinity*, Appendix.

[15] Bennett, *Richard II*, p. 155.

administratively useful, particularly during periods of uncertainty. That uncertainty had become virtually endemic to the far North by the 1380s in the form of border hostilities with the Scots and the subsequent economic and political instability that it engendered.[16] Thus, as R. L. Storey, C. J. Neville and others have shown, the region remained in an almost constant state of array in the later Middle Ages.[17] An outpost of authority in a lightly populated region, the palatinate of Durham was a critical English stronghold in the Northeast, particularly after Otterburn.

Nonetheless, Durham remained more independent by 1399 than might otherwise be supposed. Aside from the earl of Westmorland, no important member of the palatinate's political community is mentioned in the pay lists for either Henry's army or for that of the duke of York.[18] Indeed, there is little evidence that the local knights of the shire were moved to action for either the king or the pretender in 1399. In fact, royal control of Durham depended largely upon the bishop himself and his officers. While the chief responsibility for the daily maintenance of the borders lay mainly in the hands of the king's own officers, the wardens of the marches, royal control over their activities had become somewhat tenuous. Instability meant greater reliance upon the Percies, because they were best able to achieve success. But that very success had also proven politically destabilizing, as Bolingbroke's own usurpation demonstrates: much of his triumphal army was drawn from the border resources that were, at the time, under the command of Hotspur and the earl of Northumberland.[19] Thus, the Percies especially had come to pose a problem for the English government, even while rendering it the valuable service of border defence. As Professor Storey has convincingly argued, the power amassed in the later fourteenth century by the march wardens made them a fact of life with which no king could comfortably live. With their significant regional power, the Percies were doubly threatening as wardens and could provide a potent threat to royal influence in the North.[20]

For his part, Richard II had long recognized this and on various occasions attempted to exclude the Percies from service in the march, though without lasting success.[21] Percy influence in national affairs ebbed and flowed with the tides of border hostilities in the latter years of Richard's reign. In 1379, John of Gaunt was made royal lieutenant in the marches, with overarching

---

[16] DURH 3/13, fol. 137v; *CPR, 1399–1401*, p. 287.
[17] C. J. Neville, *Violence, Custom and Law: The Anglo Scottish Border Lands in the Later Middle Ages* (Edinburgh, 1998), passim; R. L. Storey, 'Wardens of the Marches of England toward Scotland, 1377–1489', *EHR* 72 (1957), 593–615.
[18] *Chrons. Rev.*, Appendices 1 and 2.
[19] *Chrons. Rev.*, Appendix 2.
[20] Storey, 'North of England', p. 137.
[21] This is outlined thoroughly in A. Tuck, 'Richard II and the Border Magnates', *Northern History* 3 (1968), 27–52.

authority over other officials there.[22] The earl of Northumberland regarded this as an intrusion into his traditional sphere of influence and thus began a state of antagonism between the two men.[23] This was confirmed when Gaunt extricated his retainer, John, Lord Neville, from his duties in France to replace Northumberland as Warden of the East March.[24] Yet Gaunt quickly realized that governing the marches without the Percies – possible in times of relative peace – was quite impossible during periods of open hostility. The following year, Northumberland became warden of a new creation, the 'Middle March', centred on Roxburgh. He later exchanged this appointment for that of Warden of the East and Middle Marches reunited, which he held in jointure with Neville and another veteran of high royal service, Walter Skirlaw, bishop of Durham.[25] For the balance of the period to 1396, the Percies and Nevilles generally shared the governance of the northern marches and the border cities of Berwick and Carlisle. Both used various local landlords to help them enforce the truce in the early 1390s and built enough support there to assemble significant military retinues, retinues that in 1399 formed the core of Bolingbroke's contingent.[26]

There was, of course, a significant change in royal policy and tactics in the North with the arrival of Henry IV. For much of the early 1390s Richard II was forced to live with the Percies and their ambitions, because of the general political situation. Yet he was uncomfortable with their control of standing armies in the marches, even as he required their services to maintain the peace and defend the country. So interested was Richard in achieving a separate peace with the Scots that, by 1394, during a period of heavy negotiation between the two governments, he sent his most experienced diplomat, Walter Skirlaw, north of the border to propose a marriage between the two royal families.[27] Nonetheless, the march remained unstable, until the

---

[22] For this and other background to what follows, see A. Tuck, *Richard II and the English Nobility* (London, 1974), pp. 200–24; Given-Wilson, *Royal Household*, pp. 171–267; and Bean, *Estates of the Percy Family*, passim.
[23] This probably came to a peak with Northumberland shutting Gaunt out of Bamburgh Castle during the Peasants' Revolt. Details regarding the political classes and their response to the Peasants' Revolt can be found in W. M. Ormrod, 'The Peasants' Revolt and the Government of England', *Journal of British Studies* 29 (1990), 1–30; and R. B. Dobson, *The Peasants' Revolt of 1381*, 2nd edn (London, 1983).
[24] Tuck, 'Richard II and the Border Magnates', p. 41.
[25] *Rot. Scot.*, II, 40–33. Skirlaw's rapid rise through the diocesan ranks began in earnest in 1386, when he was consecrated bishop of Coventry and Lichfield, only to gain a transfer to the wealthier diocese of Bath and Wells later that same year. In 1388, he was transferred to Durham, where he replaced John Fordham and took up the temporalities in September of that year. He died holding that appointment in 1406. *Handbook of British Chronology*, ed. E. B. Fryde, D. E. Greenway, S. Porter and I. Roy, 3rd edn (London, 1986), pp. 228, 242 and 253.
[26] *Rot. Scot.*, II, 105, 107 and 109.
[27] Thomas Rymer, *Foedera, Conventiones, Litterae, etc.*, 20 vols. (London, 1725–35), VII, 787. This was unsuccessful, but telling nonetheless.

end of 1396, by which time tensions between the two governments had eased somewhat, owing in part to the attainment of a separate peace with France. Having wed Charles VI's daughter, Isabella, to seal the peace, Richard then sought improved relations with the Scots. On 16 March 1398, an indenture of peace was arranged between England and Scotland as part of the agreement with the French, leaving Richard free to act against the ambitions of his march wardens.[28]

It was here that Richard's border strategy became clear. He duly replaced Hotspur as Warden of the West March with John, Lord Beaumont, one of his own courtiers; Beaumont was later succeeded by John Holland, an even more prominent courtier whose brother had married the king's sister.[29] It seems that the peace of 1398 had removed the final impediment to diluting the power of the Percies; Richard's need to placate them had finally disappeared and they could now be replaced. The king's installation of Holland – and later the ageing Edmund Langley, duke of York – as Warden of the West March showed scant regard for any lack of standing or experience in maintaining the borders. It also betrayed Richard's healthy mistrust of the Percies and his belief that the dual offices of march warden were suitable for use as royal patronage.[30]

This shift in policy was critical: it left the Percies with the prospect of being effectively shut out of border governance for the foreseeable future. In fact, by early 1399 the king felt secure enough with the situation there to allow the considerable Lucy lands in Lincolnshire and Suffolk – nominally held by the earl of Northumberland in right of his widow, Maud Lucy – to pass to her heirs rather than to the earl.[31] The king seems to have had some discretion here and found against the Percies, perhaps helping raise their ire against him. Froissart goes so far as to say that Richard summoned the Percies in 1399 to answer charges of treason and upon their refusal, exiled them by decree, though the decree was never enforced, perhaps owing to the king's impending expedition to Ireland.[32] In any case, the thrust of Froissart's message is clear: the king's feelings had hardened against the Percies, and theirs against him. Whatever the extent of their split, the spectre of long-term alienation from their coveted border offices provided all the motivation the Percies would need for seeing Richard replaced in 1399.

Anthony Tuck has outlined some of these circumstances in his important work on Richard II and the northern magnates,[33] but one cannot escape the

[28] *Foedera*, VIII, 35.
[29] Tuck, 'Richard II and the Border Magnates', pp. 48–9; *Rot. Scot.*, II, 135.
[30] For full details of this, see Tuck, 'Richard II and the Border Magnates', p. 50; and *Rot. Scot.*, II, 142–9.
[31] *CCR, 1396–9*, p. 374.
[32] J. Froissart, *Chronicles*, ed. and trans. G. Brereton (Hamondsworth, 1968), p. 441. It is far from clear whether such measures could have been enforced by that date.
[33] See above, n. 21.

feeling that this pattern of royal behaviour really supports Peter McNiven's assertion: that the Percies' primary interest lay in establishing an Anglo-Scottish lordship of some sort, combining the Douglas lands and others in Scotland with their own holdings in Cumberland and Northumberland. This they could do by manipulating the king's policy towards Scotland and by using royal resources – principally via the offices of march wardens – to achieve this.[34] This would certainly explain their withdrawal from North Riding affairs (especially in Richmondshire) in favour of more northerly matters, and would also account for their belligerence to a recalcitrant Henry IV in 1403 and 1405. Further, such a reinterpretation of Percy aspirations in the march also calls for a reassessment of their attitudes and expectations *after* 1399.

This essay cannot fully comment on the varied motivations behind the Percy revolts, except to note that Henry IV, in spite of his early grants to the contrary, generally continued the policies of Richard II and John of Gaunt in not allowing the Percies unfettered control of the border.[35] Henry's varied use of the Percies throughout the country and his balancing of Percy power in the North with that of his own kinsman, Neville, shows this.[36] Richard II's failure to create a sustainable North without Percy assistance proved to be among the great disasters of his reign, as his actions as late as the summer of 1399 certainly indicate. In letters exchanged with the duke of Aumale beginning 11 July, in preparation for their departure for Ireland, Richard granted him permission to release control of the marches (and the large army assembled there) into the hands of the earl of Northumberland. Within a matter of weeks, that army had played a key role in his overthrow.[37] This did not escape the notice of the new king after 1399.

For that reason, early Lancastrian government in the North involved more than just managing the Percies; it operated through a network of family, friends and close confidants who all performed vital service for the new king. Through this network – which was cemented by patronage – Henry IV built coalitions, managed alliances, placed his men in positions of power and built upon his solid base of support. The greatest and most honourable Lancastrian pillar in the North was Ralph Neville, earl of Westmorland, Henry's brother-in-law. Elevated to the office of marshal of England, and granted the earldom of Richmond for life, in 1399 by Henry, Westmorland's lands extended from the city of York itself northward through the North Riding and into Durham. They included the vast lordships of Middleham, Sheriff Hutton, Richmond,

[34] P. McNiven, 'The Scottish Policy of the Percies and the Strategy of the Rebellion of 1403', *BJRL* 62 (1979–80), 498–530 (pp. 529–30).
[35] Tuck, 'Richard II and the Border Magnates', pp. 27–52.
[36] Biggs, 'Reign of Henry IV', pp. 195–210, has commented briefly on the North, but stops short of ascribing Henry with an early anti-Percy policy that favoured instead the earl of Westmorland. I would not.
[37] C 47/22/11/10.

Raby and Brancepeth, and with the grant of his earldom in 1397 came the lordships of Penrith and Sowerby in the Northwest and custody of Dacre lands in Cumberland during the minority of an heir. These last, which included the barony of Burgh-by-Sands and the manors and castles of Kirkoswald and Naworth in northeast Cumberland, were important to the earl, as the Dacres were Percy clients with great estates in a region where Neville interests were fast becoming ascendant.[38] In this way, Neville became a real rival to the Percies in the Northwest.[39]

Other royal grants to the earl of Westmorland soon followed. Sometime before 21 November, Westmorland gained certain rents from the manor, town and lordship of Boston that were not part of those held within the Richmond honour.[40] Henry also confirmed his £120 annuity from the port of Newcastle and, on 5 December, confirmed him in all of his father's lands, cleared of all accrued arrears, along with another of his royal annuities, this one for £130.[41] In July 1401, the manors of Rise and Eastburn, two estates formerly belonging to Lord Fauconberg in the East Riding of Yorkshire, reverted to the crown. Eastburn was quickly granted to Westmorland, allegedly by authority of an unrecorded (and probably dubious) bargain made between John Neville and Walter Fauconberg many years earlier.[42] Westmorland also acquired grants from the wealthy Yorkshire knight Miles Stapleton; the manor of Marton in Westmorland (formerly belonging to the earl of Huntingdon); and the manors of Burton-in-Lonsdale and Kirkby Malzeard, with the forest of Nidderdale in Yorkshire, all former Mowbray lands.[43] Collectively, these grants were important steps in the building of a stronger Neville presence, particularly in the Northwest.

However, Ralph Neville's most important acquisition was the honour of Richmond, granted to him a few days after Henry's coronation.[44] Worth perhaps £1,500 in income annually to the duke of Brittany, it may well have produced something closer to £1,700 for Westmorland, while serving as an important geographic link between his great seats of power, Raby in southwest Durham and Middleham in the North Riding.[45] The grant also brought to a close the melodrama of ownership that had surrounded Richmond for

---

[38] R. L. Storey, *The End of the House of Lancaster* (Gloucester, 1986), p. 106.

[39] The chief Percy holding in Cumberland was the lordship of Cockermouth, held by Northumberland by right of his wife, Maud Lucy. The Neville estates in Cumberland included the barony of Egremont, south of Cockermouth, which Westmorland held in right of his wife, Joan Beaufort. Storey, *End of the House of Lancaster*, p. 108.

[40] *CPR, 1399–1401*, p. 102.

[41] *CPR, 1399–1401*, pp. 254, 400.

[42] *CFR, 1399–1405*, pp. 112–13.

[43] *CFR, 1399–1405*, p. 29.

[44] Enrolled on 20 October 1399. *CPR, 1399–1401*, p. 24.

[45] M. Jones, *Ducal Brittany, 1364–1399* (Oxford, 1970), pp. 178–84, discusses the extent of the Richmond lordship and surveys its constituent estates.

some years, one that had played to the advantage of the Percies as its principal farmers in the 1380s.[46] The most valuable portion of the honour was the lordship of Richmond itself, in North Yorkshire, control of which proved somewhat contentious. From 1381 to 1388 the crown had controlled the honour and had leased out the Yorkshire lordship to the Percies.[47] In 1388, it was then leased for twelve years to Lord Lumley of Durham. But, in 1391 this agreement was nullified when Richmond came once more under the control of its feudal lord, John de Montfort, duke of Brittany. In exchange for recognizing Brittany's seigneurial rights as earl of Richmond, Richard II was to receive control of the Breton castle of Brest.

Yet the crown seems never actually to have surrendered control of the honour: later in the year, the king leased the lordship to a new tenant, Henry FitzHugh, for £433 6s 8d. FitzHugh held the lands until 1395, when they were taken over by Ralph Neville, under the same terms and conditions.[48] As a foreign, absentee landlord with powerful tenants and not a little antipathy toward the English crown, Montfort was largely unable to enjoy the extent of Richmond for most of the 1390s.[49] Only in 1398 did he finally gain reasonable control over its finances, and by then Westmorland had become more firmly established as the dominant figure in the region. In this way, the Nevilles eclipsed the Percies in Richmondshire and set the stage for the grant of the honour to Westmorland by Henry.

It seems that true overlordship of the great Yorkshire lordship remained quite uncertain for many years, leaving open the probability of profits for its farmers. Richard II valued it as a negotiating tool with the duke of Brittany, and the king's council discussed its future at length throughout the early 1390s. Queen Anne's own involvement certainly speaks to the king's level of interest in its well-being, but it is clear that Richard profited from its uncertain ownership.[50] In many ways, Henry Percy was an obvious choice to succeed to the earldom of Richmond, given that its most valuable portions were located in the North and that he had already established an interest in some of its constituent parts as a farmer. But the crown continued to hold the honour in hand, granting it out piecemeal to various northern barons. Its constituent estates of Penrith and Sowerby, for example, were granted to Westmorland in early 1397, even as they were being farmed by the Percies,[51] and even though the earl of Worcester had lobbied the king on Northumberland's behalf over

---

[46] *POPC*, I, 46.

[47] Jones, *Ducal Brittany*, pp. 189–95. For an overview of the honour and lordship of Richmond, see *VCH County of York: North Riding*, ed. W. Page, 2 vols. (1914–23); A. J. Pollard, 'The Richmondshire Community of Gentry', in *Patronage, Pedigree and Power in Later Medieval England*, ed. C. D. Ross (Gloucester, 1979), pp. 37–59.

[48] Jones, *Ducal Brittany*, p. 193.

[49] *POPC*, I, 47; Jones, *Ducal Brittany*, p. 193; *CPR, 1396–9*, p. 13.

[50] *POPC*, I, passim.

[51] *CCR, 1396–9*, p. 413; *CPR, 1396–9*, pp. 39, 267.

their fate.[52] As farmers of Richmond, the Percies had enjoyed a bargain in the 1380s, paying little rent and gaining much in terms of power, prestige and profit. Owing to its confused state of ownership, they had enjoyed wide prerogative in Richmondshire until the Neville encroachment.[53] Westmorland's involvement with the honour of Richmond began in 1395 if not earlier, and its control gave him a broad swathe of territory stretching both north-eastward into Durham and into the Northwest. Their loss of Richmondshire also spelled the end of the Percies as a strong presence in North Yorkshire and Durham, and may have focused their attention on their interests in Cumberland and Northumberland.

As Cynthia J. Neville has noted in her recent treatment of the Anglo-Scottish border in the later Middle Ages, the earl of Westmorland had become a more active player in matters of border law and administration by 1399.[54] He may well have played a role in gaining for Henry the loyalty of the Scottish earl of March, George Dunbar.[55] But, for Henry, Westmorland's elevation was little more than an intensification of the policies of his predecessor. Richard II, as Dr Neville points out, consistently elaborated John of Gaunt's power as royal lieutenant in the marches for the purpose of creating a rival to the Percies – surprisingly even reviving the position in 1398, when the duke was at a fairly advanced age.[56]

Westmorland himself had even begun to encroach on the governance of Northumberland. He granted Wark Castle on the River Tweed to his new retainer, Sir Thomas Gray of Heaton, who already held the bishop of Durham's great fortress at Norham. In addition, Westmorland granted him the constabulary of Bamburgh Castle, and by 1402 the earl would also gain custody of Roxburgh Castle, perhaps the linchpin of the English border defences. The encroachment of the Nevilles further into Yorkshire and the North-West might have been tolerable, if not palatable, to the Percies; their push into Northumberland struck at the very heart of Percy aspirations. Their eclipse along the border – in both legal and political terms – along with Henry's unwavering support for their great rivals and his wooing of the Scottish earl of March – another potential rival – may help to explain their eventual political estrangement.[57]

The Scottish campaign of 1400 changed the landscape of these deployments, and all hands were recalled to the far North in the late summer for the expedition. By that date, given their treatment in recent months and the beginnings of a rearrangement of marcher government, there can be little

---

[52] Worcester drew an annuity of £100 from Penrith, which was at risk in the change of ownership and lobbied for it on his brother's behalf. *POPC*, I, 46.

[53] *CCR, 1396–9*, p. 141.

[54] Neville, *Violence, Custom and Law*, p. 101.

[55] Westmorland was one of the men sent to treat with Dunbar by Henry: *POPC*, I, 114.

[56] Neville, *Violence, Custom and Law*, p. 78.

[57] These are admirably spelled out in some detail in McNiven, 'Scottish Policy', pp. 498–530.

doubt that the Percies and the king were already at odds over Scottish policy by 1401. Only the rashness of a Scottish raiding party in trying to take advantage of the English entanglement in Wales made possible the English (Percy) victory at Homildon Hill, a victory that, if anything, hardened Henry's thinking on the subject of the Percies. J. L. Kirby has argued that the prisoner delivery to Westminster by the Percies after the battle, with the notable absence of the earl of Douglas, was an episode that elicited Henry's open hostility and may have been illustrative of his thinking by that date.[58] Indeed, very little in the king's policy toward Scotland, or in his behaviour toward the Percies, would have convinced them that their own aims were being advanced in any meaningful way by the crown.

Whether one agrees with Peter McNiven's conclusion that the chief Percy aim was establishing an Anglo-Scottish lordship, it is nonetheless clear that their main interests now lay firmly in the borders. The wardenship of the marches was their initial reward for aiding Henry following his return to England, and it was there that they had invested so much time and energy establishing a presence during the reign of his predecessor. The Percies must therefore have been keenly aware that, at the king's behest, their time was being spent in ways inconsistent with these core aspirations. In 1401–2, Hotspur was made chief justice in North Wales, while his uncle, Thomas, earl of Worcester, left the stewardship of the royal household to become the king's lieutenant in South Wales, costing the family a valuable voice at court.[59] Moreover, in Wales, both were to be subject to the authority of the prince of Wales, a blow to Hotspur's ego and a banishment for his uncle.[60] More than that, Worcester's replacement as household steward was William Heron, Lord Say, a councillor and retainer of Westmorland.[61]

Beyond the circumstances of security, one might ask how much the king's neglect of the Percies was driven by financial constraints. Kirby has shown that Henry cycled through both money and treasurers at an alarming rate. This was not entirely of his own making, of course, as Carus-Wilson and Coleman showed many years ago in their landmark study of English trade.[62] Henry was saddled with rapidly declining revenues from the customs house, which helps explain his frequent struggle to meet certain of his financial commitments. Certainly, in the critical years 1400–2, royal revenues from the customs house fell some £4,000 per year below the sums available to Richard II during the last three years of his reign. This certainly contributed to a

[58] Kirby, *Henry IV*, pp. 147–8.
[59] Kirby, *Henry IV*, pp. 130, 134.
[60] *CPR, 1401–5*, p. 53.
[61] Kirby, *Henry IV*, pp. 134 and 259. Westmorland delivered important messages to the council through Lord Say leading up to Shrewsbury and again leading up to Scrope's rebellion; *POPC*, I, passim.
[62] E. M. Carus-Wilson and O. Coleman, *England's Export Trade, 1275–1547* (Oxford, 1963), pp. 51–6 and 122–3.

growing sense of unease among the regular members of the council,[63] and may have forced the king to prioritize his spending commitments. Yet he was anything but bereft.

One of Henry's strengths as king was in his ability to attract and maintain political support, even in times of financial trouble. In spite of his supposed shortfall in revenues at the height of his financial troubles, the king nonetheless managed to find £2,000 for the efforts of the visiting Byzantine emperor to fight the Turks. Such demonstrations of largesse remind us that the king was capable of producing sums of money, although perhaps only via the instrument of loans. And while certain types of expenses – namely those payable in cash – were more difficult to meet than those paid with future assignments, the greatest single factor in determining royal finance was the royal will. Where Henry set a priority, it was generally met. The problem encountered by the Percies was in not being among Henry's financial priorities, particularly in these difficult early years.

In some sense, the Percies were also more vulnerable to Henry's financial problems than were many others, in that they were so actively engaged in numerous, expensive endeavours on his behalf. The honours and responsibilities conferred on them following Henry's accession contained a dual edge, in that they made the Percies more vulnerable than some others to the king's financial promises. Their numerous letters to the council complaining of non-payment for services rendered, beginning sometime in 1401, certainly demonstrate this, though as Dr Neville points out, matters became more immediate after the victory at Homildon Hill.[64]

But whether Henry's treatment of the Percies contained within it elements beyond simple financial shortfall is uncertain, though the evidence would tend to suggest that this king nurtured a very specific strategy where the Percies were concerned. In the exchequer rolls for 1399, 1400 and 1401, Northumberland and Hotspur received *peacetime* wages in their capacities as wardens of the respective marches and governors of Carlisle and Berwick, even though they were frequently fully arrayed and fighting on the crown's behalf, either in Wales and Scotland.[65] Clearly, their expenses were not adequately addressed by the crown even after Homildon Hill, when then the king settled their outstanding debts mostly with assignments, a practice that also reflected his own preference for using these less tangible and reliable instruments of payment.[66] A possible explanation for this royal intractability may also be locked up in a potential agreement between them. If Peter McNiven is correct and there was an agreement – if only in principle – between Henry and the Percies over the creation of some sort of lordship in

---

[63] See for example Brown, 'The Reign of Henry IV', p. 17.
[64] BL MS Cotton Vespasian C xvi, fol. 114; *POPC*, I, 204; Neville, *Violence, Custom and Law*, p. 101.
[65] E 403/565, 566 and 567.
[66] Neville, *Violence, Custom and Law*, p. 101.

the borders, then the king may well have decided to pass along part of the cost of achieving it to them. More likely, Henry was following the examples of his predecessor and his own father, in crafting a world in which they were no longer necessary.

In this, Henry was fortunate to have other magnates in the North capable of shouldering the burden, such as the Cliffords, the Grays, the Eures and the Greystokes, all of whom produced frequent royal commissioners, either in jointure with the earls of Westmorland or Northumberland, or as their inferiors. Ralph, baron Greystoke's patrimony actually abutted the manor of Penrith in Cumberland. He was a retainer of John of Gaunt, though he seems also to have been widely available for military service in the North under other banners. He served in the Percy and Mowbray retinues in the 1380s and 1390s, and seems to have been a stalwart defender of the northwest march.[67] Gaunt clearly promised him Berwick in the mid-1380s in return for his military services and the office of march warden that accompanied it.[68] In fact, Greystoke's career seems to have been somewhat dependent upon the largesse of others, as his own territorial power was relatively modest. As a somewhat vulnerable landowner in the Northwest, self-interest probably dictated his willingness to join the various military campaigns led by John of Gaunt and the earl of Northumberland against the Scots.[69] And of course, Greystoke was present with the English forces at Homildon Hill.[70]

Probably as a result of his connection with John of Gaunt, Greystoke and his retainers joined Bolingbroke's army at Doncaster in 1399.[71] In common with other northern lords, he had refused to lend money to Richard II for the financing of his second Irish expedition in 1399, a fact which Greystoke probably felt made him a potential target of the king's ire.[72] Anthony Tuck has suggested that this rebuke led either to the fact or fear of royal retribution, and led Lord Greystoke to join with the rebels in 1399.[73] It is also likely that a strong tie to Lancaster and Percy informed his politics and his view of Richard's kingship. In any event, already vulnerable to Scottish incursions into the far North and now at odds with the crown, Lord Greystoke firmly attached himself to the natural leader of the northern magnates, Henry of Lancaster, in 1399 and remained a reliable soldier in the North thereafter.[74]

Similarly, the Cliffords, under their patriarch Roger, Lord Clifford, were

[67] Goodman, *John of Gaunt*, pp. 287–8.
[68] BL MS Harley 3988, fol. 42r.
[69] *Rot. Scot.*, II, 62.
[70] Kirby, *Henry IV*, p. 144.
[71] *Historia Vitae et Regni Ricardi Secundi*, ed. G. Stow (Philadelphia, 1977), pp. 151–2.
[72] E 34/1/40/214.
[73] Tuck, *Richard II and the English Nobility*, p. 196.
[74] Goodman, *John of Gaunt*, p. 288.

also the holders of numerous border commissions. These included joint wardenship of the West March with the Nevilles in the 1380s and the occasional constabulary of Berwick in the East March.[75] By the 1390s, though, they were clearly disquieted at what they perceived as a Neville encroachment upon their traditional standing in the Northwest. As early as 1392, the crown was studying their claim of a hereditary right to the Westmorland shrievalty, a suit filed by them in response to Neville encroachments. Yet this was also a more general response to the heightened interest in the region by the duke of Lancaster, and perhaps the development of this rivalry between the Cliffords and Nevilles was eminently predictable, the result of years of their co-governance of the West March.[76] But even these stakes were certainly raised with the elevation of Ralph Neville to the earldom of Westmorland in 1397 and with the grant of the former Clifford estate of Appleby in Westmorland to the new earl in July of the following year.[77] These led the Cliffords to lodge another (this time successful) complaint with the crown touching an inability to enjoy their traditional collection of certain taxes and fees in the county.[78] In 1397, Westmorland was criticized and brought before the king's auditors to account for his management of the forests north of the Trent, in all probability the work of Richard Clifford, who was by then Richard II's keeper of the privy seal.[79] But he seems to have achieved equilibrium when in the following year he was commissioned with John Conyers, Robert Neville (at that time sheriff of York) and others to investigate the impoverishment of Clifford's Hospital of St Nicholas in Richmondshire.[80] Although not documented especially well in modern historiography, the evolving rivalry between these two families in the 1390s serves as a reminder to historians that northern politics were a more complex business than a simple feud between Percy and Neville.

Indeed, Henry relied on the active support of numerous Lancastrian retainers for support in the North. William, who succeeded his father as Lord Willoughby in 1396, had served with Bolingbroke in Prussia and the Holy Land in the early 1390s and was paid £623 in 1399 for taking up arms against Richard.[81] Heir to the widow of the late Lord Latimer, Willoughby had close connections with the Nevilles of Raby, but may also have been dissatisfied with Richard II for other, more practical reasons. In September 1382, William Ufford, earl of Suffolk, died suddenly and without issue. In his

---

[75] E 101/68/10/242; E 101/73/2/30.
[76] C 47/14/6/43. For further information on their co-management of the West March, see E 101/483/3 and E 101/68/10/239 (the 1377 account of John Neville as keeper of Carlisle and Warden of the West March).
[77] *CPR, 1396–9*, p. 384.
[78] Tuck, *Richard II and the English Nobility*, p. 202. This suit seems to have been successful.
[79] *CCR, 1396–9*, p. 35
[80] *CPR, 1396–9*, p. 439.
[81] Kirby, *Henry IV*, p. 30; *Chrons. Rev.*, p. 252.

will, Suffolk named his nephew, William, Lord Willoughby (the elder), to succeed to all of his lands not held in tail. In spite of this, the king granted these estates to his own chancellor, Michael de la Pole, who also gained the remaining Ufford lands in Suffolk with his own elevation to the earldom of Suffolk in 1385, even though Lord Willoughby was clearly the stated heir presumptive.[82] Willoughby was an important Lancastrian retainer, but he now had further cause for his treasonable acts. Frustrated in his attempts to gain lands from the Suffolk earldom, he may have been fighting *against* Richard, as well as *for* Lancaster, in 1399.

Following Henry's elevation, Willoughby became an important member of the council, witnessing numerous charters throughout the reign and seeming always to be on hand when there was business to conduct.[83] He was among those listed in the rolls of the 1404 parliament as a 'permanent member' of the king's council and, given his long service to the house of Lancaster, and especially to Henry personally, he could probably count himself among the king's favourites.[84] Willoughby may have been hoping to gain the Suffolk lands denied his father, and perhaps even the earldom of Suffolk itself. In this, he was unsuccessful. When it came to baronial promotion and the creation of new earldoms, Henry was generally conservative, and in the area of promoting his friends, restrained in this regard. If Willoughby was disappointed in this, he showed little sign of it and remained a close intimate and counsellor to Henry until his own death in 1409.

'Lancastrianism' was certainly the driving force for William, Lord Roos. His father, Thomas, Lord Roos of Helmsley, was one of Gaunt's first retainers from the earldom of Richmond, and a steadfast supporter of the house of Lancaster.[85] William went abroad in Gaunt's service at least five times and generally took an annuity from the duchy of between £40 and £50.[86] He even held the distinction of being one of Gaunt's bannerets with John, Lord Neville, and the two subsequently formed a close relationship.[87] Indeed, they even retained many of the same men, like Sir Ralph Hastings, who took an annuity from both lords in many years.[88] Thus, while not especially dissatisfied with Richard II's rule over any specific personal issue, Roos was a Lancastrian servant of long standing and probably felt aggrieved at the

[82] The Suffolk estates were extensive. See *CIPM, 1413–18*, pp. 441–51.
[83] Brown notes his presence as a frequent charter witness up to 1406. I agree with Prof. Brown's conclusion that Willoughby was one of he king's intimates, as evidenced by his dismissal from council with 'Henry's knights' in 1406; Brown, 'Reign of Henry IV', p. 12.
[84] Kirby, *Henry IV*, p. 169.
[85] He was retained in 1370: Walker, *Lancastrian Affinity*, p. 105.
[86] *CPR, 1377–1381*, p. 246; *CCR, 1377–1381*, p. 17; Walker, *Lancastrian Affinity*, p. 280.
[87] Walker, *Lancastrian Affinity*, pp. 51, 62 and 90.
[88] Walker, *Lancastrian Affinity*, p. 109. On occasion, Roos and Neville even took annuities from each other.

treatment of his great patron. Like so many others, he almost certainly saw his future in Lancastrian terms, which in turn caused him to join Bolingbroke once a rift with the crown was apparent in 1399.

In this last presumption, Roos was not wrong, and his Lancastrian pedigree, like Willoughby's, led to immediate prominence in royal government. Like Willoughby, he became a staunch and dependable member of the king's permanent council and, along with Greystoke, Willoughby and others, was on hand at the Tower to witness Richard II's resignation in September of 1399.[89] He took his turn as treasurer in 1403 (perhaps Henry's most difficult financial year, given the state of the customs receipts), and was also present in 1404 to witness the earl of Northumberland surrender Berwick and the other royal castles in the North to the crown.[90] Along with his friend Willoughby, Lord Roos remained a frequent charter witness and an influential royal councillor, and the two frequently acted in concert, as in raising the ransom of Lord Grey of Ruthyn after his capture by the Welsh rebels in 1402.[91] Helen Castor has shown that, in granting him control of the Audley estates in Staffordshire in 1408 (during the minority of both the Audley and Stafford heirs), the king demonstrated a belief that Roos could also play a significant role in the regional politics of the North Midlands – even though his core interests lay somewhat further north.[92] He was clearly a reliable and trusted servant, as well as being a reasonably talented administrator and royal councillor.

William Heron, Lord Say, was another prominent northerner in Henry's early government. Like his brother, Sir Gerard Heron of Northumberland, he was an important royal ambassador and commissioner. And while perhaps not a Lancastrian retainer before 1399, Lord Say quickly became a member of the council and put his talents to the service of the new administration.[93] The second son in a Northumbrian family, Lord Say held his title by right of his wife and rose in government through a talent for royal service, and seems to have been especially adept at handling tricky diplomatic errands. In 1400, he was part of the party sent by the king to negotiate the return of Queen Isabella to France, and to receive confirmation of the truce between the two countries, an important component of Henry's consolidation of power.[94] A year later, he was part of the procession that accompanied Richard's widow home to France, a delicate matter that had been the subject of negotiation for some months.[95] Finally in

---

[89] C. Given-Wilson, 'Richard II and the Higher Nobility', in *Richard II: The Art of Kingship*, ed. A. Goodman and J. L. Gillespie (Oxford, 1999), pp. 107–29 (p. 114).

[90] Kirby, *Henry IV*, p. 172.

[91] Brown, 'Reign of Henry IV', pp. 12–13.

[92] Castor, *Duchy of Lancaster*, p. 209.

[93] He first shows up as a member of the council in 1401: Kirby, *Henry IV*, p. 116.

[94] *Foedera*, II, 538.

[95] *Foedera*, II, 544.

1402, Heron replaced the earl of Worcester as steward of the royal household, and by November had been commissioned to assist in Queen Joan's journey to England from Brittany.[96]

In the spring of 1403, Lord Say was commissioned to treat with the Scots over numerous transgressions of the peace. Perhaps because he was already resident in the North at the time, he was then commissioned that same September to survey and manage all of Hotspur's lands, after the latter's death at Shrewsbury.[97] These included lands sold by Sir Richard Arundel to Hotspur years before, which were now granted to Heron freely.[98] Heron had also become close to Westmorland sometime after 1399, and acted at least occasionally as the earl's representative to the council. This was most notable at the start of Hotspur's rebellion in the summer of 1403, when the earl himself was engaged in the management of the North and Heron related his advice to the council. Lord Say also performed similar service around the outbreak of Archbishop Scrope's Rebellion in 1405.[99]

Fulfilling a broadly similar role was Westmorland's younger brother Thomas, Lord Furnival,[100] who frequently acted as his brother's legate at the council. He joined with Bolingbroke from Doncaster in 1399 and, like Lord Roos, was already an established duchy retainer. Politically, he naturally associated his own fortunes with those of his elder brother and, by extension, the house of Lancaster. After 1404, he was nominated to the council by parliament and soon became Henry IV's treasurer, as well.[101] A. L. Brown is surely right to suppose that his rise was directly tied to Westmorland's withdrawal from the council,[102] and the favour shown him by the king provides further evidence of the pride of place held by the Nevilles in the Lancastrian universe. From another perspective, Westmorland must certainly have found it useful to have both his brother and William Heron tracking his interests at court, at a time when he was expanding his own interests in the North.

Henry IV also benefited from the support of key members of the northern gentry, key among them Sir Thomas Gray of Northumberland and Sir Ralph Eure of Durham. Eure especially played a key role in Lancastrian governance in the North, serving several terms as sheriff for both Yorkshire and Northumberland and acting as steward of the bishop of Durham's palatine liberty

---

[96] *CPR, 1401–5*, p. 198.

[97] *CPR, 1401–5*, p. 262.

[98] *Foedera*, II, p. 547; *CPR, 1401–5*, p. 310.

[99] *POPC*, I, 209, 253; Given-Wilson, *Royal Household*, p. 287.

[100] McHardy points out that this was a courtesy title, as Thomas married the Furnival heiress, but was generally referred to in writs and summons as 'Thomas de Nevil'. A. K. McHardy, 'Haxey's Case, 1397: The Petition and its Presenter Reconsidered', in *The Age of Richard II*, ed. J. L. Gillespie (Stroud, 1997), pp. 93–114 (pp. 105, 114n).

[101] *POPC*, I, 213–14 and 295.

[102] Brown, 'Reign of Henry IV', pp. 13–14.

for nearly thirty years.[103] Gray's father, also called Thomas, had been an important soldier and administrator in Durham and Northumberland, first as a retainer of the Mowbrays and later of the earl of Westmorland, who granted him custody of Wark Castle near his family's estates at Heaton in 1397. In addition, Gray also served as constable of Norham Castle in the bishop of Durham's North Durham liberty, an important military posting along the border.[104] Well-respected in Northumberland, he was sent up to the parliaments of 1397 and 1399 by the county's electors.[105]

Like the others in this group, Gray took various royal commissions in the years directly following the new king's coronation and was made a king's knight in 1399 by Henry and given a generous lifetime annuity of 100 marks.[106] In fact, by the time of Gray's death in 1400, he was receiving at least £200 in annuities from the crown, while simultaneously holding a number of royal commissions. In common with many of Gray's Northumbrian neighbors, his grants and annuities were far more valuable than his landed income, which, in common with those of many Northumbrians, had been falling as a result of the destruction regularly meted out by the Scots.[107] Royal commissions and service within noble affinities seem to have offered Thomas Gray the political career and financial reward that country life simply could not.

Royal commissions undertaken by the region's gentry varied greatly: some tended to the redress of infractions of the peace, others were commissions of array and still others dealt with issues of a more formal diplomatic nature, such as treating for peace with the Scots – a particular speciality of the Mitfords and Herons.[108] Many of these border knights had strong connections to the Percies and Nevilles, connections that both reinforced the influence of those grand families and positively aided these knightly commissars in the performance of their tasks. But the gentry offered the crown something else in the form of their service: stability. While the personalities of the march wardens might change frequently, in general, the make-up of royal and ambassadorial commissions staffed by the gentry did not. Thus, the make-up of commissions in the North after 1399 was much as it had been under Richard II.[109] Members of the gentry that had served Richard II tended to

---

[103] M. E. Arvanigian, 'Landed Society and the Governance of the North in the Later Middle Ages: The Case of Sir Ralph Eure', *Medieval Prosopography* 22 (forthcoming).

[104] DURH 3/32; *CPR, 1396–9*, p. 410.

[105] *House of Commons*, III, 224.

[106] *House of Commons*, III, 224.

[107] This can be seen in numerous inquisitions. See, for example, *CIPM, 1405–13*, pp. 193–4.

[108] *Foedera*, VII, 650.

[109] The Grays had early associations with the Percies, though later, after 1397, had strongly shifted to the Nevilles. Like their Northumbrian associate, Sir Gerard Heron, John and William Mitford remained prominent commissioners and ambassadors throughout the reigns of both Richard II and Henry IV.

serve Henry IV in much the same capacities, providing the new regime with stability and continuity as it began the slow process of 'Lancastrianizing' the administration.

A fine example of such continuity can be found in the career of Sir Thomas Gray the younger, who came into the service of the earl of Westmorland under roughly similar terms as his father. A captain of the standing garrisons in the Northeast and a keeper of important castles in Northumberland, his landed income, like that of his father, was tenuous given the temper of the Scots and the permeability of the various truces. Also like his father, he opted for service – to the crown, the Nevilles and the bishop of Durham. Gray was already constable and receiver of the bishop's liberty of Norhamshire in 1404, when Westmorland purchased the constabulary of Bamburgh Castle for him.[110] Soon after, the earl granted him custody of his castle of Wark-on-Tweed, thereby fully investing him with the former responsibilities of his father.[111]

However, among the gentry of the North, it was Sir Ralph Eure whose career shines above all others. Undeniably a key figure in the Lancastrian consolidation of the North, he solidified Henry's administration in the region both before and during the turbulence of the rebellions of 1403 and 1405. Probably recruited by his neighbour, the earl of Westmorland, into Lancastrian service, Eure became a great asset to the new king. Because of the tenor of Henry's northern strategy, landed support in the region was critical, and he curried Eure's support from the start. In 1399, Sir Ralph was confirmed as a 'king's knight' and was granted an annuity of £50 at the Exchequer.[112] Later that same year, he gained the extraordinary assurance from the crown that he would never be forced to undertake any commissions or serve in any official capacity against his will.[113] In spite of this, he continued to serve simultaneously as sheriff of York and Northumberland and was named to commissions of array in 1399 and 1401 for Northumberland, Durham and North Yorkshire.[114] Thus, while Eure perhaps failed to lend his full military support to Henry's bid for the throne, he certainly supported it liberally following the coronation, when the new administration was very much in the market for new friends.

That support took many forms. For example, Eure certainly played some

[110] E 326/3515; *A Descriptive Catalogue of Ancient Deeds in the Public Record Office*, 6 vols. (London, 1890–1915), II, 412.
[111] Neville purchased control of Bamburgh from the earl of Salisbury. The widow of the senior Sir Thomas retained in dower many of the constituent estates around Wark: *House of Commons*, III, 225.
[112] *House of Commons*, III, 41.
[113] *CPR, 1399–1401*, pp. 143, 146. This interesting promise indicates that Richard II may, on occasion, have coerced him into doing just that.
[114] *CPR, 1399–1401*, appendix. In his capacity as palatine steward, Eure was also charged with the array in Durham in those years.

sort of military role in quelling the Percy revolt of 1403 and probably an even greater one in dealing with Archbishop Scrope's Rebellion in 1405, while also tending to the array of the Scottish march.[115] He was charged with assisting in the maintenance of the East March during the tenure there of the king's young son, John of Lancaster, while the earl of Westmorland acted as Warden of the West March.[116] Just fourteen years old when his father sent him north to head a commission of the peace in the summer of 1403, Prince John was certainly not the real power behind the maintenance of the North and of the East March.[117] For example, it is difficult to imagine that it was he, and not Eure, who acted as the true constable of Berwick in 1404.[118] In fact, it was most likely Westmorland (who remained in the North after 1403), Eure and the bishop of Durham who monitored the truce and kept the peace with the Scots, as all were available for and experienced in such matters.[119]

From this evidence, it seems apparent that the role of the northern magnates in Henry's early reign was twofold. Their first function following the revolution of 1399 was to help Henry establish control over the kingdom, which they did by virtue of their great standing and by convincing their less committed neighbours to serve the new regime. For this was their second task: to assist in the formation of a functioning government. Their efforts contributed to Henry's success in achieving a stable transfer of power to the house of Lancaster that would last for generations. This process was demonstrably begun in the early years of his reign, with the full complicity of a group of northern nobles and powerful knights. Many of these were already members of Henry's affinity before the events of 1399, while others were attracted to royal service thereafter by the earl of Westmorland or by the king himself. In this way, Lancastrian control of the North was solid enough to withstand the revolt of the region's most famous sons, the Percies.

---

[115] He was among those employed by the king in the disposition of the prisoners after Homildon Hill, when the crown came to loggerheads with the Percies over the matter of prisoners. His inclusion indicates that he may not have been in Westmorland's retinue at the time, whose members were explicitly excluded from participation. *CPR, 1401–5,* p. 213.

[116] *House of Commons,* III, 41.

[117] The commission was announced and enrolled on 16 November: *CPR, 1401–5,* p. 518.

[118] *CPR, 1401–5,* p. 381.

[119] By February 1400, Skirlaw was already leading an inquisition into border maintenance. E 30/1616. The Durham court records are also replete with cases of trespass and violations of the truce. DURH 3/36.

8

'They have the Hertes of the People by North': Northumberland, the Percies and Henry IV, 1399–1408

Andy King

'They have the Hertes of the People by North and ever had.'[1] Thus runs the oft-quoted comment of the English chronicler John Hardyng, writing about the Percy family in the mid-fifteenth century. As a Northumbrian squire who had served in the household of Henry Percy the younger from the tender age of twelve, and who fought alongside him at Homildon Hill in September 1402, the siege of Cocklaw in the following spring and at Shrewsbury in July, it might be supposed that Hardyng was as well-placed to know the truth of this as anybody.[2] But did this assertion really hold true in Northumberland, usually regarded as the Percies' heartland? The beginning of the fifteenth century saw the Percies in open rebellion against Henry IV, the man they had been instrumental in placing on the English throne. To what extent could they count on the support of the Northumbrians in this conflict?

By 1403, the Percies had been Northumbrian landowners for less than a century. They had arrived in the county only in 1309, when Henry Percy purchased the barony of Alnwick from Anthony Bek, in circumstances that some contemporaries seem to have regarded as rather dubious. The acquisition of John de Clavering's Northumbrian estates (including Warkworth Castle, which was to become the Percies' favourite residence) and the barony of Beanley established them as the greatest landholders in Northumberland by the 1330s. Yet, in spite of these acquisitions the Percies spent much of the mid-fourteenth century fighting in France, and it was not until the end of Edward III's reign, with the acquisition of the Strathbogie and Umfraville lands, that they became truly dominant in Northumberland.[3]

---

[1] *Hardyng*, p. 378. Although 'the North' is a large area, it seems reasonable to suppose that as Hardyng was a native of Northumberland, he was including the Northumbrians among 'the People by North'.

[2] Hardyng's career is described by C. L. Kingsford, 'The First Version of Hardyng's Chronicle', *EHR* 27 (1912), 462–753 (pp. 462–6). As Hardyng states that he was twenty-five when he fought at Shrewsbury, he must have entered Percy's service in about 1390: *Hardyng*, p. 351.

[3] J. M. W. Bean, 'The Percies' Acquisition of Alnwick', *Archaeologia Aeliana* 4th s. 32 (1954), 309–14; A. King, 'Englishmen, Scots and Marchers: National and Local Identities in

Thus, at the time of Hotspur's rebellion, the Percy dominance of the marches was only of some thirty years' standing; and indeed, their Cumbrian estates had come into their possession as late as the mid-1380s.[4] This was well within the adult lifetime of many of the more prominent Northumbrian gentry, such as John de Mitford, who had served Henry Percy as the steward of Corbridge since 1370 – seven years before the latter's enoblement as earl of Northumberland.[5]

When Henry Bolingbroke seized the throne in 1399, he naturally relied heavily on the huge affinity recruited by his father to help secure his position.[6] There was, of course, already a long-standing Lancastrian strong-hold within Northumberland, and this was the barony of Embleton, which had been held by the earls and dukes of Lancaster since 1269 (a good forty years before the Percies acquired their first Northumbrian estates). This included earl Thomas's hugely impressive castle at Dunstanburgh, which had been brought up to date by John of Gaunt between 1380 and 1383, with a fashionable barbican.[7] Unfortunately, there was no ready-made Lancastrian affinity in Northumberland to go with this imposing edifice. Gaunt had certainly tried to develop one; over the five years following his appointment as the king's lieutenant in the marches in February 1379, he had retained the prominent Northumbrian knights Thomas de Ilderton, John de Fenwick and William de Swinburne (among others), two of whom (Ilderton and Fenwick) had already served as sheriff of the county.[8] These links had, in fact, involved

Thomas Gray's *Scalacronica'*, *Northern History* 36 (2000), 217–31 (pp. 224–5); G. E. Cokayne, *The Complete Peerage*, 13 vols. (London, 1901–38), X, 458–60. The Percy family's fourteenth-century Northumbrian land-acquisitions are traced by J. M. W. Bean, *The Estates of the Percy Family, 1416–1537* (Oxford, 1958), 3–11; C. Given-Wilson, *The English Nobility in the Late Middle Ages: The Fourteenth-Century Political Community* (London, 1987), pp. 132–5.

4 J. M. W. Bean, 'Henry IV and the Percies', *History* 44 (1959), 212–27 (pp. 212–13); A. Tuck, 'The Percies and the Community of Northumberland in the Later Fourteenth Century', in *War and Border Societies in the Middle Ages*, ed. A. Tuck and A. Goodman (London, 1992), pp. 178–95 (p. 179).

5 *Northumberland County History*, 15 vols. (Newcastle upon Tyne, 1893–1940), X, 451.

6 A. L. Brown, 'The Reign of Henry IV', in *Fifteenth-Century England, 1399–1509*, ed. S. B. Chrimes, C. D. Ross and R. A. Griffiths, 2nd edn (Stroud, 1995), pp. 1–28 (p. 19); H. Castor, *The King, the Crown, and the Duchy of Lancaster: Public Authority and Private Power, 1399–1461* (Oxford, 2000), pp. 25–31; D. L. Biggs, 'The Reign of Henry IV: The Revolution of 1399 and the Establishment of the Lancastrian Regime', in *Fourteenth Century England I*, ed. N. Saul (Woodbridge, 2000), pp. 195–210 (pp. 195–6 and 206–9).

7 M. Hislop, 'John of Gaunt's Building Works at Dunstanburgh Castle', *Archaeologia Aeliana* 5th s. 23 (1995), 139–44; A. King, 'Lordship, Castles and Locality: Thomas of Lancaster, Dunstanburgh Castle and the Lancastrian Affinity in Northumberland, 1296–1322', *Archaeologia Aeliana*, 5th s.29 (2001), 223–34 (pp. 227–8).

8 Ilderton was a Lancastrian retainer by 1380 (and constable of Dunstanburgh), Fenwick by 1381, while Swinburne was retained in 1384–5: *John of Gaunt's Register, 1379–83*, ed. E. C. Lodge and R. Somerville, 2 vols., Camden Society 3rd s. 56 and 57 (1937), I, 7 and no. 410; II, nos. 1096, 1102 and 1163–4; Leeds, Yorkshire Archaeological Society, MS Grantley DD 53/III/501; *Northumberland and Durham Deeds from the Dodsworth MSS. in Bodley's Library,*

Bolingbroke in Northumbrian affairs during Richard II's reign. Fenwick and Swinburne wrote to him, probably in 1388, requesting him to speak with the earl of Northumberland and Hotspur, to dissuade them from intervening in a dispute between them and Henry de Heton. They had to write to Boling-broke, because by this stage, Gaunt had lost interest in the marches, and was away on the Continent pursuing his Iberian ambitions.[9] Meanwhile, with the Nevilles temporarily eclipsed following the appeal for treason of Alexander, archbishop of York, in the Merciless Parliament of 1388,[10] the last vestiges of Gaunt's influence in the marches dissipated. By 1399, his Northumbrian affinity had long been a spent force – although annuities continued to be paid out of the ducal exchequer.[11] Gaunt did make a belated effort to revive his influence in Northumbria in March 1398 by retaining Edmund Craster, one of his Embleton tenants, at a fee of 10 marks, presumably as part of his attempt to bolster the Lancastrian affinity for the sake of his son.[12] If so, then the fee was wasted, for Craster appears to have performed no service whatsoever to Henry IV.[13] However, by this time even Fenwick and Swinburne had managed to accommodate themselves to the Percies. When Hotspur was rewarded for his role in the revolution with office in North Wales, Swinburne found employment with him, as the receiver and steward for the Mortimer estate of Denbigh, and the constable of Beaumaris. By November of that year, Swinburne was close enough to Hotspur to stand as one of the two mainpernors when the latter acquired the wardship of the lands of the deceased (but formerly prominent) Northumbrian knight, Bertram de Mon-boucher. Similarly, by 1401, the Fenwicks had been brought into the Percy affinity to the extent that John de Fenwick's grandson had the earl of Northumberland and Henry Percy de Atholl (Hotspur's cousin) as his godfathers.[14]

Oxford, Newcastle upon Tyne Record Series 7 (1929), p. 210; S. Walker, *The Lancastrian Affinity, 1361–1399* (Oxford, 1990), passim.

[9] [Newcastle upon Tyne,] N[orthumberland] R[ecord] O[ffice] ZSW, 1/105; printed in F. W. Dendy, 'The Heton-Fenwick-Denton Line of Descent', *Archaeologia Aeliana* 3rd s. 14 (1917), 173–88 (p. 187).

[10] A. Goodman, 'Introduction', in *War and Border Societies*, ed. Tuck and Goodman, pp. 1–29 (pp. 13–14).

[11] Swinburne, at least, was still regularly in receipt of his annuity as late as 1396 (NRO ZSW, 1/91, 92).

[12] Craster's indenture is calendared in Walker, *The Lancastrian Affinity*, p. 302. For Gaunt's retaining policies in the late 1390s see Walker, *The Lancastrian Affinity*, pp. 36–7, 177–8; Castor, *Duchy of Lancaster*, p. 24.

[13] In fact, Edmund Craster appears to have performed no very significant service to anybody, apart from witnessing a few deeds for Robert Harbottle (*Northumberland and Durham Deeds*, pp. 153, 155–6).

[14] NRO ZSW, 1/99, 109, 112–16; *CPR, 1399–1401*, pp. 49–50; 'Proofs of Age of Heirs to Estates in Northumberland in the Reigns of Henry IV, Henry V and Henry VI', ed. J. C. Hodgson, *Archaeologia Aeliana* 2nd s. 22 (1900), p. 124; Tuck, 'The Percies and the Community of Northumberland', p. 188.

Generally in his dealings with northern England, Henry IV set out to promote the interests and influence of the Nevilles, a family with impeccable Lancastrian connections, at the expense of the Percies, whose relations with John of Gaunt had been somewhat strained.[15] Nevertheless, the military might wielded by the Percies had been crucial to the success of the Lancastrian revolution, and the price of that support was an extension of Percy authority in the marches. Bolingbroke's gift to the earl of Northumberland of the Wardenship of the West March, made under the seal of the duchy of Lancaster on 2 August 1399 – long before he had any legal authority to make such a grant – represented a down-payment on this debt. Doubtless, once king, Henry IV would have preferred to revive the Lancastrian affinity in Northumberland and to utilize his father's retainers to govern the county; but in the difficult first year of his reign, he could ill-afford to antagonize the Percies by reneging on his promises to them.[16] Thus, when he made his first hurried round of shrieval appointments on 30 September 1399, the day of his accession, Henry ensured that a high proportion of these posts were filled by Lancastrian adherents.[17] Yet, although Northumberland already had a sheriff with Lancastrian connections, in the person of John de Fenwick, the king was obliged to appoint Hotspur in Fenwick's stead. Even within the duchy of Lancaster barony of Embleton, where he might be supposed to have had a completely free hand, Henry did not employ any of his father's retainers. Instead, 1399 saw the appointment of Robert Harbottle as constable of Dunstanburgh,[18] a Northumbrian squire with no known previous Lancastrian association, and indeed, a man of very little standing in the county (though this was soon amended through royal bounty). Harbottle's previous affinities had been with the Westmorland knight Matthew Redman, who obtained the king's pardon for him, for a murder committed in Yorkshire in 1392, and with Robert de Umfraville, with whom Harbottle was accused of stealing cattle

---

[15] R. L. Storey, 'The North of England', in *Fifteenth-Century England*, ed. Chrimes, Ross and Griffiths, pp. 129–44 (pp. 134–5); and see Mark Arvanigian's essay in this volume.

[16] R. L. Storey, 'The Wardens of the Marches towards Scotland, 1377–1489', *EHR* 72 (1957), 593–615 (pp. 603, 612); Bean, 'Henry IV and the Percies', pp. 219–20. Whether Percy realized in August 1399 that his support was actually being bought for a bid for the throne – or indeed, whether Bolingbroke realized this himself – is debatable; and has been duly debated by Bean, 'Henry IV and the Percies', pp. 215–21; J. W. Sherborne, *War, Politics and Culture in Fourteenth-Century England* (London, 1994), pp. 131–53; Bennett, *Richard II*, p. 155. Either way, the point remains that it was critical for Henry to keep the Percies happy.

[17] D. L. Biggs, 'Sheriffs and Justices of the Peace: The Patterns of Lancastrian Governance, 1399–1401', *Nottingham Medieval Studies* 40 (1996), 149–66 (pp. 152–3).

[18] Somerville, *Duchy of Lancaster*, p. 537. Harbottle was appointed keeper of the castle for life, in October 1401. For overviews of his career, see *House of Commons*, III, 285–7; A. Goodman, 'The Defence of Northumberland: A Preliminary Survey', in *Armies, Chivalry and Warfare in Medieval Britain and France. Proceedings of the 1995 Harlaxton Symposium*, ed. M. Strickland (Stamford, 1998), pp. 161–72 (p. 171).

from Isabel de Fauconberg in 1397.[19] Redman was closely associated with the Percies, and owed his position in Northumbrian society to their patronage, while Umfraville was related to them by marriage.[20] Harbottle may therefore have been carefully selected as a figure who would be acceptable to the Percies, without being significant enough to arouse concerns that the king was poaching potential Percy retainers – particularly as Dunstanburgh Castle had been one of the first Lancastrian strongholds to be secured for Bolingbroke in 1399,[21] and this could hardly have been achieved without the cooperation of the Warden of the East March, Henry Hotspur Percy. Of course, it is entirely possible that rather less subtle calculations lay behind this appointment, and perhaps the custodianship represents a reward for some notable service to Bolingbroke performed by Harbottle during the revolution of 1399. Whatever the case, Henry was mindful of Percy sensitivities in the first year of his reign, as may be seen with his treatment of Robert de Swinhoe, the son of Walter de Swinhoe, who had been appointed by Gaunt as the receiver of Dunstanburgh in 1380.[22] Robert was granted an annuity of 20 marks in September 1400, yet despite this sign of royal favour, he found no employment with the crown until he was appointed a justice of the peace for Northumberland in November 1403. The explanation for this may lie in the fact that before entering Gaunt's service Walter had been an adherent of the Percies – and his defection is unlikely to have endeared him or his family to them.[23]

After a year or so, however, Henry began to be more assertive in his dealings with the Percies, and made tentative efforts to extend his own authority within Northumberland. William de Carnaby was appointed as constable of the strategically vital border castle of Norham, after the death of Thomas Gray in November 1400. The castle was held by the bishops of Durham as part of their liberty of Norhamshire, and the office was therefore in the gift of Walter Skirlaw, bishop of Durham – and thus safely beyond the Percies' sphere of influence. There can be little doubt that the king's influence lay behind this appointment as Carnaby had served Gaunt as the constable of Dunstanburgh during the 1370s.[24] But in governing Northumberland, Henry made considerably more use of the royal affinity he had acquired from Richard than of the Lancastrian affinity he had inherited from his father. Of

[19] *CPR, 1391–6*, pp. 404, 688; *CPR, 1396–9*, p. 94.
[20] Tuck, 'The Percies and the Community of Northumberland', pp. 181–2, 185–6.
[21] Bennett, *Richard II*, p. 154.
[22] *Gaunt's Register, 1379–83*, ed. Lodge and Somerville, II, no. 1075.
[23] *CPR, 1399–1401*, p. 358; *CCR, 1399–1402*, p. 221; *CPR, 1401–5*, p. 518. Walter had held a tenement in the bailey of Alnwick Castle in 1373: *The Percy Chartulary*, ed. M. T. Martin, Surtees Society 117 (Durham, 1909), pp. 371–2.
[24] 'Durham Cursitor's Records', *The Thirty-Third Annual Report of the Deputy Keeper of the Public Records* (London, 1872), p. 49; Somerville, *Duchy of Lancaster*, 370. For Carnaby's career, see *House of Commons*, II, 490–2.

the knights retained by Richard, the two most closely associated with Northumberland were Thomas Gray and Gerard Heron; and both were immediately retained by Henry, as was another of Richard's annuitants, the experienced Northumbrian administrator and envoy John de Mitford.[25] None of the three seems to have experienced any great qualms about accommodating himself to the Lancastrian regime, despite the fact that Gerard's brother John had raised a retinue of seven archers for the army that Edmund, duke of York, had so ineffectually led in defence of Richard's throne.[26] Indeed, Gray joined Bolingbroke as soon as he landed in England, and was given a prominent role to play in the deposition as a member of the delegation that obtained Richard's formal resignation of the crown.[27] On the face of it, Gray's enthusiastic espousal of the Lancastrian cause is somewhat puzzling, for he had made an exceptionally good marriage to Elizabeth, the sister of Thomas Mowbray (then the earl of Nottingham), and was close enough to Mowbray to be the first named on the council he appointed to look after his interests when he went into exile in October 1398 – and Henry Bolingbroke was, at least in part, the author of Mowbray's downfall. But it would appear that Gray's resentment was directed solely at Richard – perhaps he was rankled more by the loss of a source of patronage than by the loss of the patron himself.[28]

Gray, Heron and Mitford were all appointed to the first commissions of the peace of the new reign issued in November 1399, as indeed they had served on the last peace commission of Richard's reign, in November 1397 (see Appendix). However, the three were so prominent in the administration of the county that Henry could hardly have afforded to offend them by not renewing their annuities; and as they were already annuitants of the king in 1399, their recruitment into Henry's affinity did not represent any encroachment into the Percies' sphere of influence. In fact, Gray and Heron were on good terms with the Percies anyway. In November 1399, Gray joined them, along with the Lancastrian stalwarts Thomas Erpingham and Hugh de Waterton, in a consortium that farmed the lucrative Mortimer estates during the minority of the heir. Heron served as Hotspur's under-sheriff in 1401, and John de Mitford had a long record of service to the Percies, serving as their steward at Corbridge and as a feoffee for the earl.[29] Similarly, the recruitment of Ralph de Eure and William Heron, Lord Say (Gerard Heron's elder brother), is unlikely to have much troubled the Percies. Eure's main interests lay in the bishopric of Durham, while Heron was employed mainly in diplomatic missions to France – though they can only have been offended

[25] *CPR, 1399–1401*, pp. 30, 41, 101 and 190; *House of Commons*, III, 222–5, 353–6 and 744–6.
[26] *Chrons. Rev.*, p. 251.
[27] *CPR, 1399–1401*, p. 287; *Chrons. Rev.*, pp. 163–5, 169 and 185.
[28] *CPR, 1396–9*, p. 422.
[29] *CFR, 1399–1405*, p. 22; *List of Sheriffs for England and Wales*, PRO Lists and Indexes 9 (repr. London, 1963), p. 98; *CCR, 1381–5*, pp. 402–4.

by his subsequent replacement of Thomas Percy as the steward of the household, in the spring of 1402.[30]

Henry's retaining of Robert Umfraville as a king's knight in December 1402, with an annuity of £40, was a different matter.[31] An effective and successful marcher warrior, Umfraville was also prominent in the administration of Northumberland, having been appointed sheriff in November 1401, and was therefore an obvious candidate for such royal patronage. But Umfraville already possessed strong links with the Percies. In addition to being related to them by marriage, Umfraville had served as their lieutenant in Roxburgh Castle, and unlike Mitford, Gray and Heron, he had no previous links with the royal household. Coming on top of the appointment of Ralph Neville as constable of Roxburgh, in place of Hotspur,[32] this must have appeared to the Percies as a further attempt to undermine their authority in the marches, and doubtless increased their sense of grievance. In fact, the Percies had good reason to be concerned about their authority in Northumberland. Henry IV's initially cautious approach in his dealings with the county, and his unwillingness to attempt to revive the Lancastrian affinity there, suggests that he shared the perception of modern historians that, with their impressive accumulation of Northumbrian estates, the Percies 'must have dominated the county to an extraordinary degree'.[33] Yet the events of 1403 and 1405 suggest that their grasp on the hearts and minds of the Northumbrians was not as firm as historians have assumed, from John Hardyng onwards.[34] Considering the unrivalled extent of the Percies' landed wealth in the county, it is remarkable just how little support they received from the gentry of Northumberland in their conflicts with the crown.

For his attempted coup, Hotspur relied largely on troops raised in Cheshire, while his father's northern retainers remained in the Scottish marches, ready for a showdown with the Scots at Cocklaws.[35] Therefore, few Northumbrians were placed in the awkward position of being requested to rebel against their sovereign by the eldest son of their lord and patron. There were undoubtedly some who did join the rebellion, and by his own account, John Hardyng fought alongside Hotspur at Shrewsbury, while a

---

[30] Eure: *House of Commons*, III, 38–43. Lord Say: Cokayne, *Complete Peerage*, VI, 492–3; Brown, 'The Reign of Henry IV', p. 13; Storey, 'The North of England', pp. 135–6.

[31] *CPR* , *1401–5*, p. 237; Given-Wilson, *Royal Household*, p. 227.

[32] *Rot. Scot.*, II, 161. Umfraville was serving as keeper of Roxburgh in June 1400, presumably as Hotspur's lieutenant: *Calendar of Documents relating to Scotland, V (Supplementary), A. D. 1108–1516*, ed. G. G. Simpson and J. D. Galbraith (Edinburgh, n.d.), no. 4601.

[33] Given-Wilson, *The English Nobility*, p. 135.

[34] A notable exception is Tuck, 'The Percies and the Community of Northumberland', pp. 178–95.

[35] P. McNiven, 'The Scottish Policy of the Percies and the Strategy of the Rebellion of 1403', *BJRL* 62 (1979–80), 498–530 (pp. 513–17); P. Morgan, *War and Society in Medieval Cheshire, 1277–1403*, Chetham Society 3rd s. 34 (Manchester, 1987), pp. 212–18.

group of six rebels given a safe-conduct and protection a week after the battle included the Northumbrians Andrew and Harvey de Trollop and John Mindrum.[36] However, these were men of little account, and other more prominent Northumbrians who served with Hotspur in Wales managed to avoid being entangled in his treason. For example, William de Swinburne was one of Hotspur's main lieutenants there, charged with recruiting men for service against Owain Dŵr,[37] but Swinburne appears to have withdrawn from his Welsh commitments in 1402, and there is nothing to suggest that he took any part in Hotspur's rising in the following year. Nevertheless, it was in Northumberland that the Percies' adherents held out against the king after Shrewsbury. As one version of the *Brut* put it, 'after this bataille was ydo, the knyghtis and squiers of the north cuntre that had be with ser Henri Percy, wente hoom ayen in to Northumbirlond, and kepte thaymself in strong holdis and castellis and wolde not truste in the kyngis grace'.[38] In fact, this is not strictly accurate, in that most of the Percy's 'north cuntre' retainers had not actually been at Shrewsbury; but it is certainly true that the captains of the Percy's Northumbrian castles proved very reluctant to open their gates to the king. According to Hardyng, 'Percy's castelles all his menne held then full strong/to tyme the kyng had graunt hym plener grace.'[39] However, it would appear that 'Percy's . . . menne' who held these castles were not actually Northumbrians.

Not surprisingly, one of King Henry's more pressing concerns following the rising was to secure these Northumbrian castles, and to reassert his authority in the county.[40] On 26 July, less than a week after the battle, he appointed his squire John Coppill as constable of the royal castle of Bamburgh, which had been in the custody of Hotspur in his capacity as Warden of the East March. Since Hotspur had 'gone the way of all flesh' (as the commission coyly put it), the Wardenship of the East March was now vacant, and three days later, the post was filled by the earl of Westmorland.[41] This was obviously a panic measure, for on 6 August, Westmorland was moved to the West March, replacing the earl of Northumberland – whose continued tenure of the office could hardly be countenanced – and the East March was now committed to the king's third son, John of Lancaster. On the

---

[36] *Hardyng*, p. 351; *CPR, 1401–5*, p. 249; McNiven, 'The Scottish Policy of the Percies', p. 515n. One David Trollop had served with the earl of Northumberland in *c.* 1385: BL Cotton Roll XIII 8.

[37] For instance, Swinburne retained a company of ten men-at-arms and forty archers at Chester in January 1402: NRO ZSW, 1/117.

[38] *An English Chronicle of the Reigns of Richard II, Henry IV, Henry V and Henry VI*, ed. J. S. Davies, Camden Society 1st s. 64 (London, 1856), p. 29. The passage is a translation from the Latin *Eulogium Historiarum*, III, 398.

[39] *Hardyng*, p. 361; and cf. *POPC*, II, 79–80.

[40] There is a valuable account of the suppression of the rebels in Northumberland in 1403–5 in *Northumberland County History*, V, 36–43.

[41] *CPR, 1401–5*, pp. 252, 258.

same day, Robert Umfraville and Gerard Heron were commissioned to treat with the Scots for a truce since an attempt by the Scots to exploit the situation was the last thing that Henry needed at this juncture.[42] The situation became somewhat easier on 11 August, when Henry obtained the earl's submission at York,[43] and the latter agreed to surrender his castles – although it proved somewhat more difficult to put this surrender into effect.

With the earl safely in custody, Henry judged that the continued rebellion in Wales was now a more urgent problem, and headed south. The task of pacifying Northumberland was left in the hands of the leading North-umbrian gentry, of whom the most prominent were Gerard Heron, John de Mitford, Robert de Umfraville, Ralph de Eure and John de Widdrington, under the supervision of Lords Say and Furnival (the latter being Ralph Neville's brother).[44] It was no coincidence that all of these except Widdring-ton were annuitants of the king. Bamburgh seems to have been secured with no great difficulty, perhaps because Henry Percy's lieutenant at the castle, Thomas Knayton, was dead, probably killed at Shrewsbury. At any rate, John Coppill wrote to the king from Bamburgh in January in terms which suggest he had been in control of the place for some time.[45] Warkworth, Alnwick and Berwick castles proved more troublesome, and letters were sent to their garrisons demanding their surrender, under the earl of Northumberland's 'grande seal des armes'.[46] The names of those to whom these letters were addressed are revealing: the constable of Alnwick Castle was named as William Worthington, and the other officers listed were John Wyndale, chaplain, William Roddam, John Middleham, Thomas Clerk of Alnwick and Richard Bonde. Warkworth was held by Henry Percy de Atholl, John Cresswell (the constable) and Richard Ask, and Berwick by William de Clifford.[47] Of these (and discounting Percy), only Roddam, Clerk and Cresswell were certainly native Northumbrians; and for that matter, Thomas Knayton, the ill-fated former constable of Bamburgh, was not a Northumbrian. In the main, the garrisons of the Percies' Northumbrian castles seem to have been drawn from their Yorkshire affinity rather than from Northumberland itself. Those Northumbrians who did support the

[42] *Rot. Scot.*, II, 164.
[43] 'Annales', p. 372; *The Chronicle of England by John Capgrave*, ed. F. C. Hingeston (London, 1858), p. 283.
[44] *CPR, 1401–5*, pp. 262, 284 and 296; *POPC*, I, 211–17.
[45] *A Collection of Royal and Historical Letters during the Reign of Henry IV*, ed. F. C. Hingeston, 2 vols. (London, 1860), I, 206–7. The letters patent appointing Coppill as constable of Bamburgh stated that the office was 'in the king's gift by reason of the forfeiture of Thomas Knayton, deceased, late one of the esquires of Henry de Percy' (*CPR, 1401–5*, p. 252), which implies that Knayton was actively in rebellion.
[46] *POPC*, I, 213–16.
[47] For Clifford, see *Royal and Historical Letters*, ed. Hingeston, I, 206; Given-Wilson, *Royal Household*, pp. 228–9. The head of the unfortunate Richard Ask was later to adorn York's Botham Bar, following the events of 1405: *CPR, 1405–8*, p. 69.

Percies were mainly their tenants. The Roddams held their lands of the Percy barony of Beanley, and had a history of service to their landlords stretching back to the 1330s.[48] John Cresswell came from a Northumbrian family of no very great standing, and he owed most of his wealth to a lifetime grant from the crown of an assortment of Northumbrian lands and tenements, made in settlement of the arrears of an annuity owed to his father for service to the Black Prince.[49] Many of these tenements were held of the Percies, and as Cresswell's landed wealth was decidedly precarious, he had every incentive to seek their patronage, to try to obtain a rather more durable estate. Likewise, John Hardyng, who fought for Percy at Shrewsbury, was probably a Percy tenant.[50] By contrast, those Percy adherents whose standing in Northumberland was not dependent solely on their Percy connections showed no such loyalty to the Percy cause. Robert Lisle, the constable of the Percy castle of Prudhoe, came from a family of long-standing wealth and influence within Northumberland. He had served the crown as a tax-collector and as a knight of the shire, but having so much to lose, he appears to have come to terms immediately with the king, for he was called upon merely to hold Prudhoe, rather than to deliver it up,[51] and John de Mitford was assigned the task of obtaining the surrender of Warkworth, despite his long record of service to the Percies.[52]

In fact, the efforts of Mitford and his colleagues proved singularly ineffective. Warkworth, Alnwick and Berwick were still holding out against the king in January 1404, when it was reported that Percy livery badges were being distributed by Clifford and Percy of Atholl.[53] This open defiance of the king ended only with the rehabilitation of the earl of Northumberland in March, which removed the cause of the trouble and left his garrisons still in possession of his castles. It is interesting to note that while no Northumbrians

---

[48] 'Private Indentures for Life Service in Peace and War, 1278–1476', ed. M. Jones and S. Walker, in *Camden Miscellany XXXII*, Camden Society 5th s. 3 (London, 1994), no. 36; 'Charters of Alnwick Abbey', in G. Tate, *The History of the Borough, Castle and Barony of Alnwick*, 2 vols. (Alnwick, 1868–9), II, Appendix, pp. xxi–xxii; E 101/19/36, m. 3; E 101/20/17, mm. 2, 7; BL Cotton Roll XIII 8; *Rot. Parl.*, III, 255–6.

[49] *CPR, 1385–9*, pp. 287–8. For the elder Cresswell's career as a notorious *routier* see K. Fowler, *Medieval Mercenaries I: The Great Companies* (Oxford, 2001), passim.

[50] A John son of John Hardyng held land in Trickley near Chillingham in 1358, and Trickley was part of the barony of Alnwick, albeit held by the Heton family; John Hardyng the chronicler, born in *c.* 1378, was presumably the son or grandson of this man. It is also worth noting that when Hardyng entered Hotspur's household in *c.* 1390, Chillingham was held by Henry de Heton, who had close ties with the Percies: NRO ZSW, 1/105, 2/27, 28; *Hardyng*, p. 351.

[51] *POPC*, I, 211. For Lisle's career, see *House of Commons*, III, 610–12 (note that according to this account, Lisle was given custody of Prudhoe after Hotspur's rebellion; however, the memorandum printed by Nicolas suggests that he already held the office of constable at the time of the rebellion).

[52] *POPC*, I, 211.

[53] *Royal and Historical Letters*, ed. Hingeston, I, 206–7.

of any real standing were prepared to fight for the Percies, they seemed to have exhibited no great enthusiasm to fight against them either. John de Middleham, at least, had made some contacts among the Northumbrian gentry, being invited to accompany Thomas Gray and William de Swinburne on a 'private enterprise' cross-border raid, bringing with him 'all the men of our noble lord the earl of Northumberland', with the added stipulation that he act 'as privately as you can best do' (and so presumably without the knowledge of Percy himself).[54] It would hardly be surprising if there was a degree of reluctance among the marchers to turn against those who had fought alongside them against the Scots.[55] Nevertheless, in the wake of Hotspur's rebellion, there was only one significant change in Northumberland's administration, when Richard Cliderowe replaced William de Mitford as the escheator for the county, in August 1403. But despite the timing, there is no reason to suppose that this stemmed from any doubts over Mitford's loyalties. He was the eldest son of John de Mitford, one of the king's main agents in dealing with the recalcitrant constables of the Percy castles in the county; and William was anyway appointed to a commission of the peace for Northumberland in November. At a time when Percy's adherents were still holding out in his Northumbrian castles, this peace commission was obviously crucial to the reassertion of royal authority in the county. As such, it is interesting to note the degree of continuity with the previous commission of the peace issued for Northumberland, in May 1401, which had been headed by the earl of Northumberland and his son. Of course, by November 1403, Hotspur was dead, and his father was – unsurprisingly – conspicuous only by his absence from the new commission. They were replaced by John of Lancaster, the earl of Westmorland and Thomas Neville of Halomshire; but of the seven Northumbrian knights and esquires appointed to the commission of 1401, only one, Gerard Heron, was not reappointed in 1403. Two other Northumbrians were appointed for the first time in 1403, but only one of these, Robert Swinhowe, had any previous Lancastrian connections; the other was Robert Lisle, the erstwhile Percy adherent whose rapid capitulation at Prudhoe was now rewarded by crown office (see Appendix).

A more assertive approach to controlling the county administration of Northumberland by the king can be seen in the appointment of Thomas de Rokeby as sheriff in January 1405, in place of John de Clavering. This was surely a calculated attempt to counter the influence of the earl of

---

[54] 'auxi privatement come vous purrez bonement': NRO ZSW, 1/104, printed by Tuck, 'Richard II and the Border Magnates', p. 31. Unfortunately, this letter is not dated; but it may safely be assumed that it was written before Gray's death in November 1400 (*CIPM*, XVIII, no. 433). As Warden of the March, it was Percy's job to stamp out such raids.

[55] In this context, it is interesting to note that when Lord Say died in 1404, he left £20 to the earl of Northumberland in his will, adding 'I have been a soldier under the said earl and received more than I deserve': *Northumberland County History*, V, 37n.

Northumberland, for the appointment was made on the 21st of that month, undoubtedly in reaction to the earl's letter of the 12th, written at Warkworth, in which he excused himself from attendance at a meeting of the council on the grounds of 'grand age et fieblesse' and the difficulty of travelling in the winter; an excuse that was evidently regarded with suspicion.[56] Rokeby's lands lay in the far north of Yorkshire, making him the first sheriff of Northumberland not to hold substantial lands in the county since the appointment of the Irishman John de Caunton, in 1311. He was therefore safely removed from Percy's web of affinity, and – perhaps more pertinently – he was affiliated with the Neville family.[57] That Rokeby was seen as a loyal supporter of the king is demonstrated by his recruitment as a king's knight in the same year; and his reliability as an agent of royal authority in the north was subsequently proved when he led the Yorkshire levies against Earl Henry in his last rebellion, which ended at Bramham Moor, in February 1408.[58] Following Northumberland's attempted murder of the earl of West-morland in 1405, Henry IV took a much harder line in pacifying the county of Northumberland, by marching up with a large army with a fully equipped siege train, including guns. Prudhoe submitted at once, but the captain of Warkworth (apparently John de Middleham, the constable of Alnwick in 1403) was made of sterner stuff, replying to demands for its surrender by pointing out that the castle was well garrisoned and supplied, and would hold out in the name of the earl. Given the king's conciliatory policy in 1403, Middleham had little reason to suppose that he would be any less con-ciliatory now.[59] But he may also have been relying on Warkworth's value to the king as an important border fortress – which would obviously not be enhanced by a destructive siege. Sixty years later, when another king of England (Edward IV) was again besieging English rebels in a Northumbrian castle (Bamburgh), he is said to have specified that 'seing it marcheth so nygh hys awncient enemyes of Scotland, he specially desirethe to have it hoole, unbroken with ordennanuance'. In 1405, those who held out in Warkworth may have made hoped that Henry would show a similar reluctance.[60] If so,

---

[56] *POPC*, II, 103–4. For Rokeby's career, see *House of Commons*, IV, 228–30.

[57] *VCH Yorkshire: The North Riding I*, ed. W. Page (London, 1914), pp. 49–50, 111–12; *House of Commons*, IV, 228. For Caunton's appointment, see A. King, 'Jack le Irish and the Abduction of Lady Clifford, November 1315: The Heiress and the Irishman', *Northern History* 38 (2001), 187–95 (p. 194).

[58] *The St Albans Chronicle, 1406–1420*, ed. V. H. Galbraith (Oxford, 1937), p. 28; Given-Wilson, *Royal Household*, pp. 229, 289. Rokeby was then sheriff of Yorkshire.

[59] 'Annales', p. 411; *POPC*, I, 275–6. Middleham was described as 'late keeper of the castle of Warkworth' when he was discovered to be in treasonable communication with the exiled earl of Northumberland in August 1407: *CPR, 1405–8*, p. 428.

[60] *A Chronicle of the First Thirteen Years of the Reign of King Edward the Fourth, by John Warkworth*, ed. J. O. Halliwell, Camden Society 1st s. 10 (London, 1839), p. 37. Incidentally, although the great tower at Warkworth undoubtedly looked impressive enough, its huge traceried chapel windows and none too thick walls must have made it virtually

seven shots from the royal canons were enough to disillusion them, and they surrendered on 1 July. Even so, perhaps in order to end the siege before the castle was too badly damaged, they were granted generous terms: 'the casteleyns to pass free wher they would,/With horse and harnes without chalenge more', according to Hardyng.[61] Alnwick capitulated immediately afterwards, but Berwick, apparently held with the assistance of a Scottish force led by the earl of Orkney, required further exertions from the king's gunners to bring about its surrender.[62]

Although the earl of Northumberland may have been able to gain the support of the Scots, he again failed to attract the support of the North-umbrian gentry. The only notable exception was Alexander Blenkinsop, a second son of a minor gentry family who held land in the south of North-umberland and in Westmorland. Blenkinsop held a lease of lands in Alnwick, which perhaps led to his recruitment by the Percies. However, he was also in receipt of an annuity from the king; and this unfortunate conflict of interests was resolved by his beheading after the fall of Berwick.[63] Otherwise, and with the exception of the ring-leaders, Henry demonstrated his customary clemency. There were a few Northumbrians among those pardoned for 'treasons, insurrections, rebellions and felonies', such as Robert de Hall, John Preston, John de Warkworth, John Rothbury and William Chatton, while the border 'surnames' were represented by numerous Johnsons, Atkinsons and Dixons. There were even a couple of scions of Northumbrian gentry families: Henry Fenwick, chaplain, and Hugh Swinhoe.[64] Neverthe-less, none of these men were of any account in the political society of the county, which remained almost entirely unaffected by the earl's rebellion. After the execution of Archbishop Scrope, the king took the opportunity to extend his authority into Hexhamshire (a liberty held by the archbishops of York, and so conveniently in the king's hand), by appointing William Carnaby as steward and bailiff of the liberty for life.[65] But, even in the absence of the Percies, Henry still made very little use of his Lancastrian affinity. A case in point is that of Edmund Hastings, who had accompanied Henry on his crusade to Prussia in 1390. By means of a good marriage, and the failure in the male line of the Felton family, he subsequently acquired

---

indefensible; Middleham's prompt surrender in the face of Henry's cannonade is not therefore surprising.

[61] *Hardyng*, p. 363; *POPC*, I, 275.

[62] *Hardyng*, p. 363; 'Annales', p. 414; *Rot. Parl.*, III, 605; *Royal and Historical Letters*, ed. Hingeston, II, 61–3. The bombardment inflicted severe damage on the walls of Berwick, which was not repaired for years: S. B. Chrimes, 'Some Letters of John of Lancaster as Warden of the East Marches towards Scotland', *Speculum* 14 (1939), 3–27.

[63] *CPR, 1401–5*, p. 59; *CCR, 1405–9*, p. 161; *Hardyng*, p. 363; *House of Commons*, II, 250–1.

[64] *CPR, 1405–8*, pp. 76–7; and see the comments of P. McNiven, 'The Betrayal of Archbishop Scrope', *BJRL* 54 (1971–2), 173–213 (p. 199). Preston and Hall had served in Percy's retinue in 1384: E 101/40/5.

[65] *CPR, 1405–8*, p. 69.

their extensive Northumbrian estates, centred on Edlingham.[66] Hastings was obviously regarded as dependable by the king, for he was employed extensively on crown commissions and in crown office in Yorkshire, where his family resided, and was awarded an annuity of £20 in 1405. Yet although the bulk of his lands lay in Northumberland, and he proved acceptable enough to Northumbrian political society to be elected as knight of the shire for the parliament of October 1407, the king made very little use of his services in Northumbrian government.[67]

Percy's defection to the Scots can only have served to discredit him within Northumberland, but even so, there was some lingering sympathy for the Percy cause. In August 1407, John de Middleham received a letter from the exiled earl, which he forwarded to William Alnwick, a canon of Alnwick Abbey and the vicar of Chatton (a former Percy manor). When Middleham was caught and condemned to death for this treason, William fled in terror to Scotland where he joined the earl – though he did manage to obtain a pardon after the earl's death.[68] On the other hand, William's superior, the abbot of Alnwick, took a distinctly more practical view of political realities; in April 1407, he granted an annuity of two marks to Robert Harbottle 'for his good service and counsel given and to be given'.[69] The removal of the Percies did not leave a total vacuum of power in its wake, and most of their former adherents were able to find alternative sources of patronage within Northumberland. Less than six months after the earl's forfeiture, William Roddam was associated with Robert de Swinhoe and Edmund de Craster as a witness for one of Harbottle's property deals. John Hardyng, despite his subsequent avowal of the heartfelt loyalty of 'the people by north' to the Percies, acquired himself another good lord in the shape of Robert Umfraville, who appointed him as his constable at Warkworth – a striking, if somewhat ironic, example of continuity. Even John Cresswell, the recalcitrant constable of Warkworth in 1403, was able to reconcile himself to the new regime, and in February 1409, took out letters of protection for service in the garrison of Berwick with Prince John.[70]

---

[66] *Expeditions to Prussia and the Holy Land Made by Henry Earl of Derby*, ed. L. Toulmin-Smith, Camden Society 2nd s. 52 (London, 1894), p. 132; *CIPM*, XVIII, nos. 756–7.

[67] *House of Commons*, III, 317–19. Hastings' sole appointments in Northumberland by Henry IV were to commissions to uncover concealments and to raise loans for the king, both on the same day (18 June 1406: *CPR, 1405–8*, pp. 155, 201); he did, however, obtain rather more employment in the county under Henry V.

[68] *CPR, 1405–8*, p. 428. Incidentally, this is not the William Alnwick who subsequently achieved national eminence as bishop of Lincoln: R. C. E. Hayes, 'The Pre-episcopal Career of William Alnwick, Bishop of Norwich and Lincoln', in *People, Politics and Community in the Later Middle Ages*, ed. J. Rosenthal and C. Richmond (Stroud, 1987), pp. 90–107 (p. 91).

[69] *Northumberland and Durham Deeds*, p. 156.

[70] *Northumberland and Durham Deeds*, p. 156; *Hardyng*, p. 361; *Cal. Docs. Scot. V*, ed. Simpson and Galbraith, no. 4696.

The decade from 1397 to 1408 had seen profound political upheaval, on both a national and local level; yet throughout this period, the composition of the clique that comprised Northumbrian political society remained remarkably stable. Perhaps the only significant changes in its make-up that can be directly attributed to the political turbulence of these years were the upwardly mobile career trajectories of Robert Harbottle, whose new-found social advancement was marked out in stone, for all to see, by the impressive tower house he constructed at Preston;[71] and, to a lesser degree, of William Carnaby. The only outsiders to be imposed on the county by Henry were Thomas de Rokeby and Thomas Neville of Halomshire; and of these two, Rokeby's tenure of office lasted for less than a year. Notably, there were no significant losers among the Northumbrian gentry, who were far more likely to be removed from crown office by natural causes than by the vagaries of politics. The gentry families who dominated the government of Northumberland after the overthrow of the Percy family were still the same families who had dominated it before the overthrow of Richard II (see Appendix).[72]

All of this begs a rather obvious question: if the Percies really did wield so little authority over the Northumbrian gentry, then why did John Hardyng claim that 'they have the hertes of the people by north', and why did Henry V consider it necessary to reinstate them just ten years after their forfeiture?[73] In 1405, the Percies were replaced as the greatest landowners in the county by John of Lancaster, who was granted part of their estate on 27 June, while his father was preparing to besiege Warkworth. But Prince John received only part of the Percy lands. The grants to him excluded the Northumbrian baronies of Warkworth and Langley, along with many of the Yorkshire lands and the wealthy manor of Petworth.[74] Given the undoubted Percy sympathies of many of their Yorkshire tenants (demonstrated by the willingness of many of them to follow Percy in a doomed cause in 1408), John was unlikely to have extracted the optimum returns from the lands that he did receive. Prince John was therefore unable to match the Percies in one vital

---

[71] The 'turris de Preston Roberti Herbottille' was first recorded among the *fortalicii* in a survey of Northumbrian fortifications made in 1415: C. Bates, *The Border Holds of Northumberland, Archaeologia Aeliana* 2nd s. 14 (1891), p. 16.

[72] The careers of John de Mitford and the Grays of Heton are particularly telling in this context.

[73] In fact, Hardyng's comment should be read as pro-Percy propaganda reflecting the politics of the early 1460s, rather than as an objective historiographical thesis (a point I owe to Tony Pollard), but he presumably considered this a credible claim to make on their behalf.

[74] *CPR, 1405–8*, p. 40. Langley was granted as a well-earned reward to Robert Umfraville, for life, with reversion to John (*CPR, 1405–8*, p. 50). It should be noted that although Ralph Neville held considerable estates in the south of the county (Tuck, 'The Percies and the Community of Northumberland', pp. 188–9), and was regularly appointed to commissions of the peace after 1403, he took no great interest in Northumbrian affairs and made no effort to acquire an affinity there.

matter – and this was the prompt payment of wages. The Percies may have had difficulty in obtaining payment of the fees owed to them by the crown, but they were wealthy enough to pay their own retainers in the meantime, effectively subsidizing the defence of the marches from their own estates. John received a substantially smaller fee, and had even greater difficulty extracting the money from Henry's cash-strapped government – as he complained frequently and bitterly[75] – and with a greatly reduced estate, he could not draw on his own landed wealth to the same extent as the Percies to off-set the crown's tight-fistedness. As a result, the garrisons of vital border fortresses were often left unpaid and unsupplied, with the consequent threat of desertion, and the defences of Berwick remained in the ruinous state wreaked by Henry's cannons in 1405, rendering it indefensible – or so John claimed. Intended as they were to elicit a financial response, his complaints may have painted an exaggeratedly pessimistic picture; however, their desperate tone is altogether different from the earl of Northumberland's well-known letter of June 1403, in which he vaguely warned of the possible dishonour of 'le bone renome du chivalerie de vostre roialme' if money was not forthcoming. It would appear that John's ability to defend the marches was genuinely and seriously hampered by a lack of resources. Certainly, he would have been hard-pressed to repeat the expedient adopted by Percy in 1384, when the Scots briefly captured Berwick, of buying off its captors for 2,000 marks of his own money.[76]

John's problems were largely of the making of his own father. On coming to the throne, Henry had adopted a more aggressive policy towards Scotland, inspired partly by the provocation of the Scottish attack on Wark Castle, while its owner, Sir Thomas Gray, had been in Westminster helping to depose Richard II; and partly by the need to appease the ambitions of the Percies. He revived English claims to the overlordship of Scotland, demanding that King Robert and his magnates do homage to him; and this stance was maintained, at least nominally, even after his expedition to Scotland in 1400 predictably failed to enforce these demands.[77] However, the logical corollary of a hostile policy towards Scotland was massive expenditure on soldiers and garrisons in the marches (as John of Lancaster appreciated all too clearly), expenditure that Henry was politically quite unable to raise the taxes to pay

---

[75] Chrimes, 'Some Letters of John of Lancaster', passim; Storey, 'The Wardens of the Marches', pp. 603–4. The Scottish marches were accorded a much lower priority for crown spending than Calais or Wales: E. Wright, 'Henry IV, the Commons and the Recovery of Royal Finance in 1407', in *Rulers and Ruled in Late Medieval England. Essays Presented to Gerald Harriss*, ed. R. E. Archer and S. Walker (London, 1995), pp. 65–81 (pp. 77–8).

[76] Chrimes, 'Letters of John of Lancaster', passim; *POPC*, I, 204–5; *Westminster Chron.*, p. 104.

[77] C. J. Neville, *Violence, Custom and Law: The Anglo-Scottish Border Lands in the Later Middle Ages* (Edinburgh, 1998), pp. 97–8; A. L. Brown, 'The English Campaign in Scotland, 1400', in *British Government and Administration: Studies Presented to S. B. Chrimes*, ed. H. Hearder and H. R. Loyn (Cardiff, 1974), pp. 40–54.

for; and in practice, the marches were increasingly left to fend for themselves, though the rhetoric of overlordship continued.[78] Fortunately, the defection of the Scottish earl of March, followed by the spectacular English victory at Homildon Hill, served to obviate the worst potential consequences of this muddling. The removal by desertion, death or captivity of a large section of the Scottish border nobility, coupled with the political instability surrounding the Scottish crown, ensured that the threat of any major Scottish invasion was greatly reduced – although it was precisely these circumstances that allowed Hotspur to contemplate the luxury of rebellion in the first place.[79] But these same conditions also served to undermine the whole system of march law. For its effective implementation, this required a degree of cooperation between magnates on both sides of the border; and with the eclipse of the Percies, there was simply nobody left on the English side with the requisite authority.

However much he may have coveted lands in Scotland, the earl of Northumberland had been an effective warden of the marches. He was thoroughly experienced in the precarious workings of the march tribunals, and while the Percies may not have commanded the allegiance of the Northumbrian gentry, they certainly had the authority and standing to restrain and punish the cross-border crime perpetrated by them – as William Heron or William de Swinburne could have testified.[80] The teenaged John of Lancaster had neither the practical authority nor the experience to be an effective replacement; and in any event, his father's hawkish line on Anglo-Scottish relations precluded the necessary cross-border cooperation. This left a permanent state of low-level cross-border hostility, which served to undermine the maintenance of order in Northumberland, as uncontrolled cross-border raiding spilled over into uncontrolled internal feuding. An interesting indication of the increasing level of lawlessness is provided by an indenture of September 1407, by which the widow of John de Dalton leased various properties around Hexham to William Ellison for life, at a rent of 5 marks a year. The agreement included a clause that made allowance in case any of the properties were destroyed by the Scots, but also in case William was prevented from taking his profit by 'any other lieges of the lord king whatsoever'.[81] Leaving aside the implication that the Scots should be

---

[78] A telling indication of the rapid decline of crown interest in the marches is that between 1296 and 1400, every king of England personally led an expedition against the Scots; after 1405, the only Lancastrian king to visit the marches was Henry VI, who took refuge there after Towton.

[79] A J. Macdonald, *Border Bloodshed: Scotland, England and France at War, 1369–1403* (East Linton, 2000), pp. 157–60.

[80] *Rot. Parl.*, III, 255–6; NRO ZSW, 101, 102; Neville, *Violence, Custom and Law*, p. 87 and passim.

[81] 'Et si contingat predicta terras tenementa uel aliquam parcellam eorundem destrui per Scotos siue dictum Willelmum esse impeditum *per quoscumque alios ligeos domini regis* de

numbered among the 'lieges of the lord king', this suggests a serious loss of confidence in the ability of the crown to control the situation. Although there are plenty of surviving fourteenth-century lease agreements from Northumberland that make provision for the attentions of the Scots, rather fewer make any provision for damage by the English.[82] This loss of confidence was by no means unjustified. Northumberland faced a virtual breakdown of order that was reflected to an unprecedented degree of concern in parliament. Typical of the disturbances that beset the county was a violent feud between the brothers Robert Ogle and John Bertram over Bothal Castle in 1410, which rapidly escalated into a armed siege, involving 200 Scots brought specially across the border. This was just the sort of dispute the Percies could have settled, by either force or arbitration, before it reached such a dangerous level of violence; and it eventually became clear that in the continued absence of crown interest in the marches, the only alternative means of restoring order was to establish a local magnate who could do the job for them – and in practice this meant the Percies.[83]

At the time of Henry Percy's creation as earl of Northumberland, the Percy affinity was drawn largely from their Yorkshire lands, and their authority in Northumberland was far from complete.[84] It has been said of Henry IV's England that 'the county "establishment" was almost a law unto itself and difficult to control from Westminster';[85] but the Percies seem to have trouble enough controlling Northumberland from Warkworth. They could undoubtedly bring the gentry of Northumberland out against the Scots – Ralph de Eure, Sir Robert Umfraville and Robert Harbottle all fought alongside Hotspur at Homildon Hill;[86] but they could not bring them out against the king. Hotspur's reliance on disaffected Cheshiremen to support his rebellion may have been due to well-founded doubts as to the dependability of his Northumbrian supporters; and it is certainly suggestive that his father's revolt of 1408 was based in Yorkshire rather than Northumberland. The Percies' perceived dominance of the county at the beginning of Henry's reign rested largely on their success in keeping out rival magnates; they were

profitus suo inde capiendo quod tunc debita allocatio fiet dicto Willelmo de firma predicta': NRO ZMI, B1/VII/2 (my emphasis).

[82] A lease from the troubled days of November 1313, recorded in Durham Cathedral, Muniments of the Dean and Chapter, Reg. II. fols 34v–35r, is the only other example I have come across.

[83] Neville, *Violence, Custom and Law*, pp. 102–9; Macdonald, *Border Bloodshed*, pp. 231–5; C. Allmand, *Henry V* (London, 1992), pp. 311–12. For an example of arbitration involving the Percies see NRO ZSW, 1/107. This is a subject I hope to deal with at greater length elsewhere.

[84] Tuck, 'The Percies and the Community of Northumberland', passim.

[85] Brown, 'Reign of Henry IV', p. 23.

[86] Macdonald, *Border Bloodshed*, p. 155; *CCR, 1399–1402*, p. 552. Note that Harbottle is not mentioned by name in the latter reference, but can safely be identified as the anonymous 'constable of Dunstanburgh'.

able to draw erstwhile Lancastrians such as William de Swinburne and John de Fenwick into their orbit owing to the lack of any viable alternative to their good lordship. However, it was obviously much more difficult to keep out the influence of the crown. Indeed, it proved so difficult that Hotspur resorted to attempting to change who wore the crown instead. Henry IV successfully exerted his authority over Northumberland by working with the grain of Northumbrian political society rather than against it, by retaining the service of the most influential Northumbrians, rather than attempting to impose his own men. Perhaps if the Percies had done the same, they might not have needed to resort to the desperate expedient of rebellion. But once the crown had lost interest in Scotland and the marches, this ceased to be a problem. If, during the course of the fifteenth century, the Percies did gain 'the hertes of the people by north', it was perhaps because there were so few rivals for their affections.

Appendix

Office-holding in Northumberland, 1397–1408

	1397	1398	1399	1400	1401	1402	1403	1404	1405	1406	1407	1408
GENTRY												
John Mitford	J, K		J	K	E, J	K, S	J		J		J	
Thomas Gray de Heton	J, K		J, K	d.								
Ralph Eure	J, S		J		J		J		J		J	
Sampson Harding	J		J, K	E	J		J, K		J		J	
Gerard Heron	J, K		J	K, S	J	K	J	d.	J			
Robert Lisle	K						J	K	J	K, S		
John Fenwick		S			d.							
Thomas Gray de Horton					J		J		J			
William Mitford					J	E	J		E, J		J	
Robert Umfraville					J, S		J		S			
Richard Cliderowe							E					
John de Clavering							S			K		
Thomas Neville							J		J			
Robert Swinhowe							J		J		J	

John de Widdrington		K		J	
William de Carnaby				d.	
Thomas Rokeby			S	J	S
Thomas Gray de Heton				J	K
Edmund Hastings					K
Robert Harbottle					K, S
MAGNATES					
John of Gaunt	d.			J	
Henry Percy	J			J	
Henry Hotspur	J, S		f.	J	
John of Lancaster	J			J	J
Ralph Neville	J			J	

Key

E Escheator (note that the escheatry included Northumberland and Cumberland in 1397–1401)
K Knight of the shire
J Justice of the peace
S Sheriff
d. died
f. forfeited

9

The Yorkshire Risings of 1405:
Texts and Contexts

Simon Walker

Early in May 1405 Henry Percy, earl of Northumberland, attempted to ambush his great rival for pre-eminence in the north of England, Ralph Neville, earl of Westmorland, as he dined with Sir Ralph Eure. Westmorland was forewarned of the plot and managed to make good his escape to the safety of Durham Castle but the incident was, as Thomas Walsingham justly remarked, 'the beginning of great evil'.[1] Within a fortnight, sporadic disturbances throughout the North and East Ridings had gathered sufficient momentum to attract the leadership of some prominent local gentry. A substantial force was assembled in Cleveland and began advancing south through the North Riding towards York, until it was dispersed at Topcliffe, apparently after a brief armed encounter, by Westmorland and John of Lancaster, the king's son. Although the areas most directly affected by these disturbances are conventionally identified as Cleveland, Allertonshire and the area around Topcliffe itself, it is clear that the disruption associated with this movement spread over a much wider area. Malton and the vale of Pickering saw considerable disturbances, as did the liberties of Ripon and Beverley; the keepers of the town of Beverley were still concerned enough at the situation on 5 June, when most of the trouble was over, to order the sparring of the town gates.[2] In York, meanwhile, the discontent that the citizens and local clergy felt at the heavy financial burdens placed upon them by the new Lancastrian regime found articulate expression in the preaching of the archbishop, Richard Scrope. Alarmed at the disorder he saw around him and especially concerned, it seems, by the evidence of dissension among the great magnates of his archdiocese – Percy, Neville and Mowbray – Scrope allied himself with Thomas Mowbray, the earl marshal, and led a mixed body of York citizens and clergy, afforced by the household men of the two captains, out to Shipton Moor. There they remained for three days, demanding the public redress of their grievances that the parliamentary process

---

[1] 'Annales', p. 400. The date conventionally assigned to the outbreak of the revolt in official records, 1 May, may also represent the actual date of Northumberland's attempted ambush: *CIPM*, 1399–1405, nos. 451, 1152.

[2] Beverley, Humberside Record Office, BC II/6/4, Expense communis pecunie.

seemed no longer to offer, until, on 29 May, the assurances of the earl of Westmorland that their complaints would be addressed persuaded them to disband. It proved a fatal error: Scrope and Mowbray were immediately detained to await the king's pleasure and, some ten days later, both were executed as traitors. Within a month, Henry IV could write with satisfaction to his councillors, reporting the final reduction of the Percy strongholds in Northumberland to royal obedience.[3]

These events are well attested and their significance for the reign of Henry IV is obvious: the king's suppression of the Yorkshire risings and his successful reassertion of royal authority on the northern march proved to be vital turning-points that allowed a crisis-ridden regime to assume, at last, some appearance of permanence. The motives and ambitions of the insurgents have proved more debatable. Polydore Vergil's change of heart, which led him to cast Sir William Plumpton, rather than Archbishop Scrope, as the ring-leader of the Yorkshire rising in the second and subsequent editions of his *Anglica Historia*, is only one instance of the explanatory dilemma the episode has posed, both to contemporaries and to later commentators.[4] Among current professional historians, however, a considerable degree of consensus about the nature and causes of the rising has emerged, largely fashioned around the valuable reconsideration of the evidence undertaken, some thirty years ago, by Peter McNiven.[5] His argument, in summary, was that the 'clerical prejudice' of the chroniclers had led to an undue emphasis upon the agency of the archbishop in the Yorkshire risings when it was, in fact, the earl of Northumberland who was 'the active leader of a single, greater conspiracy'. Northumberland's ambush of his rival was to be the opening move in a carefully concerted plan; with the Lancastrian regime's chief partisan in the region safely in his grasp, Northumberland would move down from the far North, systematically consolidating the troops that his allies and retainers had collected into a single great army. Archbishop Scrope

---

[3] *POPC*, I, 275–6.

[4] D. Hay, *Polydore Vergil, Renaissance Historian and Man of Letters* (Oxford, 1952), p. 193; his account is most readily accessible in *Plumpton Correspondence*, ed. T. Stapleton, Camden Society old s. 4 (London, 1839), p. xxiv. Compare with J. H. Ramsay, *Lancaster and York: A Century of English History, 1399–1485*, 2 vols. (Oxford, 1892), I, 88: 'What Scrope hoped to effect it is not easy to divine . . .'.

[5] P. McNiven, 'The Betrayal of Archbishop Scrope', *BJRL* 54 (1971), 173–213. P. McNiven, *Heresy and Politics in the Reign of Henry IV: The Burning of John Badby* (Manchester, 1987), pp. 123–5 offers a similar interpretation. General accounts of the period that clearly base their account of the rising upon McNiven's include M. H. Keen, *England in the Later Middle Ages* (London, 1973), pp. 311–13; A. Tuck, *Crown and Nobility 1272–1461* (London, 1985), pp. 230–2; P. Heath, *Church and Realm 1272–1461* (London, 1988), pp. 240–3; A. J. Pollard, *Late Medieval England, 1399–1509* (London, 2000), pp. 49–51. J. A. F. Thomson, *The Transformation of Medieval England, 1370–1529* (London, 1983), p. 168 offers a more neutral formulation, while A. Goodman, *A History of England from Edward II to James II* (London, 1977), p. 207 provides an analysis that preserves the independence of the Yorkshire risings.

was not, therefore, acting on his own initiative but was brought into the conspiracy as a subordinate, whose principal role was 'to lend a spurious air of religious mission to the earl's rebellion'. Even in this respect, his performance was not judged to be impressive: his 'activities' on Shipton Moor – the repeated preaching to his followers, the celebration of mass – were 'futile and dangerous time-wasting', while the programme of reform he set out was 'naive nonsense', suggesting only the defective political sensibilities of his audience.[6]

It should be emphasized that, in many respects, McNiven's article retains its value; but I shall argue in this study that it is mistaken in most of its principal conclusions. If Scrope was 'betrayed', it was not by Northumberland; the archbishop was an independent political actor, whose demands were informed and politically astute. Conversely, the earl of Northumberland had little direct association with the disturbances in Yorkshire; there was, indeed, no 'great conspiracy', organized by the Percies or anybody else, but rather a series of loosely connected and largely spontaneous risings, united in a common idiom of protest. The events of May 1405 are best treated as three separate, and perhaps sequential, episodes: Northumberland's failed *coup de main*, which sent him in rapid retreat towards Berwick; an armed demonstration among some of the North Riding gentry and their tenants, inspired both by their sympathy with the Percies and by apprehension at the broader consequences of Northumberland's failure; and a movement of protest at the disorder prevalent in the region, led by the archbishop, which sought to articulate the grievances of the citizens and clergy of York in politically acceptable terms. In order to demonstrate this, I shall first look at the narrative sources for the risings and seek to show that a close and informed reading of them, which pays due attention to their rhetorical structure and polemical purpose, can support such an interpretation of events. In the second half of the essay, I shall assess the plausibility of this analysis by examining in more detail the contexts in which such a widespread act of political defiance, one that united significant elements of the shire's nobility, gentry, clergy and townsmen into a single movement, came to be regarded as both possible and justified.

TEXTS

The narrative sources for a study of the Yorkshire risings fall into four principal categories: judicial proceedings against the rebels; chronicle accounts of the risings; hagiographical accounts of the archbishop's martyrdom; and reports of the rebels' manifestos. I shall examine them in turn.

---

[6] McNiven, 'Betrayal', pp. 186, 192, 209 and 185.

Simon Walker

Judicial proceedings

Two strong commissions of *oyer et terminer* to punish participants in the rising were issued early in June 1405 but, if the commissioners ever acted under their powers, no record of their sessions has survived. It may well be that the general pardon issued a week later rendered their work otiose.[7] The evidence for any common-law proceedings against the rebels is, in fact, very sparse. The only incident associated with the Yorkshire risings to appear in the records of King's Bench, the killing of Sir Thomas Colville in the forest of Galtres by George Darell of Sessay and others, was brought there on a writ of error as late as April 1409.[8] This is because the main work of judicial retribution was done in the Court of Chivalry, where judgement was rendered upon the king's record.[9] Fortunately, the most important of these proceedings is preserved in the 'record and process' of Northumberland and Bardolf's attainder recited during the Long Parliament.[10] This recalls how the temporal Lords, assembled before the king on 19 June, had been asked by Prince Henry the previous week to render judgment against Henry Percy *et autres de sa covyne*, in the light of the process formerly begun against them in the Court of Chivalry, according to the laws and usages of arms.

This is an important document for our understanding of the Yorkshire risings, supplying a better chronology and a more detailed account of its course than any other source, but its nature and contents need to be studied quite carefully for their full significance to become apparent. The record starts by reciting how Sir John Fauconberg, Sir Ralph Hastings, Sir John Fitzrandolf and Sir John Colville assembled a force of 7,000–8,000 men at Topcliffe, Allerton and Cleveland, falsely declaring that the intent of their insurrection was to address certain mischiefs and defaults in the kingdom, and to punish certain malefactors around the person of the king and his council, without informing the king either of the alleged mischiefs or of the names of the malefactors, as the custom of the realm required (articles 2–3). Fauconberg, Hastings and the others subsequently assembled their forces together at Topcliffe, until John of Lancaster, with Westmorland and Lord Fitzhugh, dispersed them (*fesoit voider le champ*) and captured them in their flight (article 4). Afterwards (*Item puis apres*), Richard Scrope, archbishop of York,

---

[7] *CPR, 1405–8*, pp. 65, 40; *CCR, 1402–5*, p. 517.

[8] KB 27/592 Rex, m. 14; KB 27/594 Rex, m. 2.

[9] BL MS Additional 9021, fols. 8–9 (Sir Henry Boynton); *Rot. Parl.*, III, 633 (Sir Ralph Hastings).

[10] *Rot. Parl.*, III, 604–7; M. H. Keen, 'Treason Trials under the Law of Arms', *TRHS* 5th s. 12 (1962), 85–103, and J. G. Bellamy, *The Law of Treason in England in the Later Middle Ages* (Cambridge, 1970), pp. 159, 180 and 182–3, deal with some of the legal issues the document raises, while A. L. Brown, 'The Commons and the Council in the Reign of Henry IV', *EHR* 79 (1964), 1–30 situates the process it reports within the chronology of the Long Parliament (pp. 12–25).

Thomas Mowbray, earl marshal, Sir William Plumpton, Sir Robert Lamplugh and Sir Robert Persay assembled forces in several places within the county, falsely declaring that their intent was to amend and redress certain grievances within the realm and to punish certain evil-doers who were of the king's council. Assembling together on Shipton Moor, with a force of 8,000–9,000 men, Scrope and Mowbray continued in their traitorous purpose, until they were taken on the moor on 29 May (article 5).

It is at this point that the judicial record turns to the culpability of the earl of Northumberland, reciting and, in some cases, documenting a whole string of potentially treasonable actions: the detention of the king's messenger, Robert Waterton; seditious correspondence with the Scots and French; the capture and sack of Berwick; the defiance of the Northumbrian castellans; Northumberland's subsequent residence in Scotland and his continued contact with the rebels in Wales (articles 6–12). The transition from one set of alleged treasons to the other is effected by the statement that Northumberland conspired with and counselled (*estoit conspirant, conjectant et conseillant*) Scrope and Mowbray, as well as with Fauconberg, Hastings and their accomplices. This is, of all the sources we shall examine, the strongest statement of direct Percy involvement in either the North Riding gentry risings or in Scrope's York-centred protest. Yet it is clearly an assertion of a very different order from the other charges against the earl, lacking either the detailed substantiation provided for his treasonable correspondence or the public notoriety of his capture of Berwick and detention of Waterton. In assessing it, a degree of scepticism is in order; the clear purpose of the narrative that supports it is to reformulate several distinct acts of resistance as a single, and unquestionably treasonable, conspiracy to rebel, disguising the unsubstantiable nature of its pivotal assertion of complicity by a carefully detailed rehearsal of times, names and places. An alternative reading would suggest that the Yorkshire rebels were pursuing an agenda quite distinct from Northumberland's declared purpose. Northumberland is very clear, in his letter to the duke of Orleans (article 9), that his struggle is a dynastic one: his intention and firm purpose is to sustain the rightful quarrel of King Richard, if he is still alive, and to avenge his death if he is not, for which reason he has moved war against Henry of Lancaster, currently regent of England. This is consistent with the strain of legitimist defiance evident in most of the other Percy manifestos issued in and after 1403 but quite at odds with the consistently reformist nature of the demands made by the Yorkshire rebels, as reported by the chroniclers and tacitly acknowledged, in the 'Record and Process' itself, by reference to the 'falsely' moderate nature of the insurgents' demands. Questions about the Lancastrian authority to rule were easier to resist and marginalize when they were couched in terms of self-interested loyalty to an absent and unpopular predecessor than when they were expressed as a series of widespread protests at the excessive demands and inadequate responses of a new and fragile dynasty. In conflating the two idioms, the 'Record and Process' was performing one of the characteristic rhetorical manoeuvres of the nascent Lancastrian regime, exaggerating the threat posed by a real but manageable danger in order to justify a disproportionately rigorous response.[11]

The principal judicial record relating to the Yorkshire rising provides important evidence, then, for the actions and demands of the insurgents, but its assertion of Percy complicity needs to be treated with caution, for it serves a clear polemical purpose, and it is supported, as we shall see, only very equivocally in the other narrative sources for the rising. In this respect, it should be noted that, although the official version of events won credence over time,[12] the government's tendentious narrative of the risings had still to gain full conviction in 1406, when significant sections of the political nation showed themselves anxious to preserve some distinction between the actions and intentions of Northumberland and his immediate associates, on the one hand, and the rest of the Yorkshire rebels, on the other. Asked for their verdict on the process initiated in the Court of Chivalry, the peers replied that certain actions of the earl of Northumberland were treasons and that Thomas, Lord Bardolf, was of his counsel and alliance; they were therefore to be summoned to appear before the king and, if they failed to respond, were to be held convicted and attainted of the aforesaid treasons. Asked the same question with regard to Scrope and Mowbray, the peers temporized: according to the information given to them by the Constable, it seemed to them that the case was treasonable; nevertheless, they wished for further deliberation before giving their answer to the king. There was no scope for an immediate response, for parliament adjourned for the harvest on the same day; and when it reassembled in the autumn, the question of Scrope and Mowbray's alleged treason had disappeared from view. It was the Commons who raised the issue once again, on 30 November, when they asked the king if they could know what had been done touching the late rebellions, at Shrewsbury and elsewhere; the answer was to finalize the attainder of Northumberland and Bardolf alone, with no further reference made to the guilt of the earl marshal and the archbishop.[13]

Chronicle accounts

The disturbances in the North, and particularly Archbishop Scrope's part in them, attracted considerable attention from contemporary chroniclers. The events they recounted were clearly important in themselves but they were

---

[11] P. Strohm, *England's Empty Throne: Usurpation and the Language of Legitimation, 1399–1422* (London, 1998), pp. 34–6 and passim.

[12] 'John Benet's Chronicle for the Years 1400 to 1462', ed. G. L. Harriss and M. A. Harriss, *Camden Miscellany XXIV*, Camden Society 4th s. 9 (London, 1972), pp. 175–6.

[13] The unexpected nature of the Commons' intervention is clear in the original enrolment, where it required the hasty addition of another membrane: C 65/69, m. 2.

also dramatic and invited reformulation within certain clearly recognizable narrative conventions: the stratagem by which Scrope and his allies were allegedly persuaded to disband their forces belonged to the world of *fabliaux* and folk-tales, while the execution of the archbishop was readily rendered as a martyrdom. There is a great deal to be gained from a close reading of these accounts, not least a series of explanations for the rebels' actions largely at odds with the official account, though their understandable concentration on the person of the archbishop tends to simplify a more complex picture. The accounts that particularly concern us are those either written close in time to the events they describe or given a particular authority by their northern provenance: the various recensions of Thomas Walsingham's chronicle; the Franciscan continuation of the *Eulogium Historiarum*; John Strecche's Kenilworth chronicle; the narrative preserved in the compilation known as *Giles' Chronicle*; and the divergent accounts of the rising given by John Hardyng.

The most circumstantial of these, and the account that agrees most closely with the official narrative of the 'Record and Process', is Thomas Walsingham's. For Walsingham, the Yorkshire risings presented particular difficulties of organization and interpretation, for they brought two of the guiding principles of his historical writing, loyalty to the Catholic Church and support for the Lancastrian dynasty, into direct conflict. A rebellion led by an archbishop could not easily be reduced to his favourite narrative formula, 'the objectification of opponents in a sufficiently vivid form to permit a reciprocal stabilisation of the Lancastrian king as the guarantor of civil order and ecclesiastical orthodoxy'.[14] For this reason Walsingham seems to have devoted considerable care to his account of the 1405 rebellion. At least three versions survive: the long narrative of the *Chronica Majora*, most probably composed within a couple of years of the events it describes, and two shorter versions for his *Chronica Minora*, one – the earlier? – substantially longer than the other.[15] This extended process of composition creates, in certain respects, an 'open text', constantly subject to revision. For some particularly sensitive issues, such as whether the king played any direct part in the archbishop's condemnation, Walsingham provides three different answers. Whereas the *Chronica Majora* version specifically states that Henry refused to see Scrope, one recension of the *Chronica Minora* describes an interview between them, during which the archbishop's staff is snatched

---

[14] Strohm, *England's Empty Throne*, pp. 81–2; R. G. Davies, 'After the Execution of Archbishop Scrope: Henry IV, the Papacy and the English Episcopate, 1405–8', *BJRL* 59 (1976–7), 40–74 examines in detail the ecclesiastical difficulties created by Scrope's execution.

[15] 'Annales', pp. 402–12; *Historia Anglicana*, II, 268–71, 422–3. The account in *Ypodigma Neustriae, a Thoma Walsingham, quondam monacho monasterii S. Albani, conscriptum*, ed. H. T. Riley (London, 1876), pp. 412–15, follows the shorter *Chronica Minora* version. For the relationship and dating of these accounts, see *The St Albans Chronicle, 1406–1420*, ed. V. H. Galbraith (Oxford, 1937), pp. liii–lxvi.

from his hand; the shorter text of the *Chronica Minora*, perhaps Walsingham's final version of events, avoids committing itself on the issue entirely and seeks to distance the king as far as possible from the execution.[16]

It is within this context of indeterminacy that Walsingham's assertion of collusion between Scrope and Northumberland – one of the mainstays of McNiven's argument – should be viewed. For Walsingham, the explanatory considerations were finely balanced: associating Scrope's initiative with the activities of a proven traitor like Northumberland was discreditable to the archbishop, but provided a stronger justification for the king's harsh action. The earlier account of the *Chronica Majora* appears to concur in the accusation of conspiracy made by the 'Record and Process': far away in Wales, the king hears how the archbishop of York and the earl marshal, on the one hand, and the earl of Northumberland and Lord Bardolf, on the other, have gathered together *an* army. As the Lancastrian kings secured themselves more firmly on the throne, Walsingham's growing confidence that they enjoyed the mandate of heaven allowed him to shift the burden of culpability a little and take a more questioning stance towards the issue of treasonable collusion. The later *Chronica Minora* account is substantially less dogmatic: the earl and the archbishop have, *it is said*, received comfort from Northumberland; the rest of the narrative treats Percy resistance to Henry's authority in the far North as a parallel but entirely separate set of developments.

The well-informed account in the continuation of the *Eulogium Historiarum*, one apparently composed in a Franciscan house, in all likelihood before the end of Henry IV's reign, takes this interpretation of events one step further, by treating the Yorkshire rising quite separately from its account of the king's campaign to return the Northumbrian castles to royal hands.[17] It is supported in this respect by the Whalley Abbey continuation of the *Polychronicon*, a text that displays a particular and knowledgeable interest in the deeds of the Percy family between 1400 and 1408, but makes no connection between the Yorkshire risings and its tale of the relentless royal pursuit of Northumberland.[18] John Strecche's chronicle, too, treats the rebellions of Scrope and the earl of Northumberland as two

---

[16] Note also that Scrope's rebellion was one of the episodes where Walsingham's readers felt most free to criticize his conclusions. Compare the outraged exclamations at the earl of Westmorland's deception in Oxford, Bodleian Library, MS Bodley 462, fol. 278v (*falsum est*) with Thomas Otterbourne's careful exculpation of Ralph Neville's actions: *Duo Rerum Anglicarum Scriptores Veteres*, ed. T. Hearne (Oxford, 1732), p. 256.

[17] *Eulogium Historiarum*, III, 405–8; this is the basis for the vernacular account of the rising in *An English Chronicle of the reigns of Richard II, Henry IV, Henry V and Henry VI written before 1471*, ed. J. S. Davies, Camden Society old s. 64 (London, 1856), pp. 31–4.

[18] C. L. Kingsford, *English Historical Literature in the Fifteenth Century* (Oxford, 1913), pp. 279–91 (p. 282). Note the similar interpretation of events in BL MS Additional 29504, a northern roll chronicle that pays close attention to the doings of the Percies but makes no connection between their rebellions and Scrope's rising.

entirely separate movements, linking Scrope's protest, instead, to the forth-right criticism of Henry's government voiced in previous parliaments.[19] Finally, the compilation known as *Giles' Chronicle* casts doubt upon Henry Percy's complicity from another angle. Notable both for its strong connections to York and its access to official documents, the account in *Giles* is especially sympathetic to Scrope, whom it clearly treats as a saint undergoing martyrdom, and suggests the king's treatment of Thomas Mowbray, earl marshal, as the original cause of the rising. 'Ancient hatred' between Mowbray and certain other lords had led Henry to deprive the earl marshal of his hereditary offices and persuaded Scrope, taking into account as well many other grievances, to exhort the people to fight for justice.[20]

The last, and in some ways most problematic, of the chronicle accounts that need to be considered are those of John Hardyng. Hardyng is in some ways a prime witness: a Northumbrian by birth, he had spent many years in the household of Henry Percy, the earl of Northumberland's eldest son. Although he had left Percy employment by 1405, it was only to take service with Sir Robert Umfraville, one of the earl of Westmorland's most reliable lieutenants, and a man who played a significant part in the suppression of the Yorkshire rising itself. Hardyng was, however, writing with the benefit of half a century of hindsight, and successive recensions of his chronicle present significantly different versions of events. His second recension, completed in 1463 and intended for presentation to Edward IV, is the only unequivocal witness for the view that the Yorkshire risings involved a deliberate collaboration between Scrope and Northumberland. Hardyng explains that the rising was part of a broader conspiracy among the lords to regain royal favour for the earl and describes how the army Scrope and Mowbray assemble on Shipton Moor is made up:

> Of their owne and their frendes also,
> Of therles menne of Northumberland that were
> To the nombre of twenty thousand tho,
> Afore the daye assigned that was so
> By therle then of Northumberland,
> That there cheften with theim should have stand.[21]

---

[19] BL MS Additional 35295, fols. 263v–264; for the date of this passage (*c.* 1417–22), see 'Chronicle of John Strecche for the reign of Henry V (1414–1422)', ed. F. Taylor, *BJRL* 16 (1932), 137–87 (pp. 139–40).

[20] *Incerti Scriptoris Chronicon de regnis . . . Henrici IV, Henrici V, et Henrici VI*, ed. J. A. Giles (London, 1848), pp. 43–8; M. V. Clarke, *Fourteenth Century Studies* (Oxford, 1937), pp. 82–6.

[21] *Hardyng*, pp. 362–4 (quotation at p. 362); the relationship between Hardyng's career and his writings is further discussed in C. L. Kingsford, 'The First Version of Hardyng's Chronicle', *EHR* 27 (1912), 462–82 and F. Riddy, 'John Hardyng's Chronicle and the Wars of the Roses', in *Arthurian Literature XII*, ed. J. P. Carley and F. Riddy (Cambridge, 1993), pp. 91–108.

He then emphasizes the Percy connection further by describing the gentry leaders of the North Riding insurgents as 'knightes . . . full manly/ To therle of Northumberland openly'. Such an interpretation of the rising is, however, wholly absent from his first recension. Completed in 1457 and intended for presentation to the Lancastrian royal family, this presents a substantially different account, which disclaims all knowledge of Scrope and Mowbray's motivation – 'for what cause or encheson / I know no thynge what so was their reson' – although it does imply that their agenda was a reformist rather than a dynastic or legitimist one. The earl and archbishop are persuaded to disband their forces:

> Supposyng than in parlement of Recorde
> All shulde bene wele and putte in gode accorde
> Reformed hole as most to gode myght plese
> For thair worship and for the comon ese.

At one point, Hardyng describes how John of Lancaster and the earl of Westmorland were at Durham when they first heard news of the Yorkshire rising and asserts that they initially intended to stay there and garrison the castle in strength 'for dread then of the earl of Northumberland', but this refers to the existing disruption in the far North created by Percy's castellans rather than to any preconcerted plan on Northumberland's part to join with the Yorkshire insurgents. No connection is alleged between the earl and the rising's gentry captains.[22]

There are, of course, no clear criteria by which one version of Hardyng's narrative can be privileged over another but, in assessing the strong assertion of Percy involvement in the Yorkshire risings that he makes in the second recension of his chronicle, it is important to consider the context in which it was made. At his accession, Edward IV made some effort to encourage the cult of Archbishop Scrope, representing his execution as one of the chief demonstrations of the injustice and illegitimacy of Lancastrian rule. Hardyng was alert to this current of opinion and did his best to conform to it, adding to the second recension of his chronicle the claim that Henry Hotspur had rebelled in 1403 'by the good advice of Master Richard Scope'.[23] His emphasis on the further collaboration of Scrope and Percy in 1405 had the effect of uniting the two most substantial acts of resistance to Henry IV's rule into a single movement and conferring the authority of the saintly archbishop upon

---

[22] BL MS Lansdowne 204, fols. 206v–207.

[23] *Hardyng*, p. 351; S. Walker, 'Political Saints in Later Medieval England', in *The McFarlane Legacy: Studies in Late Medieval Politics and Society*, ed. R. H. Britnell and A. J. Pollard (Stroud, 1995), pp. 77–106 (pp. 84–5). One consideration exercising Hardyng in the composition of his second recension was a desire to promote the case for the restoration of Percy influence in the North: A. J. Pollard, *North-Eastern England during the Wars of the Roses* (Oxford, 1990), pp. 285–300.

the Percies' legitimist protests, couched in terms that directly anticipated the Yorkist claim to the crown.

In considering the various chronicle accounts of the Yorkshire risings, I have sought to show that our sense of scepticism about the motives imputed to the rebels in the official version of events, and specifically the claim that the insurgents acted in collusion with the earl of Northumberland, can be both sharpened and informed by the stories they have to tell. The chronicles provide very little support for the claim of Percy involvement, preferring to treat Scrope's rising and Northumberland's continued defiance as two separate episodes. They do, however, direct our attention to some alternative lines of inquiry, suggesting that the grievances of the earl marshal played a significant part in bringing the archbishop's own sense of disillusion with the Lancastrian dynasty to the point of action and associating his protests with the criticisms of royal government voiced by the Commons in parliament.

Hagiographical narratives

Richard Scrope was the first English archbishop to be executed after condemnation before a secular court and, even in an era of notably close collaboration between the secular and ecclesiastical authorities, his death was bound to attract attention. A cult of the martyred archbishop was soon in evidence at York, and several hagiographical accounts were composed to encourage and confirm this devotion.[24] With one exception, they have little to say about the rising that preceded the archbishop's death, preferring to dwell upon the signs of sanctity the victim displayed and the miracles that followed his execution. The exception is the theologian Thomas Gascoigne's account of Scrope's death, which was subsequently worked up by the Bridgettine monk, Clement Maidstone, into the *Historia de martyrio Ricardi archiepiscopi*.[25] Gascoigne had kinsmen among the rebels and was the great-nephew of William Gascoigne, chief justice of King's Bench, who was said to have refused the king's order to pass judgment upon the archbishop. His sources of information were unusually good, therefore, and, while his rendering of Scrope's address to his followers on Shipton Moor may be too fluent to carry

---

[24] *The Historians of the Church of York and its Archbishops*, ed. J. Raine, 3 vols. (London, 1879–94), II, 429–32; *Political Poems and Songs relating to English History*, ed. T. Wright, 2 vols. (London, 1859–61), II, 114–18; J. W. McKenna, 'Popular Canonisation as Political Propaganda: The Cult of Archbishop Scrope', *Speculum* 45 (1970), 608–23; J. Hughes, *Pastors and Visionaries: Religion and Secular Life in Late Medieval Yorkshire* (Woodbridge, 1988), pp. 305–15.

[25] *Historians of the Church of York*, ed. Raine, III, 288–91; Thomas Gascoigne, *Loci e libro veritatum*, ed. J. E. Thorold Rogers (Oxford, 1881), pp. 225–9 (Gascoigne's account); *Anglia Sacra*, ed. H. Wharton, 2 vols. (London, 1691), II, 369–72 (Maidstone's). The relationship between these accounts is discussed in S. K. Wright, 'The Provenance and Manuscript Tradition of the *Martyrium Ricardi Archiepiscopi*', *Manuscripta* 28 (1984), 92–102, though none of the conjectures offered is entirely convincing.

full conviction, it provides some insight into what informed gentry opinion considered the rising to be about.[26] In it, Scrope protests against the financial oppression of the clergy but calls God to witness that he intends no harm against the king; he has gathered his followers together because he needs their support in his endeavour to mediate in the many quarrels of the magnates, most especially that between the Neville family and Thomas Mowbray – 'quia jam quis dominus poterit equitare sine multitudine?'[27] The profession of loyalty is to be expected, but the emphasis on the archbishop's desire to be a peacemaker between the lords is an interesting amplification of the statement in *Giles' Chronicle* that it was the hostility between Mowbray and certain other lords that first lured Scrope into rebellion.

Manifestos

There are three sets of articles traditionally associated with the Yorkshire rising, though only one of them can plausibly be dated to 1405. These are the 'York articles', included by Walsingham in his *Chronica Majora* and said to be a literal translation of the original English manifesto affixed by the archbishop and his supporters to the doors of the churches of York. There seems little reason to doubt that this is what they are; the digest of Scrope's demands given in several other chronicles is close enough to Walsingham's text to suggest that the chroniclers had the same document in front of them.[28] In these articles, Scrope calls for a freely elected parliament to be held in London, at which several issues for reform will be addressed: alleviating the insupportable burdens being placed upon the clergy; finding a remedy for the subjection and annihilation to which the lords of the land have been subject; ordaining a remedy for the excessive taxation imposed on all the estates of the realm and punishment for those who have put the wealth of the commons to their private use. On several of these demands, the account in the continuation of the *Eulogium Historiarum* provides a further gloss, complaining particularly of the Lancastrian regime's dependence on loans and frequent recourse to household purveyance, while identifying as the principal target of the insurgents the 'avaricious and greedy counsellors around the king, gorging themselves on the wealth ordained for the common good (*ad commune subsidium ordinata*)'. If all this is done, Scrope's manifesto continues, better resistance can be made to the country's enemies and, in particular, to those rebelling in Wales, who have promised they will return to their former obedience if these reforms are implemented.

---

[26] W. A. Pronger, 'Thomas Gascoigne', *EHR* 53 (1938), 606–26 (pp. 607–10).
[27] *Historians of the Church of York*, ed. Raine, III, 288.
[28] 'Annales', pp. 403–5; *Eulogium Historiarum*, III, 405–6; *Incerti Scriptoris Chronicon*, ed. Giles, p. 44.

Of the other manifestos associated with Scrope, one clearly dates from before the rising and one from after his execution. A list of ten Latin articles, issued by the 'proctors and defenders of the republic', was erroneously ascribed to Scrope's authorship during the Yorkist era.[29] The articles rehearse at length Henry of Lancaster's perjury and treachery in 1399, and detail the many deaths for which he has subsequently been responsible, ending with the recent (*novissime vero*) death of Henry Hotspur. They pay particular attention to Henry's oppressions of the church, including among these the Lancastrian regime's continued use of the Statute of Provisors, which is said to be especially destructive of the well-being of the universities. Apparently the work of a group of clerical Ricardian loyalists, they can be dated on internal grounds to the period between July 1403 and May 1405. Although a verbose and academic production, the articles have some value in demonstrating the degree of hostility that existed towards the new dynasty among some sections of the clergy.[30] It is worth noting that the proctors finally state as their intentions, besides the restoration of the right heir to the English throne, the creation of peace with the Welsh and other enemies of the kingdom and an end to all unjust fiscal exactions: two promises that also appear in Scrope's York articles. Finally, there is a list of reasons for Scrope's execution, said by Thomas Gascoigne, plausibly enough, to have been circulated by the earl of Northumberland and his allies in 1406. It faithfully rehearses most of the demands made in the York articles but adds to them a strain of legitimist criticism that is notably absent from Scrope's own manifesto; the archbishop is said to have been executed because he wished the crown of England to be restored to the right line of blood, and counselled the king to do penance for the perjury he committed in forcing the late king Richard to resign.[31]

In assessing the motives of the Yorkshire insurgents, then, it is the York articles that are of most direct concern. They display several striking features. One of the most obvious is their strict adherence to the hierarchical ideology of the three orders; the grievances of each order – clergy, nobility and commons – are dealt with in successive articles. Equally noticeable is the estate rhetoric that the manifesto employs, presenting the three separate orders of society as united in their concern for the commonwealth: the articles

[29] E 163/6/16 is the earliest extant version, but cannot be the text on which later copies, printed in *Anglia Sacra*, ed. Wharton, II, 362–8 and *Historians of the Church of York*, ed. Raine, II, 292–304 are based. The ascription to Scrope appears to have originated with the compiler of BL MS Cotton Vespasian E VII (at fols. 96v–103v). L. A. Coote, *Prophecy and Public Affairs in Later Medieval England* (York, 2000), pp. 225–6, emphasizes the Percy connections of this manuscript.
[30] Compare the denunciation of Henry's usurpation and exhortation to the English to rise against his rule preserved in Oxford, Bodleian Library, MS Ashmole Rolls 26 and MS Bodley 623, fols. 96–7.
[31] *Historians of the Church of York*, ed. Raine, II, 304–5; Gascoigne, *Loci e libro veritatum*, pp. 229–31. The heading, 'Articuli Nobilium' is an editorial insertion; Oxford, Bodleian Library, MS Auctar. 4. 5, fols. 102–3.

are issued 'by the assent of the commons'; reforms are demanded to redress the injuries and harms done to the 'estates, both temporal and spiritual'; if accomplished they will be for the salvation of the kingdom and the 'redress of the estate of the faithful commons'.[32] Such an idiom of protest seems to place the Yorkshire risings of 1405 squarely within the 'rising of the commons' tradition – risings that sought to defend a traditionally articulated social hierarchy from the damage inflicted upon it by a ruling regime seemingly unmindful of its own responsibilities. Such protests, stretching from the rebellion of 1381 to the Pilgrimage of Grace, possess a series of common features that the 1405 rising also displays: an articulate and politicized agenda, objecting to particular royal policies while continuing to profess loyalty to the person of the king; a broad social composition, expressing the confluence of disparate grievances; and a clear plan of campaign, in which a centre of regional or national government becomes the goal and muster-point of the insurgent forces. They were, in general, attempts to express dissent within a context of obedience, both to legitimate political authority and to the demands of the existing social order.[33] Within Yorkshire, elements of this tradition are already apparent in the disturbances around Doncaster and Beverley in 1392, and are more fully articulated in the 'Robin of Redesdale' agitation in 1469 and the 1489 rising, in which the fourth earl of Northumberland lost his life.[34]

Considered as a whole, therefore, the narrative evidence suggests that the part played by the earl of Northumberland and his ambitions in the Yorkshire risings was not a dominant one. It points, instead, to the independence of the disturbances in the county and emphasizes the significance of the earl marshal's grievances in prompting Archbishop Scrope to take up the cause of reform. An examination of the rebels' demands suggests that their movement had as its object much the same set of concerns as animated the parliamentary Commons: the complaint about purveyance and the attack on the malign influence of Henry's intimates had both, for example, been anticipated in Sir Arnold Savage's frank exchange with the king in the parliament of Hilary 1404.[35] In the second section of this essay, I shall examine in more detail the composition of the insurgents, in order to specify

[32] 'Annales', pp. 403–4.

[33] M. James, *Society, Politics and Culture: Studies in Early Modern England* (Cambridge, 1986), pp. 4–5, 259–69; M. Bush, 'The Risings of the Commons in England, 1381–1549', in *Orders and Hierarchies in Late Medieval and Renaissance Europe*, ed. J. Denton (Basingstoke, 1999), pp. 109–25, 187–9.

[34] *Select Cases in Court of King's Bench under Richard II, Henry IV and Henry V*, ed. G. O. Sayles, Selden Society 88 (London, 1971), pp. 83–7; C. Ross, *Edward IV* (London, 1974), pp. 126–7, 439–40; M. Hicks, *Richard III and his Rivals: Magnates and their Motives in the Wars of the Roses* (London, 1991), pp. 395–418.

[35] C. M. Fraser, 'Some Durham Documents relating to the Hilary Parliament of 1404', *BIHR* 34 (1961), 192–9 (p. 198).

more precisely the nature of their grievances against the rule of Henry of Lancaster.

CONTEXTS

The feature of the Yorkshire risings that most struck contemporaries was the considerable degree of clerical involvement.[36] Comparison with the Great Revolt of 1381 suggests that it was less the sheer number of clerical insurgents that set the 1405 rebellion apart than their higher social status. Scrope was supported in his protest by members of his own household, including his nephew, Geoffrey Scrope; his chancellor, Richard Conyngston, archdeacon of York; and Robert Wolveden, one of his vicars-general.[37] Several other members of the York chapter also feared for their position in the aftermath of the revolt, while five vicars-choral and a chaplain in the Minster were pardoned for their part in the rising.[38] If this was the core of Scrope's clerical following, the support of the secular clergy of York, such as John Whitwell, the rector of All Saints', North Street, was significant in giving additional impetus to the rising in the city. The part played by one chaplain in particular, William Forster, in rousing the citizens was acknowledged by the display of his head on Ouse Bridge.[39] Beyond York, the evidence for clerical participation is more difficult to determine. Very few mendicants sought pardons, although the continuator of the *Eulogium Historiarum* claimed that all four orders were involved in the rising and included a graphic account of the humiliation of a group of eighteen Franciscans among Scrope's forces.[40] Among the rest of the religious, the impoverished house of

[36] *Eulogium Historiarum*, III, 406: 'Et collecto exercitus de burgensibus, villanis, presbyteris, et religiosis . . .'; *The Register of Philip Repingdon, 1405–1419: Memoranda, 1405–1411*, ed. M. Archer, Lincoln Record Society 57 (Lincoln, 1963), p. 136: '. . . nonnullos potentes et proceres dicti regni ac eciam alios inferioris status necnon viros ecclesiasticos seculares et regulares . . .'.

[37] *CPR, 1405–8*, p. 19; *A Calendar of the Register of Richard Scrope, Archbishop of York, 1398–1405*, ed. R. N. Swanson, 2 vols., Borthwick Texts and Calendars: Records of the Northern Province 8 and 11 (York, 1981–5), I, 38 (Scrope); *Register of Richard Scrope*, ed. Swanson, I, 15, 47 and 334 (Conyngston); *Register of Richard Scrope*, ed. Swanson, II, 956, 963 (Wolveden); *Fasti Ecclesiae Anglicanae, 1300–1541: Northern Province*, ed. B. Jones (London, 1963), p. 18.

[38] R. L. Storey, 'Clergy and Common Law in the Reign of Henry IV', in *Medieval Legal Records*, ed. R. F. Hunnisett and J. B. Post (London, 1978), pp. 342–408 (pp. 394–5); *CPR, 1405–8*, pp. 71–2.

[39] *CPR, 1405–8*, pp. 79, 69; *Register of Richard Scrope*, ed. Swanson, II, 966 (Whitwell). John de Burton, rector of St Helen on the Walls, was also implicated in the rising: *CPR, 1405–8*, p. 44, *Register of Richard Scrope*, ed. Swanson, II, 766.

[40] *Eulogium Historiarum*, III, 407. The participation of the mendicants is also especially emphasized in the 'Waltham annals': BL MS Cotton Titus D XV, fol. 51. Fr John Tokhost and Fr William Thorpe are the only mendicants whose pardons are enrolled: *CPR, 1405–8*, pp. 76, 193.

Austin canons at Warter supplied the archbishop with some adherents, and a
former prior of the Gilbertine house at Malton also appears among the list of
those who sought pardons.[41] The pattern of participation appears slightly
different among the secular clergy, where those beneficed priests identifiable
among the rebels tended to come from parishes dominated by one of the
gentry insurgents.[42]

Naturally, a whole variety of grievances exercised this disparate gathering of the clergy. As a substantial local landowner, the York chapter
cultivated good relations with the neighbouring gentry and shared many
of the concerns that animated landed society. The vicars-choral depended
on an overwhelmingly urban portfolio of rents for their prosperity and had
interests as well as grievances in common with the citizens of York, while
among the mendicants doubts as to the legitimacy of Henry IV's title to rule
remained particularly strong.[43] The issue of most general and immediate
concern to the clergy of the diocese was, however, the unaccustomed weight
of royal taxation. Discontent at the king's demands had been growing for
some time throughout the northern province. A combination of administrative confusion and Lancastrian insolvency meant that, between Henry
IV's accession and the outbreak of the Yorkshire rising, the northern clergy
had already been called upon to pay four clerical tenths and were
committed to finding the resources for a further tenth within the next
twelve months.[44] The most recent of these grants had, in addition, been
extended to apply to benefices customarily exempted on the grounds of
poverty: in June 1404 the contribution threshold had been lowered from £10
to 10 marks, and in the following December it was, for this grant only,
removed altogether. The imposition of unaccustomed fiscal burdens upon
the poorest members of the clerical estate inevitably evoked protests from
an already recalcitrant Convocation. This fact was most forcibly expressed
in June 1404, when a grant was made with the attached condition that
inquisitions and distraints carried out by royal commissioners 'against the
liberty of the Church and ancient custom of the Church in England' should

---

[41] *CPR, 1405–8*, pp. 55, 287; *Register of Richard Scrope*, ed. Swanson, II, 708, 726 for Warter's
poverty.
[42] *CPR, 1405–8*, pp. 34, 196 (Thomas Anlaby, rector of Spofforth); *CPR, 1405–8*, pp. 1, 14, 49;
Register of Richard Scrope, ed. Swanson, I, 391 (Simon Wentislaw, rector of Cowlam); E 28/
22/27 (William Gibson, rector of Slingsby).
[43] York, York Minster Library, E 1/38 shows the chapter paying fees to several local lawyers
and administrators for Easter term 1405; *Charters of the Vicars Choral of York Minster: City of
York and its suburbs to 1546*, ed, N. J. Tringham, Yorkshire Archaeological Society Record
Series 148 (Leeds, 1993), pp. xxiii–xxxix; D. W. Whitfield, 'Conflicts of Personality and
Principle: The Crisis in the English Franciscan Province, 1400–1409', *Franciscan Studies* 17
(1957), 321–62.
[44] I. R. Abbot, 'Taxation of Personal Property and of Clerical Incomes, 1399 to 1402',
Speculum 17 (1942), 471–98 (pp. 489–98); A. Rogers, 'Clerical Taxation under Henry IV',
BIHR 46 (1973), 123–44 (pp. 127–33).

cease.[45] Although this stipulation may have been no more than an expression of the general sense of secular oppression prevalent among the clergy in the early fifteenth century, it is significant that it also articulated a specific grievance of the archbishop himself, over the crown's evident disinclination to recognize the full immunities enjoyed by the see of York. Conflict had centred on the liberty of Beverley: the archbishop's claim to deliver his own gaols there and at Ripon had been overridden, apparently for the first time in more than a century, as recently as 1403, while in August 1404 Scrope had found it necessary to procure an additional royal grant, preventing the steward and marshal of the household from exercising their jurisdiction within the liberty of Beverley.[46] In choosing, in his manifesto, to demand remedies for the insupportable burdens placed upon the clerical estate and for the injuries done to the liberties of Holy Church, Scrope was addressing issues of immediate concern to himself and his *familia* but calculated also to create a broad platform of support among the clergy of his province.

A second distinctive feature of the Yorkshire risings was the whole-hearted participation of the townsmen of York, who, as nearly all the chronicle accounts emphasize, formed a major part of Scrope's host. Walsingham describes 'almost all the citizens of York who could bear arms' as joining the archbishop, while the king's reported anger towards the city, which he threatened to raze to the ground, and the dramatic abasement of the citizens, 'lying on the earth as though it was another Judgment Day' as they sought the king's pardon, substantially confirms this analysis.[47] The individual pardons issued by chancery supply very few names of York townsmen involved in the rising, most of whom sought protection under the terms of the general pardon the city purchased, at a cost of 500 marks, in early August.[48] The context within which they chose to embark upon such an unprecedented act of defiance can, however, be suggested. One element must be the appreciable downturn in the volume of wool and cloth exports through the city's outport at Hull in the years immediately after 1400, although York's status as a regional market centre, and its consequently diversified economic structure, indicate that this was unlikely to have been a decisive consideration.[49] A more

---

[45] *Register of Richard Scrope*, ed. Swanson, II, 767, 773.

[46] JUST 3/82/1–3; CPR, *1401–5*, p. 95; R. B. Pugh, *Imprisonment in Medieval England* (London, 1968), pp. 297–8; E. G. Kimball, 'Commissions of the Peace for Urban Jurisdictions in England, 1327–1485', *Transactions of the American Philosophical Society* 121 (1977), 448–74 (pp. 466–7).

[47] 'Annales', pp. 405, 408; *Incerti Scriptoris Chronicon*, ed. Giles, p. 44; *Chronicle of Adam Usk*, p. 202.

[48] CPR, *1405–8*, p. 40; E. Miller, 'Medieval York', in *VCH Yorkshire: The City of York*, ed. P. M. Tillot (Oxford, 1961), pp. 25–116 (p. 58).

[49] J. Kermode, *Medieval Merchants: York, Beverley and Hull in the Later Middle Ages* (Cambridge, 1998), pp. 167–72; P. J. P. Goldberg, *Women, Work and Life Cycle in a Medieval Economy. Women in York and Yorkshire c. 1300–1520* (Oxford, 1992), pp. 23–6.

immediate grievance was the heavy fiscal demands made upon the city by the new Lancastrian regime. York had provided vital assistance to Henry of Lancaster with a loan of 500 marks, 'delivered to him in his necessity before he undertook the government of the realm', and continued to prove a reliable lender: in the six years between Henry's return to England and the outbreak of the 1405 rising, the city's loans to the crown averaged £265 per annum.[50] York's governors clearly entertained hopes of swift repayment, agreeing to allow the mayor a small commission on any sums he recovered, but there is little sign that their efforts met with success. The string of murages and pontages that the city secured in these years had to serve as inadequate recompense.[51]

Allied to the heavy national taxation of these years, and the regular commitment of the fee farm, this was a substantial financial burden for the city to bear, made all the more galling by the knowledge that some of York's subsidy payments were being put to meet the costs of an unpopular royal household.[52] The natural resentment that many civic corporations felt at the level of crown demands upon their resources was accentuated, in York's case, by the revival of dissension within the city's governing groups and given a particular focus by growing discontent at the predominance enjoyed by the mayor, William Frost, throughout the early years of Henry IV's reign. In December 1399 a panel of twelve influential arbitrators had been appointed to consider the grievances set out in a bill exhibited by Thomas Santon, one of the city's chamberlains. Santon's bill was sufficiently controversial for the arbitrators to be unable to agree among themselves, and he was required, instead, to enter into a recognizance that he would not again transgress against the peace 'either by insurrections, confederations, illegal congregations, or by treacherous threats'. A month later, an 'ordinance' of the commons of the city, criticizing the aldermanic policy on admission to the freedom and asking that the crafts be given sufficient time to consult before responding to any request for taxation, 'without being rebuked or compelled against their will to grant any such tax', was repealed (or, perhaps more likely, rejected).[53]

William Frost, the mayor who quashed the commonalty's initiative, was a

---

[50] *CPR, 1399–1401*, p. 354; *CPR, 1401–5*, pp. 251, 403, tabulated in L. Attreed, *The King's Towns: Identity and Survival in Late Medieval English Boroughs* (New York, 2000), p. 159. This is a minimum figure, as the city received further requests, to which the response is unclear.

[51] [York,] Y[ork] C[ity] A[rchives] MS D 1, fol. 10; *CPR, 1399–1401*, p. 224; *CPR, 1401–5*, pp. 166, 333 and 352.

[52] E 101/512/23.

[53] YCA MS D 1, fols. 349v, 348; *House of Commons*, IV, 304–5; S. Rees Jones, 'York's Civic Administration, 1354–1464', in *The Government of Medieval York. Essays in Commemoration of the 1396 Royal Charter*, ed. S. Rees Jones, Borthwick Studies in History 3 (York, 1997), pp. 108–40 (pp. 121–2).

controversial figure in early Lancastrian York. Drawn from a local gentry family, and with little direct involvement in overseas trade, his proven ability to mediate successfully between York and Westminster must have made him an obvious choice to guide the city through the uncertain years of a new dynasty.[54] Frost proved highly adept at this task but his services did not come cheap: for his first year in office (February 1400–1), the customary mayor's fee of £50 was augmented with an additional remuneration of £20 and two pipes of wine. In the following year, the city agreed to meet the expenses of the man-at-arms Frost had sent on the king's Scottish expedition, and by the time of his fifth successive election as mayor in February 1404, his additional remuneration had climbed to £50. Frost's vice-regal conception of the mayoralty was not only expensive; it also ran counter to a more collegial approach to the office, embodied in a neglected ordinance of 1393, that limited both the mayor's emoluments and his length of tenure. By February 1405, when Frost was unexpectedly replaced as mayor, his activities had clearly provoked a reaction in the city. His successor, Adam del Bank, was no radical: a wealthy dyer, he had long since run through the *cursus honorum* of civic office. He was, however, prepared to adopt a less lavish approach towards the mayor's office, accepting the 'customary' mayor's fee of £50 and immediately effecting further economies within the mayor's household.[55] The implication of these changes seems clear. Within the city of York, an internal power-struggle preceded the outbreak of rebellion. Discontent with the burdensome and authoritarian regime of William Frost served to crystallize a more general sense of dissatisfaction with the new Lancastrian dynasty and created a climate of opinion in which the citizens were willing to give voice to their grievances. In choosing to complain of the impoverishment of the merchants' estate through the insistent royal demand for loans, as well as by the raising of excessive tolls and customs, Scrope had read the anxieties of his urban followers well.

Analysis of the gentry insurgents, the majority of them engaged in the North Riding rising, throws up a different set of issues. The names of many of the major figures are easily recovered, but identifying a common context for their decision to rebel remains problematic. While it is clear that some of the Percy affinity in Yorkshire was directly involved in the rising, privileging the agency of the earl of Northumberland and his followers does not provide a sufficient explanation for the composition and concerns of the rebels. One reason for this lies in the actions of the earl himself; the earlier version of Hardyng's chronicle makes it clear that, after the failed ambush at Sir Ralph

[54] *House of Commons*, III, 138–41; R. B. Dobson, 'The Crown, the Charter and the City, 1396–1461', in *The Government of Medieval York*, ed. Rees Jones, pp. 34–56 (pp. 41–4).

[55] YCA MS D 1, fols. 10r–10v; J. Kermode, 'The Merchants of York, Beverley and Hull in the Fourteenth and Fifteenth Centuries' (unpublished Ph. D. dissertation, University of Sheffield, 1990), Appendix 1; R. B. Dobson, *Church and Society in the Medieval North of England* (London, 1996), pp. 267–84 (pp. 278–9).

Eure's residence, Northumberland withdrew rapidly northwards, taking a number of his most prominent Yorkshire retainers with him.[56] This meant that, although a number of Percy adherents and well-wishers were implicated in the rising, including two of the captains of the North Riding insurgents, Sir John Colville and Sir John Fauconberg, their influence upon the rebels' actions and demands was never a decisive one.[57] Another of the leaders of the North Riding rising, Sir John Fitzrandolf, took a fee from the earl of Westmorland, for example, while several of the insurgents enjoyed some form of royal patronage: Sir John Colville was a king's knight, as well as a Percy retainer; Sir Robert Lamplugh, a royal annuitant; Sir Robert Persay was forester of the duchy of Lancaster forest of Pickering.[58] Indeed, one striking characteristic common to some of the gentry insurgents was the strength of their family connection to the duchy of Lancaster. Sir Ralph Hastings, executed for his part in the rising, was the son of one of John of Gaunt's most favoured retainers; another ring-leader, Sir William Plumpton, was the son of a duchy annuitant; Sir Alexander Metham, his brother Thomas and Gerard Usflete the younger, all subsequently pardoned, were also the sons of Lancastrian servants.[59] There were, in addition, strong ties of association among some of the participants, quite independent of the claims of lordship. A significant nucleus among them were active local administrators within the North Riding: Persay, Colville, Fitzrandolf and John Percy of Kydale were all frequently commissioned to collect the parliamentary subsidy and to administer the various fiscal experiments attempted by the new Lancastrian regime; Persay and George Darell of Sessay had also acted as coroners within the riding.[60]

Such men make unlikely revolutionaries. It suited the Lancastrian regime

[56] BL MS Lansdowne 204, fol. 206v; these included Sir Henry Boynton, Sir Gerard Salvayn, John Aske and Randolph del See: *Rot. Parl.*, III, 605; *CPR, 1405–8*, pp. 24, 67 and 69.

[57] *CPR, 1401–5*, p. 297 (Colville); *CPR, 1388–92*, p. 513; *CPR, 1399–1401*, p. 24; *CCR, 1399–1402*, p. 366; G. E. Cokayne, *The Complete Peerage*, 13 vols. in 12 (London, 1910–57), V, 276–81 (Fauconberg). Other members of the Percy affinity involved in the rising included Richard Fairfax, John Percy of Kydale and Nicholas Tempest: *CPR, 1401–5*, p. 297; *CPR, 1405–8*, p. 79 (Fairfax); *CIM, 1399–1422*, no. 451 (Tempest); *CPR, 1401–5*, p. 297; *CPR, 1405–8*, p. 48 (Percy). Robert Vavasour of Rudstan had more distant links with the Percies: *CIPM, 1405–13*, no. 341.

[58] *CCR, 1405–8*, p. 194 (Fitzrandolf); *CPR, 1401–5*, p. 42 (Colville); *CPR, 1399–1401*, p. 135; *CFR, 1399–1405*, p. 162 (Lamplugh); *CPR, 1405–8*, p. 57; *CCR, 1409–13*, p. 10 (Persay).

[59] *CPR, 1405–8*, pp. 69, 478 (Hastings); *CPR, 1405–8*, p. 63; *CCR, 1402–5*, p. 469 (Plumpton); *CPR, 1405–8*, pp. 78, 79 (Metham); *CPR, 1405–8*, p. 71 (Usflete). For their duchy connections, S. Walker, *The Lancastrian Affinity, 1361–1399* (Oxford, 1990), pp. 271, 275, 278 and 283; DL 29/738/12096, m. 4.

[60] *CFR, 1383–91*, pp. 70, 159 and 265; *CFR, 1391–9*, pp. 27, 141 and 264; *CFR, 1399–1405*, pp. 115, 148, 190, 256, 286 and 291; *CCR, 1396–9*, p. 262 (Persay); *CCR, 1402–5*, p. 439 (Darell). For Persay and his fellows acting under these commissions, *Inquisitions and Assessments relating to Feudal Aids*, 6 vols. (London, 1899–1920), VI, 261–2; E 359/19, rots. 2, 4, 6; E 179/211/41, 43.

to represent their armed protest as a real threat to the maintenance of social and dynastic order, forcing the king to resist the restless demands of the multitude lest the whole kingdom perish, but the violence of the rebels was restrained and relatively discriminating.[61] At the heart of their concerns was the sharp readjustment in the traditional alignments of county society precipitated by the Neville family's permanent acquisition of the honour of Richmond in 1399 and confirmed by Ralph Neville, earl of Westmorland's, emergence as Henry IV's chosen lieutenant in the North.[62] Some of the insurgents had already suffered in the cause of the Nevilles advance: as early as 1372, Sir John Fauconberg's father, the unstable Thomas, Lord Fauconberg, had been persuaded to surrender two East Riding manors to John, Lord Neville.[63] Among their companions, resentment towards the beneficiaries of this emergent new order was strong. The chief – and perhaps the only – victim of the rebels was Sir Thomas Colville, who embodied in his own person the coalescence of the Neville and Lancastrian affinities that defined it, while lesser servants of the Nevilles also suffered: John Norton complained that, although he had purchased the office of warrener of Ripon from Archbishop Scrope for 20 marks, he had subsequently been ousted from his post, at the suit of Sir John Scrope and Sir William Plumpton, 'because he was of the livery, and in the service, of the earl of Westmorland'.[64] Royal lands and servants were also targeted: the king's tenants at Kilburn reportedly sustained great losses at the hands of the insurgents, while a royal esquire, John Haukswell, had his haystacks and granges plundered.[65]

Yorkshire had suffered considerable disruption in the aftermath of Hotspur's defeat at Shewsbury, with the continued show of strength made by Percy partisans around Beverley and York considered threatening enough to require the king's presence in the shire. The consequent disorder had been called to Henry's attention by the parliamentary Commons at Hilary 1404, when they requested the king to charge the earls of Northumberland and Westmorland, on their return to their countries, to impose upon their servants, tenants and familiars the same unity and concord that they had themselves sworn to observe. 'Lying rumours' were, nevertheless, still reported to be stirring the county to strife and discord.[66] It was against this

---

[61] *Register of Philip Repingdon, 1405–19*, ed. Archer, pp. 136–8.

[62] *CPR, 1399–1401*, p. 24; C. D. Ross, 'The Yorkshire Baronage, 1399–1435' (unpublished D. Phil. dissertation, University of Oxford, 1950), pp. 10–14; R. L. Storey, 'The North of England', in *Fifteenth-century England, 1399–1509*, ed. S. B. Chrimes, C. D. Ross and R. A. Griffiths (Manchester, 1972), pp. 129–44 (pp. 134–7).

[63] *CFR, 1399–1405*, pp. 112–13; *CIPM, 1399–1405*, no. 427. Thomas, Lord Fauconberg, may himself have been involved in the rising: *CPR, 1405–8*, pp. 123, 282.

[64] *House of Commons*, II, 638–9 (Colville); E 28/22/19 (Norton).

[65] *CPR, 1405–8*, pp. 43, 55 and 56.

[66] *POPC*, I, 209–10; *Rot. Parl.*, III, 525; *CCR, 1402–5*, p. 515.

background of regional disorder that the crown was proving powerless to control that the Yorkshire gentry insurgents chose to make their protest. In their eyes, it was Henry IV's partisan deployment of his considerable influence within the shire that, by fuelling the fire of magnate rivalries, had created the disorder that plagued the region. Their solution was to reassert a threatened local solidarity, taking direct action against the most prominent agents of the new order while demanding a return to a more familiar pattern of lordship – 'that the heirs of noblemen be wholly restored to their honours and inheritances, according to the condition of their birth'.[67]

It was consequently his status as the most prominent casualty of Neville aggrandizement that conferred upon Thomas Mowbray, earl marshal, the significance in the outbreak of the Yorkshire rising that most of the chroniclers acknowledge. Although he held substantial estates around Epworth and the Isle of Axholme, on the southeastern borders of the county, Mowbray could not be counted as a major regional magnate: his Yorkshire estates yielded approximately £160 per annum in 1399 and delivered a lump sum of only £80 to his coffers in 1403–4.[68] On the evidence of those pardoned, he had few clients among the shire gentry but relied, principally, upon the resources of his household and estate administration to provide his forces.[69] It was rather the nature of his grievances that placed the young earl marshal at the centre of the 1405 rising. The Mowbrays were hereditary marshals of England but, since Thomas Mowbray had been too young to exercise the office at Henry IV's coronation in 1399, it had been granted, instead, to Ralph Neville, earl of Westmorland, for life.[70] Mowbray was permitted the style earl marshal but not the substance of the marshal's authority. The subordination of the young Mowbray's rights and claims to the consolidation of a new Neville ascendancy was further underlined by the commitment of Mowbray manors in Yorkshire to the keeping of Westmor-

[67] *Eulogium Historiarum*, III, 406.

[68] SC 6/ 1087/14; BL Additional Charter 16556, m.9.

[69] Mowbray followers implicated in the rising include his cousin, Ivo, son of John, Lord Welles; Sir Robert Lamplugh; Sir Nicholas Colfox; John Burgh, receiver of his Yorkshire lands; William Fencotes, steward of Thirsk; William Bachelor, his cook; Robert Botvelayn; John Haldeburgh; Nicholas Hall; John Holbourne; and 'Yeven'. CPR, *1405–8*, pp. 38, 99; *Complete Peerage*, XII, ii, 443 (Welles); CPR, *1405–8*, p. 73; BL Add. Ch. 16556, m.12 (Lamplugh); CPR, *1405–8*, p. 80; *Anglo-Norman Letters and Petitions*, ed. M. D. Legge, Anglo-Norman Text Society 3 (Oxford, 1941), no. 386 (Colfox); CPR, *1405–8*, pp. 73, 110; BL Add. Ch. 16556, m.9 (Burgh); CPR, *1405–8*, p. 70; SC 6/1087/14 (Fencotes); CPR, *1405–8*, pp. 38, 73; BL Add. Ch. 16556, m.22 (Bachelor); CPR, *1405–8*, pp. 68, 80; CPR, *1401–5*, p. 335 (Botvelayn); CPR, *1405–8*, p. 32; BL Add. Ch. 16556, m.8 (Haldeburgh); CPR, *1405–8*, p. 41; BL Add. Ch. 16556, m. 4 (Hall); CPR, *1405–8*, p. 41; CPR, *1401–5*, p. 335 (Holbourne); BL Add Ch. 16556, m. 16 (Yeven).

[70] CPR, *1399–1401*, p. 9; R. E. Archer, 'Parliamentary Restoration: John Mowbray and the Dukedom of Norfolk in 1425', in *Rulers and Ruled in Late Medieval England*, ed. R. E. Archer and S. Walker (London, 1995), pp. 99–116 (pp. 104–5).

land during his minority.[71] Although he was granted early livery of his inheritance in November 1403, Thomas Mowbray's continuing disaffection had rendered him a known malcontent by February 1405, when he admitted concealing his knowledge of the duke of York's intention to abduct the heirs of Roger Mortimer from the court. His animosity towards the Lancastrian regime intensified when his claim for precedence in parliament over Richard Beauchamp, earl of Warwick, was rejected by the council.[72] Mowbray's complaints against the government of Henry IV were particular and personal but they attracted considerable support in the region, where they replicated the concerns of the coalition of interests opposed to the rise of the Nevilles and their clients that imparted to the Yorkshire rising some sense of common purpose.

What remains to be explained is why the earl marshal's grievances evoked so strong a response from Scrope himself, prompting the archbishop to preach against the evils that afflicted the kingdom, both in his own cathedral and in the surrounding churches, and then to issue his manifesto, calling on every man to lay out his strength for justice and to be strong in zeal for reform.[73] One element in Scrope's actions was clearly his concern for ecclesiastical liberties. He had associated himself with Archbishop Arundel's blunt defence of the Church against the threat of disendowment, made at the Coventry Parliament in October 1404.[74] The king's subsequent proposal, that stipendiary chaplains, and others customarily exempt from the subsidies granted by Convocation, should now be called upon to contribute to the defence of the realm, can only have increased his anxieties; it was perhaps to discuss the implementation of this demand that Scrope was summoned to meet with the king at Worcester in late April 1405.[75] But while there was an established tradition of clerical advice and admonition on the ills of the kingdom, exemplified in the open letter addressed by Philip Repingdon to Henry IV in 1401, it offered no sanction for Scrope's decision to seek popular support for his chosen remedies.[76]

There is, as we have seen, little contemporary evidence that Scrope was

---

[71] *Anglo-Norman Letters and Petitions*, ed. Legge, nos. 383, 386; *CPR, 1401–5*, p. 322; *CCR, 1402–5*, pp. 68, 225 and 250; *CFR, 1399–1405*, p. 29.

[72] 'Annales', pp. 398–9; *POPC*, II, 104–5. Mowbray may have feared that defeat on the precedence issue would also jeopardise his tenure of the lordship of Gower, where his family had been in dispute with the Beauchamps for half a century: J. B. Smith and T. B. Pugh, 'The Lordship of Gower and Kilvey in the Middle Ages', in *Glamorgan County History*, ed. G. Williams, 6 vols. (Cardiff, 1936–80), III, 205–65 (pp. 249–56).

[73] *Incerti Scriptoris Chronicon*, ed. Giles, p. 44.

[74] 'Annales', p. 392.

[75] *POPC*, II, 100–1; *Signet Letters*, no. 328; *Register of Richard Scrope*, ed. Swanson, II, 993. Henry was acting against the advice of several of his councillors in seeking this additional grant: *POPC*, II, 101–3.

[76] *Chronicle of Adam Usk*, pp. 136–42, discussed in F. Grady, 'The Lancastrian Gower and the Limits of Exemplarity', *Speculum* 70 (1995), 552–75 (pp. 552–5).

encouraged to do so by the earl of Northumberland, and there is no sign, in the York articles, of sympathy with the legitimist arguments that formed an important part of the Percies' platform: Scrope's ecclesiastical advancement had owed more to papal patronage, and his own considerable abilities, than to the favour of Richard II, while he had played an active part in securing the late king's resignation.[77] The narrative accounts seem, rather, to indicate that Scrope's intention was to offer himself as a mediator, initially between the feuding northern magnates, and then between the king and his critics. As the son of a Yorkshire nobleman, Henry, first Lord Scrope of Masham, the archbishop's lineage allowed him to contemplate the first part of this plan; his nephew, Henry, third Lord Scrope of Masham, was to display a similarly misplaced confidence in his ability to manage and resolve a major political crisis in 1415.[78] The language of his manifesto might also suggest that, in aspiring to extend the scope of his mediation to the kingdom as a whole, Scrope was responding, as primate of England, to an imperative that was as much pastoral as political. Impelled by an active and ascetic piety, he had already sought to reform the public worship of his province; now he turned to the spiritual health of the nation, calling upon his people to follow the path of truth and justice, to be 'helpers (*adjutores*) in your salvation, and in ours'.[79] His hopes proved vain but he managed, by imposing structure and purpose upon the unresolved grievances thrown up by six years of Lancastrian rule, briefly to rally around himself a regional coalition of protest as broadly based as any in fifteenth-century England.

[77] M. Harvey, *The English in Rome, 1362–1420* (Cambridge, 1999), p. 138; R. G. Davies, 'Richard II and the Church in the Years of "Tyranny"', *Journal of Medieval History* 1 (1975), 329–62 (pp. 345–9); *Chrons. Rev.*, pp. 163–6, 169, 171–2. The fullest recent account of Scrope's career is in B. Vale, 'The Scropes of Bolton and Masham, c. 1300–1450: A Study of a Northern Noble Family', 2 vols. (unpublished D. Phil. dissertation, University of York, 1987), I, 143–90.

[78] T. B. Pugh, *Henry V and the Southampton Plot of 1415*, Southampton Record Series 30 (Southampton, 1988), pp. 109–21.

[79] *Index Britanniae Scriptorum. John Bale's Index of British and Other Writers*, ed. R. L. Poole and M. Bateson (Oxford, 1902), p. 358; *Catalogue of the Library of Syon Monastery, Isleworth*, ed. M. Bateson (Cambridge, 1898), p. 76; Hughes, *Pastors and Visionaries*, pp. 73, 203 and 267; 'Annales', pp. 403, 405.

10

The Politics of Health:
Henry IV and the Long Parliament of 1406

Douglas Biggs

'The history of Parliament', Stanley Chrimes wrote in 1936, 'is essentially paradoxical. In origin it was of royal creation; in time it came to limit and at last to control the king himself.' 'The great problem in Parliamentary history,' Chrimes continued, 'is to trace and explain these paradoxes.'[1] One of the most intriguing of these 'parliamentary paradoxes' centres on Henry IV's relationship with the parliament of 1406, and many historians have sought to solve its conundrum. Viewing the parliament from the safety and security of Victorian Britain, William Stubbs perceived the parliament of 1406 as representing the epiphanal expression of Lancastrian Constitutionalism, that nascent medieval democracy, as the Commons forced their programme of government reform upon the king.[2] Although Stubbs's successors, led primarily by K. B. McFarlane,[3] vigorously attacked the bishop's conclusions, they could not quite escape the core of the Stubbsian paradigm that Henry IV's relations with his parliaments were adversarial.[4] A. L. Brown noted that in 1406 Henry jealously guarded his royal rights and would only yield to the humiliating restraints of the Commons with a fight.[5] J. L. Kirby,[6] Peter McNiven[7] and Alan Rogers[8] all echoed this view, and Chris Given-Wilson noted that, in Henry's relations with parliament, 'one is entitled to wonder

[1] S. B. Chrimes, *English Constitutional Ideas in the Fifteenth Century* (Cambridge, 1936), p. 66. Much of the work on this paper was undertaken during the term that I served as Visiting Fellow at the Centre for Medieval Studies at the University of York. I would like to thank my colleagues there, and those at the symposium, along with Tony Pollard, Mark Ormrod, Gwilym Dodd and Peter McNiven, for their kind and constructive comments.

[2] W. Stubbs, *The Constitutional History of England in its Origin and Development*, 3 vols. (Oxford, 1898), III, 54–9.

[3] *LKLK*, p. 99; K. B. McFarlane, 'The Lancastrian Kings', in *The Cambridge Medieval History VIII* (Cambridge, 1936), pp. 363–416 (pp. 371–4); K. B. McFarlane, *The Nobility of Later Medieval England* (Oxford, 1970), p. 1.

[4] A. L. Brown, 'The Commons and the Council in the Reign of Henry IV', *EHR* 79 (1964), 1–30 (p. 29).

[5] Brown, 'Commons and the Council', p. 19 n.6.

[6] Kirby, *Henry IV*, p. 257.

[7] P. McNiven, 'The Problem of Henry IV's Health', *EHR* 100 (1985), 746–72 (pp. 760–1).

[8] Alan Rogers, 'Henry IV, the Commons and Taxation', *Mediaeval Studies* 31 (1969), 44–70 (p. 44).

whether [the king] really needed any enemies'.[9] Few historical traditions seem more firmly grounded than the perception that in 1406 a combination of foreign and domestic crises coupled with a strong, unified Commons drove Henry IV from most of the daily routine of government and then placed government in the hands of a continual council who were beholden to them. '[I]t was,' as McFarlane noted, 'the greatest surrender of the reign.'[10]

But was this indeed the case? It seems to some at least that we have been beguiled by a largely Victorian historiography where reiteration of historical opinion has become accepted as historical fact. In 1995 A. J. Pollard offered some 'preliminary conclusions' regarding what took place in 1406 in his study of the Long Parliament. He showed that there were a large number of Lancastrian retainers in the Commons, and offered the suggestion that perhaps the king's health may have been responsible for the political situation, but did not elaborate on his suggestion. He also commented that perhaps a group of 'independent' knights and some burgesses led an alliance of determined opposition to the king.[11] As I have stated elsewhere, and as Gwilym Dodd has argued, parliament in Henry IV's reign was not full of enemies but rather functioned as a Lancastrian forum.[12] Membership to this forum was carefully controlled and was a place where open debate was tolerated and even encouraged by the king, who stood 'face to face' with his subjects. Parliament in Henry IV's reign was a thing of his creation – he dominated it and packed it with his supporters both in the Commons and the Lords – and parliament in return did his bidding. Within this forum taxation and matters of policy were debated, often heatedly, but when the time came to vote for subsidies parliament did so with alacrity that even McFarlane found impressive.[13]

If then, parliament was a Lancastrian forum, packed with Henry's friends and supporters, how do we interpret the Long Parliament? It seems to me, that following on from what Pollard and Dodd have already suggested, it was Henry's poor health and not opposition to his policies or crises abroad, that was the coin on which all the events of 1406 turned. An examination of the Long Parliament along these lines reveals an evolution of historical tradition. Parliament opened in March but had to be recessed in early April after conducting little business. In late April the crisis of 1406 broke. The king suffered a serious attack (a stroke?) that left him near death in early June. Henry recovered, but not sufficiently to govern, and conceded the

[9] Given-Wilson, *Royal Household*, p. 253.
[10] *LKLK*, p. 91.
[11] A. J. Pollard, 'The Lancastrian Constitutional Experiment Revisited: Henry IV, Sir John Tiptoft and the Parliament of 1406', *Parliamentary History* 14 (1995), 103–19.
[12] G. Dodd, 'Conflict or Consensus: Henry IV and Parliament, 1399–1406', in *Social Attitudes and Political Structures in the Fifteenth Century*, ed. T. Thornton (Stroud, 2001), pp. 118–49 (p. 141).
[13] *LKLK*, p. 101.

government of the realm to his council on 22 May and more formally on 22 December. Throughout the process, as Professor Pollard suggests, parliament acted as an *ad hoc* great council, and through the last eight months of the year moved from panic, to trepidation, and finally to cautious action in response to the difficulties that faced it. Against the backdrop of the king's failing health we shall first briefly discuss the composition of the Long Parliament, both in terms of the Commons and also of the Lords. Secondly, we shall determine the significance of the first session within the context of the Long Parliament. Finally, we shall discuss the king's health itself and how it affected the last two sessions and the 'constitutional documents' of 1406 – the bill of 22 May, the succession act of 7 June and the 'Thirty-one Articles' of 22 December.

To begin with the membership of the Long Parliament. Within the parliament that met at Westminster on 1 March 1406 it is difficult to find many members opposed to the king or his policies. The Lords, especially after the rebellions of 1403 and 1405, formed a Lancastrian bastion: the lords who served as triers of petitions were among Henry's closest friends and supporters, and quite probably had much to say when it came to taxation.[14] Certainly no opposition or acquiescence in any opposition would be brooked from this portion of the political community. Likewise the Commons contained a substantial Lancastrian presence. The Speaker, Sir John Tiptoft, was a staunch Lancastrian and a knight of the king's chamber.[15] Of the seventy-five knights of the shire (there was one by-election) at least thirty-six, or 49 per cent, were either royal retainers or tenants of the duchy of Lancaster. These Lancastrians, when added to the retainers of the prince of Wales and pro-Lancastrian peers, yields at least forty-six out of the seventy-five knights of the shire, or 62 per cent, who may be counted as supporters of the royal cause (Appendix 1). Many of these men, such as the Pelhams in Sussex, had risen to the pinnacle of political and social prominence in their counties through association with Henry of Bolingbroke. They largely monopolized the legitimate power structures in their localities, and to suggest these men would oppose their friend, or sit by and allow a minority of members to drive their benefactor from government, is highly unlikely. Professor Pollard, however, suggests that some burgesses and a group of 'independent' knights of the shire opposed the king. It is clear that the role of burgesses in parliament is not well understood and that they were not passive observers in the proceedings, but to ascribe leadership of the opposition to them is difficult to support. A brief analysis of the burgesses from the major towns

---

[14] *House of Commons*, I, 124; G. Dodd, 'The Lords, Taxation and the Community of Parliament in the 1370s and Early 1380s', *Parliamentary History* 20 (2001), 287–310.

[15] It is also to be doubted if Tiptoft's supposed assaults on household extravagance actually rang true, considering he had just received on 31 December 1405 the keeping of certain lands during minority, 'notwithstanding that such wardships have been assigned to the expenses of the king's household': *Signet Letters*, p. 115; *CPR, 1405–8*, p. 109.

reveals their pro- rather than anti-royalist leanings. William Standon, a burgess from London, was among a group of Londoners who loaned £200 to the king in 1402, and followed this loan with another of £133 in 1407.[16] Nicholas Wotton, Standon's fellow London MP, thought so much of the king that he joined with his friends in 1407 to loan Henry £1,200.[17] Although the identity of the MPs for York in 1406 is lost, Henry Bokerell, burgess from Bristol, was high enough in royal favour to receive appointment as alnager for Bristol in May 1406 and continued in office for the next five years.[18] Gilbert Joce, Bokerell's fellow Bristol burgess, received royal appointment in April 1406 as a customer for a number of West Country ports,[19] and John Fitling, burgess from Hull, received appointment as collector of customs for his city after the parliament.[20] These were among the most influential and wealthy burgesses in parliament. It is doubtful that an alliance of royal opponents strong enough to force the king from government could have existed without some of their number. Since clearly these wealthy burgesses enjoyed the king's grace before and after the Long Parliament, it is doubtful any of them stood in opposition. Parliament did not vote a new subsidy during the first session, but considering all of the extraordinary taxation that parliament had given in 1404 this is not surprising. The parliament of January 1404 voted a special income tax, while the Coventry (or 'Unlearned') Parliament of October 1404 delivered two full tenths and fifteenths and a special land tax. In fact, collection for the last portion of these taxes began only on 2 February 1406.[21] Quite possibly popular opinion ran against another tax coming so soon because in 1406 the king again sought extraordinary subsidies to finance wars he seemed incapable of winning. There is no doubt that in 1406, as earlier in the reign, parliament was critical of the government's handling of the war, of purveyance and the size of the royal household, but as McFarlane suggested comments such as these, which historians have long viewed as opposition were, in fact, not opposition at all: they possessed 'no other object but the achievement of economy'.[22]

Parliament assembled for the first time in the Painted Chamber at Westminster on 1 March 1406, and is supposed to have met under a cloud of foreign crises: Wales, Scotland, Guienne and even threats from the sea. Although all of these were trouble spots, it is difficult to label them as crises. The rebellion in Wales continued, but even with the addition of Henry Percy, Lord Bardolf and their small band of followers who joined Glyn Dŵr from Scotland, the Welsh rebellion lost ground, and the 1406 campaign saw the

[16] *House of Commons*, IV, 447–50.
[17] *House of Commons*, IV, 905–7.
[18] *House of Commons*, II, 273.
[19] *House of Commons*, III, 493.
[20] *House of Commons*, III, 76–7.
[21] Wylie, *Henry IV*, II, 416.
[22] McFarlane, *Nobility*, p. 294.

English successful at every turn.[23] Although the northern marches and Guienne were of concern in 1406, troubles on these fronts shrank in significance. Even before the death of the Scottish king, Robert III, in April, Henry possessed an impressive array of Scottish hostages, including the duke of Albany's son Murdoch. Any real threat from Scotland, save for the ubiquitous border raiding on the northern marches,[24] was nullified when Prince James fell into English hands in March.[25] The threat to the English position in Guienne seemed great, and on 22 May Speaker Tiptoft claimed that ninety-six towns and castles had been lost to the French in the last year alone, though this was more than likely an exaggeration.[26] From the middle of spring a number of diplomatic negotiations took place with the French not only for extending the truce between England and France but also for the marriage of Prince Henry to a French princess.[27] Guienne was a stalwart Lancastrian bastion during Henry IV's reign, and the willingness of the communes to withstand the duke of Orleans' invasion of 1406 was largely responsible for the French military failures there.[28] Perhaps the best measure of the seriousness of these supposed crises, however, may be seen by the fact that parliament dealt directly with only one of them: the keeping of the seas. The French 'fleet' that periodically preyed on English shipping in the Thames estuary throughout the winter months of 1405–6 was nothing more than pirates. Although parliament charged local merchants with the keeping of the seas, they were not to take up their duties until 1 May – a full four months after the supposed threat of invasion. In September, nearly a full year before their commission for defence ran out, these same merchants asked to be let out of their responsibility because they were unable to carry out their charge effectively. Such a lethargic response to this 'threat of invasion' suggests parliament itself did not view this 'crisis' with any great alarm.[29] Professor

---

[23] 'Annales', p. 418; R. R. Davies, *The Revolt of Owain Glyn Dŵr* (Oxford, 1997), pp. 122–4; C. Allmand, *Henry V* (London, 1992), pp. 34–8; J. E. Lloyd said that 1406 was the year Glyd Dŵr's rebellion was 'brought to a standstill': J. E. Lloyd, *Owen Glendower* (Oxford, 1931), p. 126.

[24] The last truce of which there is good record expired on Easter day, 19 April 1405: *Foedera*, 20 vols. (London, 1725–35), VIII, 363, 368. It appears that another truce was concluded shortly thereafter, but no one paid any attention to it because no conservators were appointed: J. H. Ramsay, *Lancaster and York*, 2 vols. (Oxford, 1892), I, 97.

[25] For his capture see *Johannis de Fordun Scottichronicon*, ed. T. Hearne, 5 vols. (Edinburgh, 1871–2), IV, 1161.

[26] *Rot. Parl.*, III, 573.

[27] Z. El-Gazar, 'Politics and Legislation in England in the Early Fifteenth Century: The Parliament of 1406' (unpublished Ph. D. thesis, University of St Andrews, 2001), p. 130.

[28] M. Vale, *English Gascony, 1399–1453* (Oxford, 1970), p. 53. *Chronique du Religieux de Saint-Denys*, ed. M. Bellaguet, 8 vols. (Paris, 1839), III, 450–60.

[29] Issue Rolls from 27 February 1406 show that the French fleet was under command of an Italian mercenary named Charles de Savoisi; E 403/586. The merchants were not to take over defence of the seas until 1 May, nearly four months after the supposed threat of invasion. In September, very nearly a full year before their commission for defence of the

Pollard argues that contemporaries had no way of knowing that the greatest crises of the reign were over by 1406,[30] but by the same token contemporaries could tell that the problems facing them in early 1406 during this first session of parliament were no worse than they had already encountered. None of these previous crises, or even all of them put together, had been enough to force Henry to back away from government. Thus, if there were no foreign or domestic crises of sufficient weight, and no opposition in parliament, some other cause must have been responsible for driving Henry from government in 1406. This cause was Henry's declining health.

Perhaps more significantly the parliament roll is void of any of the language of opposition found in times of crisis. The parliament of 1406 made no issue about statements of constitutional principle, which were normal in difficult times during the fourteenth and fifteenth centuries.[31] It seems rather that the Commons went to the opposite extreme. Between the opening of parliament on 1 March and its adjournment on 22 December the Speaker, Sir John Tiptoft, made no fewer than seven protestations before the king and the Lords for the actions of the house – hardly the actions of the leader of united opposition.[32] Just as the Commons led no opposition in 1406, neither did the Lords because there were no peers so inclined to lead them. The triers of petitions for both the British Isles and those parts beyond the seas were made up of men who had long service in Henry's cause, in addition to being some of his closest friends and even some family members. All of these men, both in the Lords and in the Commons, were in Henry's good graces before, during and after the Long Parliament, and it is extremely doubtful that they would have remained so if they had worked forcibly to remove him from government, no matter how congenial he was towards criticism.

The parliament roll and other documents seem to suggest that, rather than trying to drive Henry from government, the king's supporters were closing ranks to support him. On the king's council, for example, the fluctuating membership of the past ceased. All those, and only those, who were members of the council now attended the meetings.[33] The seventeen members of the council initially named on 22 May were among the king's closest friends and supporters, as were the councillors named on 27 November and those twelve who took oaths before parliament on 22 December and who swore to the

---

seas was to cease, these same merchants were let out of their responsibility for defence because they were unable to carry out their charge efficiently, *Rot. Parl.*, III, 602; *Foedera*, VIII, 455; *CCR, 1405–9*, pp. 156–7; Ramsay, *Lancaster and York*, I, 97.

[30] Pollard, 'Parliament of 1406', p. 105.

[31] J. Watts, 'Ideas, Principles, and Politics', in *The Wars of the Roses*, ed. A. J. Pollard (New York, 1995), pp. 110–33 (pp. 110–11).

[32] These were made on 2 March, 23 March, 3 April, 15 May, 7 June, 19 June and 18 November.

[33] Brown, 'Commons and the Council', p. 22.

'Thirty-one Articles'.[34] These councillors were not part of any opposition or the pawns of such. The majority of these councillors were the exact same men who had been sitting at council for a number of years. If indeed the Commons attempted to drive the king from government for ineffective policy it seems unlikely that they would have then placed government in the hands of the very men who had helped to carry out the ineffective policies of the past. The councillors named to each of these councils did not undertake their duties with great alacrity.[35] No one liked serving on continual councils and, as several abject lessons from the previous reign demonstrated, being on the wrong council at the wrong time could prove problematic if the king turned vindictive.

A similar closing of a protective ring may also be seen in the charter witness lists for the same period. For the eighteen months prior to the second session of the Long Parliament, royal charters contained an average of ten witnesses. These ten witnesses often represented an eclectic mix including William Heron, Lord Say and even Thomas, Lord Bardolf, and excluded some of Henry's closest friends such as William, Lord Willoughby and William, Lord Roos.[36] With the charter dated 24 May 1406, however, the witness lists undergo a rapid change. The number of witnesses rises from about ten to near fourteen, and the personnel contained in the lists becomes rigid and regular, containing only Henry's closest friends and supporters throughout the remainder of the year.[37]

As Peter McNiven suggests, Henry IV's health is a shadowy topic to discuss.[38] It seems that even early in the reign Henry suffered from bouts of illness,[39] but he suffered the first in a long series of serious attacks (strokes?) on 8 June 1405.[40] Though the exact symptoms of the malady will likely never be known,[41] for the last half of his reign Henry faced extended periods where he found himself incapable of governing. Unfortunately, sources are often silent on Henry's health and offer only fleeting glimpses into his physical condition. The reasons for this silence are easy to understand since the vitality of a king provided one sure measure of his political strength.

[34] J. L. Kirby, 'Councils and Councillors of Henry IV, 1399–1413', *TRHS* 5th s. 14 (1964), 35–65 (pp. 54–6, 63–4).
[35] J. Watts, *Henry VI and the Politics of Kingship* (Cambridge, 1996), pp. 74–80, 86.
[36] C 53/174–5.
[37] C 53/175–6.
[38] McNiven, 'The Problem of Henry IV's Health', p. 746.
[39] Clearly Henry suffered a bout of illness in 1399, but this has been seen as a case of food-poisoning; McNiven, 'Problem of Henry IV's Health', p. 747. Nevertheless, Henry did make a number of purchases of medicines from early in the reign; Wylie, *Henry IV*, IV, 269.
[40] Thomas Gascoigne is the only chronicler to relate a story of the attack of June 1405 that supposedly occurred after the execution of Archbishop Scrope as punishment from God. T. Gascoigne, *Loci e Libro Veritatum*, ed. J. E. Thorold Rogers (Oxford, 1884), p. 228.
[41] For a discussion of these, McNiven, 'Problem of Henry IV's Health', pp. 746–52.

Almost certainly, Henry hoped this illness would quickly pass and he would return to good health. More importantly, public knowledge of his infirmity could have had disastrous consequences. Rebellions had already come in bewildering succession and his most inveterate opponents remained at large. If news that Henry was ill and incapable of governing became public, a new round of civil disorder could result and perhaps end in the overthrow of the Lancastrian dynasty.[42] It seems that Henry himself understood this and worked to keep up appearances. Royal letters from late 1405 often over-stressed Henry's improving physical condition and increased vigour.[43] But at the same time, the king sent letters to sheriffs ordering the arrest of vagabonds spreading rumour of his prolonged sickness, and bishops received letters requesting prayers for Henry's physical recovery and con-tinued good health.[44]

Yet, in spite of royal claims and episcopal prayers, the king's health took a turn for the worse in the spring of 1406. On 28 April a signet letter came to the council detailing Henry's intention to come to London, but he had been suddenly stricken with a malady in his leg and 'une grand accesse'.[45] His doctors forbade him to travel by horseback,[46] and he told the council that he hoped to arrive by river within the next few days.[47] A second letter arrived on the afternoon of 28 April in which Henry told the council his 'dis-ease' kept him from travelling, and there would be a further delay before he could attend parliament.[48] Quite possibly Henry did not arrive in London until 4 May.[49] While the king tarried owing to his health for four days, parliament assembled but could conduct no business. Finally, on 30 April, with the archbishop of Canterbury, the duke of York and many other lords present, parliament began again.[50]

It is not only significant that Henry failed to attend parliament, but also that he bypassed Westminster and continued on to London where he resided at the palace of bishop-elect Thomas Langley – out of sight of

---

[42] Watts expresses a similar view for the political situation in 1422 following the death of Henry V: J. L. Watts, 'When Did Henry VI's Minority End?', in *Trade, Devotion and Governance*, ed. D. J. Clayton, R. G. Davies and P. McNiven (Stroud, 1994), pp. 116–39 (p. 121).

[43] Wylie, *Henry IV*, II, 21. Henry caused at least one tract on urnology to be translated into English: C. Rawcliffe, *Medicine and Society in Later Medieval England* (Stroud, 1995), p. 47.

[44] Wylie, *Henry IV*, II, 252 n. 4; Rawcliffe, *Medicine and Society*, p. 92.

[45] *Signet Letters*, p. 126.

[46] The exact number of physicians caring for Henry at any one time is difficult to determine. It seems in 1406 that he was attended by as many as five doctors. This was an unusual number since the king usually had only one physician about him.

[47] *POPC*, I, 290; *Signet Letters*, pp. 125–6.

[48] *POPC*, I, 291; *Signet Letters*, p. 126.

[49] *POPC*, I, 275. Henry's signet letters demonstrate that he did not reach London until at least 4 May: *Signet Letters*, p. 126.

[50] *Rot. Parl.*, III, 571.

parliament and inaccessible. The best, though hardly foolproof, way to demonstrate his inaccessibility is through the use of signet letters that show the king did not leave the bishop's palace between 4 May and 7 July.[51] The only references to him being anywhere else during this period are on the parliament roll, the veracity of which may be doubted. Parliament rolls were not only written after the event, but were also a highly formulaic, 'official' version of events. Henry had 'spun' the roll of the 1399 parliament to reflect the deposition as he wished it portrayed. In 1406 it is beyond question that the roll underwent 'spin-doctoring'. For example, the 'official' version for the delay in opening the second session 'spun' on to the parliament roll was because the Garter feast at Windsor delayed the king and many nobles.[52] The real reason for the delay, as revealed in the signet letters, was the result of the king's ill health.

Also indicative of Henry's incapacity and inaccessibility in May and June is the increased volume of signet letters from the king to council, since in normal times they would have usually communicated verbally.[53] McFarlane perceived this flurry of signet correspondence as Henry's attempt to circumvent the council and maintain an active hand in government by communicating royal wishes directly to the chancellor.[54] It seems more probable that the increased use of the signet resulted from Henry's sickness rather than out of political concerns. Richard II's use of the signet caused much political resentment and Henry IV severely restricted its use, only employing it when he could not communicate verbally with his council. The letters under the signet during this period are very ordinary in content and format, and nothing in them suggests anything subversive. This unusual reliance on his personal seal suggests Henry was indeed inaccessible and thus a cause for political concern.

Clearly, kings had to be accessible to members of the political community; the success of their government depended on it.[55] Kings were also expected to be accessible when parliament was in session to conduct both ordinary and extraordinary business.[56] Richard II's withdrawal from the Merciless

---

[51] All of the signet letters in this period show the king in London. Though there are gaps of several days in some groups of letters they all state Henry's location as London in the dating clause, which suggests he never went anywhere. *Signet Letters*, pp. 126–33.

[52] *Rot. Parl.*, III, 571.

[53] McFarlane noted that more signet letters appeared in this three-month period than in any other comparable period throughout the reign. It cannot be doubted that the council took up heavy duties, and the percentage of privy seal warrants ordering payments or assignments made 'with the advice of the council' rose from 20 per cent in 7 Henry IV up to 22 May, to 60 per cent from 22 May to the end of the regnal year on 29 September; Brown, 'Commons and the Council', p. 23.

[54] *LKLK*, p. 91.

[55] Watts, *Henry VI*, pp. 81–90.

[56] Peter McNiven suggests something similar: McNiven, 'Problem Henry IV's Health', p. 752.

Parliament drew a stern rebuke for the young king from the duke of Gloucester and the earl of Arundel, who reminded Richard that where parliament sat the king should be.[57] At every other parliament of the reign Henry IV's itinerary shows him to be where the parliament sat.[58] Even in 1406 Henry stayed at Westminster during the first session and almost all of the third session; only during the second session was he tucked away in Bishop Langely's London residence near Dowgate.[59] Henry's inaccessibility is also suggested by the length of the second session. Although business was only recorded on eight days on the parliament roll, the session lasted from 30 April to 19 June, a total of fifty-one days. Taking away the seven Sundays in this period, when business would not normally be conducted, yields a total of forty-three days, dangerously close to the point laid down in the *Modus tenendi parliamentum* when members could lawfully leave parliament if the king were not present and had not explained his absence.[60]

This inaccessibility may be the reason behind the Commons' legislation against aliens enacted in the second session of the Long Parliament. Historians have long been puzzled by this series of events, and in interpreting them it is important to remember that this legislation is of different character than the usual round of parliamentary complaints against foreigners.[61] In the first session the Commons asked for the removal of all alien Bretons and Frenchmen from the kingdom, but it is not clear what had been achieved by the time the second session opened.[62] Yet, on 8 May, parliamentary assaults on aliens resurfaced with new urgency. Rather than reiterate their earlier plea, the Commons produced a list of named aliens who, together with any Bretons or Frenchmen that had entered the country since the beginning of parliament, were to leave the country by 24 May.[63] In addition, these departing aliens were to show all letters of grants they had received since the beginning of parliament to the proper authorities.[64] The list of names on the parliament roll gives the appearance of being hastily assembled and contains reference to forty-three individuals, only twenty-five of whom are named in full. For the remaining men and women, thirteen are mentioned only by their first name; two are only referred to as 'the wife of . . .' and one as 'the brother of . . .'; and finally there are mentioned simply 'two washerwomen'.[65] Apparently, these

[57] *Knighton's Chron.*, pp. 356–8.
[58] Wylie, *Henry IV*, IV, 269–302.
[59] For a rough idea of Henry's itinerary during this period see Wylie, *Henry IV*, IV, 294–5.
[60] *Parliamentary Texts of the Later Middle Ages*, ed. N. Pronay and J. Taylor (Oxford, 1980), pp. 26 (n. 48), 72.
[61] Political poems of the first years of the reign were full of complaints against foreigners and flatterers at court who sought royal largess, and the first parliament of 1404 had dismissed four such 'hangers-on': *Eulogium Historiarum*, III, 411; *Rot. Parl.*, III, 523, 525.
[62] *Rot. Parl.*, III, 569.
[63] *Rot. Parl.*, III, 571–2.
[64] *CPR, 1405–8*, p. 120.
[65] *Rot. Parl.*, III, 572.

'named' foreigners were not the only ones under suspicion, because on 7 June the Commons noted that a number of rascals still served the king and sought their removal and replacement with good men of substance.[66] Exactly how many aliens quit the country is unknown, but the panic caused by their presence abated to the point in July that licences were issued for eighty-five aliens to remain in the country.[67]

Exactly what parliament hoped to accomplish by these endeavours is not clear, but it leaves the impression of a panic – possibly over the king's health. The members of parliament, certainly the eight MPs who were members of his household, knew the reasons behind Henry's failure to attend the opening of the second session of parliament, and his inaccessibility in London probably made matters worse. With the popular bias against foreigners so prevalent in political poetry, it is not difficult to believe that rumours regarding Henry's health and mental competence circulated and fuelled this panic. Only those aliens who had entered the kingdom since the beginning of parliament were the focus of parliament's attacks for the remainder of the year. This, when combined with the demand that any royal grants given to them during this period be examined, suggests that perhaps such gifts had been given by a king with impaired judgement. The removal of aliens, coupled with parliament's demand that only men of substance be allowed to serve Henry, was possibly an attempt to stave off the same kind of disaster that befell Edward III in his last years. No doubt many in 1406 would have known the stories – true or otherwise – of how the incapacitated Edward III found himself surrounded by self-promoting scoundrels who preyed on his illness to secure lavish grants and finally stole the rings and jewels from his dead hands.[68]

In the midst of this panic over aliens, a more serious situation arose as the king's health declined even further, and on 22 May Henry removed himself from most of the daily functions of government. He informed the Commons of his inability to pay sufficient attention to affairs of government and transferred much of his power to the council. The king reserved to himself only control over appointments of officers and pardoning offenders.[69] Although certain historians have long debated how the eleven sections of this document are to be interpreted,[70] it seems the most obvious interpretation may be the best: that the king withdrew from government because he could not spend as much energy on government as he would like and because his councillors could easily relieve him of the work. The councillors

---

[66] *Rot. Parl.*, III, 577.

[67] *CPR, 1405–8*, pp. 220–2.

[68] W. Longman, *The Life and Times of Edward III*, 2 vols. (London, 1869), II, 290; Given-Wilson, *Royal Household*, pp. 209–14; T. F. Tout, *The Collected Papers of T. F. Tout*, 3 vols. (Manchester, 1934), II, 173–90.

[69] *Rot. Parl.*, III, 572.

[70] Brown, 'Commons and the Council', pp. 14–19

nominated by the king were among his closest friends and supporters. Certainly any governmental body which contained Archbishop Arundel and the king's two half-brothers would do nothing to harm Henry's reputation or image or have any part in removing him from government by force.

Last but not least, the bill stated that if the councillors thought of anything which they could remember or add to the bill for the betterment of the kingdom, then they could do so.[71] Thus, the bill was 'left open' and suggests a king in ill-health. Although Professor Brown believed this bill represented a significant piece of reform-minded legislation, there is evidence enough to suggest a different interpretation.[72] All other attempts at reform-minded legislation, from 1215 to the attacks on Richard II in the 1380s, and even the 1399 'Record and Process', clearly defined abuses of government and explicitly stated how government should and/or would operate. The bill of 22 May is an extremely amorphous document. The king's place in governance, save for several clauses regarding the movement of writs and signet letters,[73] is hardly defined. Nor was the council's place or its duties as the sort of 'collective sovereign' clearly delineated. The bill gave both the lords of the council and the king an extremely wide range of governmental motion, which could be amended or withdrawn if necessary. The amorphous nature of the bill further suggests it was intended as a temporary arrangement, which, when coupled with the succession act that followed two weeks later, perhaps represents an expectation that the king would die.

Probably this fear drove the production of Henry's third declaration on the succession that came before parliament on 7 June.[74] It is not remarkable that Henry's thoughts should have turned to the succession. His health was poor and the succession had never been far from his mind. He had already made two public declarations of the succession, one in 1399 and another in 1404. The 7 June document differed from the previous two in that the succession now descended to each of Henry's sons in tail-male. It is instructive to the king's mind at this time. Had Henry died in the summer of 1406 the end result could have been another round of civil disorder. Against this background one can readily see why Henry and his supporters would find a more detailed and more legally binding description of the succession desirable and even necessary. It is important to remember that, although Henry had four healthy sons in the summer of 1406, three of them were yet to reach the age of majority and Prince Henry was still only eighteen. Such a clarification of the

---

[71] *Rot. Parl.*, III, 572–3.

[72] Brown, 'Commons and the Council', p. 16.

[73] For a discussion on the importance of these instruments and how their use was limited see Brown, 'Commons and the Council', pp. 16–17.

[74] *Rot. Parl.*, III, 574–6. For another interpretation on the succession act see P. McNiven, 'Legitimacy and Consent: Henry IV and the Lancastrian Title, 1399–1406', *Mediaeval Studies* 44 (1982), 470–88 (pp. 484–6).

succession exclusively in tail-male was intended to help ensure political stability for an uncertain future. Such statements were not unusual within the English royal family. Henry II had done so and Edward I had ordered the succession following the death of three of his sons in 1290.[75] Perhaps the blueprint for Henry's succession act was Edward III's settling of the succession in 1376.[76] The situation facing Edward in that autumn was similar to the one facing Henry in June 1406: a sick king whose death might have led to civil disorder. The succession acts of 1376 and 1406, while not near copies, are similar in form and suggest, as Michael Bennett has argued, that John of Gaunt secured a copy of his father's succession act and that Henry then used this copy as a model in 1406. In addition, at the end of the succession document of 1406, the parliament roll records that the Speaker lavished almost gratuitous praise on the person and exploits of the prince of Wales, whose succession might have seemed close at hand.

Yet Henry of Bolingbroke did not die in the summer of 1406 and it seems that no one knew quite what to do next. Henry recovered enough strength to travel in early July, but he was still not completely well. The king's continued heath problems led to the lengthy prorogation of parliament from 19 June until 13 October. Despite the recess, Henry remained in London for the rest of June, which was 'a most unusual procedure for him'.[77] The most instructive evidence regarding Henry's health in this period rests in his itinerary. Historians have noted the slowness of Henry's progress through East Anglia and Lincolnshire in the summer,[78] but no one has made a detailed inquiry into Henry's movements during this period (Appendix 2). When one totes up the journey from 7 July to 13 October, one finds a trip of approximately 355 miles travelled over 98 days, an average of about 3.62 miles per day. This is a slow pace, even by medieval standards, and hints at a monarch whose health impeded his ability to travel.[79]

Investigation into the places visited reveals there was more to this journey than merely aimless wandering about the countryside, since many of the stops housed holy places and/or relics that were specifically associated with healing.[80] For example, Bury St Edmunds by 1400 had developed as a thriving medical community, which attracted many people to the town to

---

[75] F. M. Powicke, *Henry III and the Lord Edward*, 2 vols. (Oxford, 1947), II, 732–3, 788.

[76] M. J. Bennett, 'Edward III's Entail and the Succession to the Crown', *EHR* 112 (1998), 580–609.

[77] Kirby, *Henry IV*, pp. 126, 201.

[78] Wylie, *Henry IV*, II, 448–9; Kirby, *Henry IV*, pp. 201–4; Pollard, 'Parliament of 1406', p. 114.

[79] C. A. J. Armstrong, 'Some Examples of the Distribution and Speed of News in England at the Time of the Wars of the Roses', in *Studies in Medieval History Presented to Frederick Maurice Powicke*, ed. W. A. Pantin, R. W. Hunt and R. W. Southern (Oxford, 1948), pp. 429–54.

[80] This route of pilgrimage through East Anglia had been used before. Richard II had made a similar journey to similar places on what was referred to as a pilgrimage in 1383, *Westminster Chron.*, p. 42.

take advantage of its services.[81] In addition, Bury housed the shrine of St Edmund the Martyr, which, along with the cup of St Edmund that the abbey also possessed, had the power (many believed) to heal the sick.[82] Thetford housed St Thomas Becket's comb and a number of relics 'found' in the fourteenth century that attracted many pilgrims to its doors in the latter years of that century.[83] Wyndmonham Abbey possessed a piece of the True Cross.[84] St Albans had be renowned for healing miracles since the time of Bede.[85] Bardney contained relics of St Oswald,[86] while Walsingham housed two holy wells and relics holy to the Virgin, which in the late fourteenth century had been held responsible for a number of miraculous cures.[87]

Perhaps most instructive evidence as to the recuperative nature of this journey rests in a description of Henry's visit to Bardney Abbey in Lincoln- shire. Upon his arrival at the abbey, Henry dismounted and, with great humility, knelt and kissed a holy cross and received a sprinkling of holy water from the abbot.[88] The king then attended services within the abbey church and stopped to kiss the holy relics housed in the abbey.[89] Henry came to Bardney not as a king but rather as a pilgrim. It was not normal for a king to dismount and kneel before the abbot for a blessing,[90] nor was it normal to receive an application of holy water. But Henry's veneration of the relics is of most significance. Even given Henry's high station, it was most unusual for him to hold relics – and kissing them was extraordinary. Most pilgrims who came to such shrines never saw the relics they travelled so far to venerate, and they were almost never allowed to touch them.[91] Holy relics, convention

---

[81] R. S. Gottfried, *Bury St Edmunds and the Urban Crisis: 1290–1539* (Princeton, 1982), pp. 192–207.

[82] *VCH Norfolk*, 2 vols. (London, 1901–6), II, 393.

[83] When an old statue of the Blessed Virgin was placed in a newly constructed stone chapel the head was found to contain relics that conferred miraculous powers of healing. For a discussion of this see, L. Butler and C. Given-Wilson, *Medieval Monasteries of Great Britain* (London, 1979), pp. 378–9, and also G. McMurray Gibson, *The Theater of Devotion: East Anglian Drama and Society in the Late Middle Ages* (Chicago, 1989), p. 213 n.14.

[84] *VCH Norfolk*, II, 337.

[85] Bede, *A History of the English Church and People*, trans. L. Sherley-Price (New York, 1985), p. 47.

[86] Bede, *History*, pp. 155–63; J. Leland, *Antiquarii de Rebus Britannicus Collectanea*, 6 vols. (London, 1770), VI, 300–1.

[87] Butler and Given-Wilson, *Medieval Monasteries*, pp. 378–9.

[88] '& visa processione serenissimus Rex Henricus ab equo suo desiluit, & flexis genibus sanctam Crucem humiliter est osculatus, & sancta aqua aspersus', Leland, *Collecteana*, VI, 300.

[89] '. . . reliaquias sacras oscalatus est. . . .', Leland, *Collecteana*, VI, 300.

[90] There were only twenty-one Benedictine monks in the 1370s at Bardney, and this number had fallen to sixteen by 1437: D. Knowles and R. N. Hadcock, *Medieval Religious Houses: England and Wales*, 2nd edn (London, 1971), pp. 52, 59.

[91] J. Sumption, *Pilgrimage* (Totowa, N.J., 1975), p. 82. See also Rawcliffe, *Medicine and Society*, pp. 21–4. R. Finucane, *Miracles and Pilgrims: Popular Beliefs in Medieval England* (Totowa, N.J., 1977), pp. 26–7.

held, radiated holy energy so that mere proximity sufficed to cure most diseases. The touching of a holy object allowed more holy energy to flow into the body. Kissing the relic was a way in which the greatest amount of holy energy could be transferred and was therefore reserved only for the great, and when especially powerful acts of healing were necessary.[92]

Exactly how effective this pilgrimage was in restoring Henry's health is debatable, especially since the third session of parliament had to be postponed for five days in succession.[93] More puzzling is the fact that, following the opening on 18 October, there were no recorded meetings until 18 November. A. L. Brown argued that parliament 'must' have met daily during this period, and the silence of the roll to such meetings is indicative of continuing conflict between the king and the Commons. More recently, Dr El-Gazar has argued that the duke of Burgundy's threat to Calais was the cause for the lack of business.[94] Yet the available evidence does not seem to support the weight of either suggestion. There was no continuing conflict between the king and the Commons, and although Burgundy and Henry did indeed make preparations for war over Calais in the final months of 1406, both king and duke were involved in diplomatic negotiations to resolve their differences, which suggests that their military preparations were little more than posturing. In spite of Henry's expressing his intention to lead troops to Calais, no commissions of array were issued, no captains received indentures for war, and no ships were pressed for passage of the army. Such a lack of regular and effective military preparation, combined with the fact that parliament was neither recessed nor prorogued, suggests that something more than war lay at the heart of the month-long parliamentary hiatus.

Something more than war also lay at the heart of the last constitutional document of 1406 given on 22 December, usually called the 'Thirty-one Articles'.[95] Although A. L. Brown concentrated his interpretation on the administrative side of the articles, taken as a whole, they demonstrate a parliament often marking the fine line between mistrust and political necessity. Here is a clearly delineated series of articles that sets the patterns of governance for the next ten months, until parliament met at Gloucester in October 1407. Historians have long seen these articles as placing a large number of restrictions on the king, although they placed greater restrictions on the council whose powers as a sort of 'collective sovereign' were now clearly defined. Power of filling offices and disposing of grants now lay so

---

[92] A good example of this comes from the French court. In August 1321 an ailing Philip V kissed a piece of the True Cross, one of the nails of the Crucifixion and some of St Simeon's relics, and felt restored to good health; E. A. R. Brown, *The Monarchy of Capetian France and Royal Ceremonial* (New York, 1991), p. 273.

[93] *Rot. Parl.*, III, 579.

[94] El-Gazar, 'Politics and Legislation', p. 136.

[95] *Rot. Parl.*, III, 580–2.

firmly under the council's control that it was left in a position similar to the one its predecessors had enjoyed in Richard II's minority. Indeed, the council's power for this time was even greater since they were now not limited to making temporary grants. A number of the 'Thirty-one Articles' expressly ordained that the great officers of state would perform their duties in accordance with the statutes. Other articles demanded that all officers, even clerks in the Chancery, Exchequer, judicial system and the royal household, should follow the appropriate statutes in the performance of their daily duties – as if to suggest, or guard against the possibility, that they were not. This same kind of mistrust or fear of wrongdoing may also be seen in the articles that specifically related to the council. No councillor was to show any favouritism in the debates on grants; the king was only to govern with the advice and consent of the council; and some were to be about him at all times. The members of council were to acquaint themselves with every part of government from the household to the chamber to the wardrobe and to the county offices; and matters passed by the council had to be passed by the *entire* council in person unless there was great need to the contrary. Sheriffs, escheators and other officers should be appointed according to statute and not by personal application to the king, and sheriffs were to notify the people of the place and day of elections to parliament at least fifteen days before they took place. Parliament even demanded that no one take a gift from the king from the revenues, profits or other commodities of the kingdom that were not already granted before the beginning of parliament on pain of being forfeit to twice their value.

A number of articles also dealt directly with the king, and it is clear that access to him and the type of business he could conduct were closely controlled. The council was not to bring before him matters which the common law might solve. No one in the royal household was to bring supplications before the king. Any disputes among the king's entourage were to be settled by the council or via the common law, not by the king himself. If any member of the royal household were to 'cause the mind of the king to be swayed for their particular advantage', they were to be removed. In addition, Wednesdays and Fridays were publicly proclaimed as the only days on which the king, always in the presence of some of his council, would conduct public business and would be accessible to the political community.

These articles, when viewed through the lens of an infirm Henry IV, allow the situation at the end of 1406 to come into sharper focus. A number of the articles were directed at the council and mandated that everyone who would be involved in governance had to 'follow the rules' laid down by statute and not play favourites, as happened so frequently in medieval governance. Such items not only display a general mistrust of the council and government on the part of parliament, they are also suggestive of the fact that the king was in no condition to oversee their actions and correct their abuses if he found any. Among the most important articles of this group is number seven: the demand that no money from the subsidy that parliament just voted be used for any new grants. This article represents how effective the Commons were at controlling their taxation. Fearing that their subsidy might be squandered, they attempted to vote a tax only on condition that it would be entirely repaid if the council misused the funds, but the anger of the king forced them to retract this demand.[96] Royal wrath notwithstanding, parliament placed the vast bulk of royal finance squarely in the hands of the continual council. Not only did the council have control over the subsidies voted in June and December 1406, it also appropriated the last portion of the tax due from the Coventry Parliament of 1404.[97] Parliament allocated only £6,000 to Henry for his personal use, hardly a vast sum of money and probably what parliament believed it could afford to lose.[98]

The group of articles that specifically dealt with the king were perhaps the most significant and the most illustrative as to Henry's physical and possibly even mental state. The article ordering that Henry set aside two days a week for public business in the presence of councillors was not an attempt to restrict his role in government, but rather to demand his presence within it. As John Watts suggests, it was imperative for the king to be accessible to the members of the political community; the very success of the monarchy depended on it.[99] Further, the article's demand that these days be publicly proclaimed as occasions when Henry IV would be personally accessible suggests there had been a time in the past when he had not. The demands that the king should not be burdened with business that could be solved under the common law, and warnings against anyone caught swaying his mind, speaks of a king with impaired judgement. As a group, the articles that dealt with the king's person strongly suggest that Henry was still incapacitated in late 1406. It was one thing to constrict or limit the king's role in government, but to drive him from the governance of his own household, and even to bar him from settling disputes among his own servants, were extraordinary constraints and only necessary when the king was a minor or incapable of governing.

'No king, or other lord, ruled his followers without their counsel,' John Watts wrote in 1996, 'but [the king], not his counsellors, was the locus of their government.'[100] The principal activity of the Long Parliament of 1406 was to preserve this locus. That it took parliament so long to achieve a workable solution should not surprise us, because its members hoped the king would soon get better (or that he would die) and possessed no desire that the

---

[96] *The St Albans Chronicle, 1406–1420*, ed. V. H. Galbraith (Oxford, 1937), pp. 2–3.

[97] *Rot. Parl.*, III, 568, 578.

[98] Walsingham wrote that the cost of the parliament was enormous and that it equalled the money granted in the subsidy ('Annales', p. 418; *Historia Anglicana*, II, 273). Wylie tallied the expenses for the MPs and these alone amounted to £2,499 12s: Wylie, *Henry IV*, II, 477.

[99] Watts, 'When did Henry VI's Minority End?', p. 119.

[100] Watts, *Henry VI*, p. 101.

solution they eventually cobbled together should long endure.[101] In 1406 it was the politics of health, and not parliamentary malevolence, that drove the engine of political necessity. Throughout the last eight months of the year, parliament acted as an *ad hoc* great council. It moved from panic over the presence of aliens in the household, to a temporary solution on 22 May, which allowed for great governmental latitude, to bolstering the dynasty by passing the succession act on 7 June when it was feared that the king might die, and finally to the conservative action contained in the 'Thirty-one Articles' that clearly defined the parameters of government. As such, the Long Parliament represents medieval constitutionalism at its best. But perhaps the greatest achievement of the Long Parliament does not lie so much in constitutional principles, but rather in the strength and resilience of the Lancastrian political community. Although the king had suffered rebellion after rebellion, the events of 1406 represented the most serious test of Lancastrian kingship. Henry of Bolingbroke, the vigorous knight, the noble crusader, renowned jouster, the courteous, well-liked courtier and the admired friend of many was gone. In his place lay a broken shell of a man who would never again ride in the lists or lead men to war. Henry did have four sons, but they were all young and none could match their father's reputation, his years of experience in politics, or yet command as broad a base of support and loyalty. More than sufficient opportunity existed for ambitious men in the political community to abandon what might have seemed like a short-lived dynasty for greener pastures. The young Mortimer still lived, Glyn Dŵr still remained at large, and the aged Henry Percy still gnawed at the ends of old plots. Yet, no rebellion, or even hint of rebellion, ensued. Rather, the political community rallied to Henry, and though they no doubt debated at length in regard to procedure, in the end some of the greatest members of that community even agreed to govern for him. This is perhaps the most significant aspect of 1406, and one that illustrates much about Henry of Bolingbroke's character and his kingship.

---

[101] Pollard, 'Parliament of 1406', p. 117.

Appendix 1

Lancastrian retainers and retainers of royalist nobles in the Long Parliament[1]

LANCASTRIAN RETAINERS

Berks.	Lawrence Drew	Lancs.	William Botiller
Bucks.	Edmund Brudenell[2]	Leics.	Henry Neville
Cambs.	John Hobildod[3]	Leics.	John Neville
Cambs.	William Asenhill[4]	Lincs.	John Copuldyk
Corn.	John Arundel	Norfolk	Edmund Noon
Cumb.	John Skelton[5]	Norfolk	John Reymes
Derbs.	Roger Bradshaw[6]	Northants.	John Cope
Derbs.	Roger Leche[7]	Northants.	John Warwick
Devon	Hugh Luttrell	Notts.	Thomas Chaworth
Devon	Thomas Pomeroy	Notts.	Richard Stanhope
Dorset	H. Stafford the Elder	Oxon.	Thomas Chaucer
Essex	Elmyng Leget	Staffs.	Thomas Aston
Gloucs.	Robert Whittington	Sussex	John Dalyngrigge
Herefords.	John ap Henry	Sussex	John Pelham
Hunts.	John Botiller[8]	Warwicks.	Thomas Lucy
Hunts.	John Tiptoft (Speaker)	Wilts.	Thomas Bonham[9]
Kent	Richard Clitheroe	Yorks.	Richard Redman
Lancs.	Robert Lawerence	Yorks.	Thomas Rokesby

[1] Unless otherwise referenced, see A. J. Pollard, 'The Lancastrian Constitutional Experiment Revisited: Henry IV, Sir John Tiptoft and the Parliament of 1406', *Parliamentary History* 14 (1995), 103–19.

[2] Granted stewardship of King's manor at Chiltern Langley, 4 December 1399, *CPR, 1399–1401*, p. 120.

[3] King's esquire by 20 January 1402, *CPR, 1401–05*, p. 33.

[4] Alias Harpedan.

[5] Retained by John of Gaunt, S. K. Walker, *The Lancastrian Affinity, 1361–1399* (Oxford, 1991), p. 281.

[6] Master forester in forest of Ashdown in Kent for John of Gaunt, PRO, DL 42/15, fol. 100. Rider and ranger of Ashdown Chase, 1395, PRO, DL 28/32/22, m. 12.

[7] Somerville, *Duchy of Lancaster*, p. 419.

[8] Retained by John of Gaunt, Walker, *The Lancastrian Affinity*, p. 265.

[9] Chief Steward of the South Parts of the duchy of Lancaster from 1401: DL 42/15, fol. 87v.

Douglas Biggs

RETAINERS OF ROYALIST NOBLES

Essex	Richard Baynard (duke of York)	Staffs.	Humphrey Stafford the Younger (prince of Wales)
Northumb.	John Clavering (earl of Westmorland)	Warwicks.	Thomas Burdet (earl of Warwick)
Oxon.	John Wilcotes (earl of Somerset)	Worcs.	Ralph Arderne (earl of Warwick)
Salop.	Thomas Holbache (earl of Arundel)	Worcs.	Thomas Hodlyngton (earl of Warwick)
Som.	Leonard Hakluyt (earl of March)		

Appendix 2

Henry IV's itinerary for the summer of 1406[1]

8 July	Hertford[2]	20 August	Horncastle[13]
17 July	Waltham Abbey[3]	21 August	Bardney Abbey[14]
19–20 July	Hertford[4]	24–25 August	Lincoln[15]
20 July	Barley[5]	29 August–	
21 July	Babraham,	6 September	Leicester[16]
	Newmarket[6]	8 September	Northampton,
24 July	Bury St Edmunds[7]		Huntingdon,
24 July–31 July	Thetford,		Pishobury[17]
	Wymondham,	13 September	St Albans[18]
	Norwich[8]	15 September	Smithfield[19]
1–2 August	Walsingham[9]	30 September	Worksop[20]
4 August	Castle Rising[10]	1–3 October	London[21]
7–16 August	King's Lynn[11]	8–11 October	Merton Priory[22]
17 August	Spalding[12]	13 October	Westminster[23]

[1] Henry left London on 7 July.
[2] *Signet Letters*, p. 133.
[3] *Signet Letters*, p. 133.
[4] *Signet Letters*, p. 133.
[5] Wylie, *Henry IV*, II, 448.
[6] Wylie, *Henry IV*, II, 448.
[7] *Signet Letters*, p. 134.
[8] Wylie, *Henry IV*, II, 448.
[9] Wylie, *Henry IV*, II, 448.
[10] Wylie, *Henry IV*, II, 448.
[11] *Signet Letters*, pp. 134–5; E 404/22/535.
[12] *Signet Letters*, p. 135.
[13] Kirby, *Henry IV*, p. 202.
[14] J. Leland, *Antiquarii de Rebus Britannicus Collectanea*, 6 vols. (London, 1770), VI, 300–1.
[15] Wylie, *Henry IV*, II, 461.
[16] *Signet Letters*, p. 135; Wylie, *Henry IV*, II, 461.
[17] *Signet Letters*, p. 135; Wylie, *Henry IV*, II, 461.
[18] *Signet Letters*, p. 136.
[19] Wylie, *Henry IV*, II, 461. A tournament was held here on this date: E 404/21/308.
[20] Wylie, *Henry IV*, II, 461.
[21] *Signet Letters*, pp. 136–7.
[22] *Signet Letters*, p. 137.
[23] *Signet Letters*, pp. 137–9; Wylie, *Henry IV*, II, 461.

INDEX

Albert of Bavaria, count of Hainault, 64, 65, 67
Anne of Bohemia, queen of England, 41, 44, 45
Arundel, Thomas, archbishop of Canterbury, 3, 9, 12, 13, 16–18, 20, 23, 25, 32, 33, 104, 192, 196
Arvanigian, Mark, 85
Ask, Richard, 47

Bannockburn, battle of, 86
Bardolf, Lord Thomas, 166, 168, 188, 191
Barel, John, 100
Beauchamp, Thomas, earl of Warwick, 14, 183
Beaufort, Henry, bishop of Lincoln and Winchester, 102, 104
Beaufort, John, earl of Somerset, 58, 67, 104, 107
Becket, St. Thomas, archbishop of Canterbury, 4, 12, 30, 37–8
Beaumont, Lord John, 123
Bennett, Michael, 120
Biggs, Douglas, 25, 108, 119
Blenkinsop, Alexander, 151
Bokerell, Henry, 188
Boniface IX, pope, 60
Boucicaut, Jean de, 68
Bottlesham, John, bishop of Rochester, 102
Bowet, Henry, bishop of Bath and Wells, 102
Bramham Moor, battle of, 150
Brown, A. L., 74, 95, 96, 100, 108, 117, 134, 185, 196, 199

Carnaby, William, 143, 151, 153, 159
Chamberlain, John, 100
Charles VII, king of France, 54, 57–8, 123
Chatton, William, 151
Chaucer, Geoffrey, 58–9
Cheyne, Sir John, 100, 102, 107
Clavering, John, 149, 158
Clerk, Thomas, of Alnwick, 147
Cliderhowe, Richard, 149–58

Clifford, Lord Roger, 130
Clifford, William, 147
Cobham, Lord John, 33, 104
Colville, Sir John, 164, 180
Colville, Sir Thomas, 181
Conyers, John, 131
Coppill, John, 146, 147
Court, Francis, 62, 63, 70
Craster, Edmund, 141, 152
Cresswell, John, 147, 148, 152
Creton, Jean, 16, 19, 42, 43, 51
Curson, John, 102, 107

D'Artois, Jean, 87
Dacre estates, 125
Dalton, John, 154
Despenser, Henry, bishop of Norwich, 56
DeVere, Robert, duke of Ireland, 56
Dodd, Gwilym, 186
Doncaster, oath of, 21
Doreward, John, 102, 105, 107
Douglas, Archibald, earl of Douglas (Scottish), 80, 81, 82, 128
Du Boulay, F. R. H., 60
Dunbar, George, earl of March (Scottish), 127
Dymmock, Sir Thomas, 68

Earls' Rebellion/Epiphany Rising (1400), 40, 47
Edmund, 'Crouchback', earl of Lancaster, 22, 23
Edmund of Langley, duke of York, 19, 20, 104, 121, 123, 144
Edward the Confessor, 37, 38, 39, 44
Edward I, 89, 197
Edward II, 13, 14, 31, 41, 52, 86
Edward of Woodstock, 'the Black Prince', 49, 148
Edward III, 4, 13, 20, 32, 41, 48, 64, 76, 78, 79, 81, 86, 88, 89, 99, 103, 195
Edward of York, earl of Rutland, duke of York, 81, 104, 183, 192
Ellison, William, 154
Elizabeth I, 15

Erpingham, Sir Thomas, 70, 102, 107, 118, 119, 144
Eure, Sir Ralph, 119, 134, 144, 147, 156, 158, 161, 180

Fauconberg, Isabella, 143
Fauconberg, Sir John, 180, 181
Fauconberg, Lord Thomas, 125, 164, 165, 181
Fenwick, John, 140–42, 157, 158
Fitling, John, 188
Fitzalan, Richard, earl of Arundel, 13, 14, 47, 57, 63, 194
Fitzalan, Thomas, earl of Arundel, 12, 17
Fitzhugh, Lord Henry, 126, 164
Fitzrandolf, Sir John, 164, 180
Fortescue, Sir John, 32
Freningham, John, 102
Frisby, Dr. William, 27, 29
Froissart, Jean, 11, 39, 56, 57, 63–4, 66, 67, 69, 123
Frost, William, 178–9
Frye, Robert, 97, 100

Gascoigne, Thomas, 171, 173
Gascoigne, William, 171
Given-Wilson, Chris, 118, 185
Glorious Revolution (1688), 25, 31
Glyn Dŵr, Owain, 109, 146, 188, 202
Gower, John, 12, 18, 23, 33, 43, 58
Gray, Sir Thomas, of Heton, 119, 127, 134–5, 143–4, 153, 158–9
Gray, Sir Thomas, 'the younger', 136
Grey, Lord Reginald, of Ruthyn, 104
Grey, Lord Richard, of Codnor, 104
Grey, Sir Thomas, 83, 87
Greystoke, Lord Richard, 119, 130, 133

Hall, Robert, 151
Harbottle, Robert, 142, 152, 153, 156, 159
Harding, Sampson, 158
Hardyng, John, 74, 139, 145, 146, 148, 152, 153, 167, 169, 170
Haseldene, Sir Thomas, 70, 71
Hastings, Edmund, 159
Hastings, Sir Ralph, 132, 164, 165, 180
Henry II, 197
Henry III, 12, 22, 23
Henry V/Henry of Monmouth, 36, 39, 67, 196
Henry VI, 29, 50, 61, 98

Henry of Grosmont, duke of Lancaster, 56, 59
Heron, Sir Gerard, 133, 144, 147, 149, 158
Heron, John, 144
Heron, William, Lord Say, 128, 133, 134, 144, 145, 147, 154, 191
Heton, Henry, 141
Hoccleve, Thomas, 100
Holand, John, duke of Exeter, 123
Holy Oil of St. Thomas, 4, 12, 16, 37, 38
Homildon Hill, battle of, 128, 129, 130, 155, 156

Ilderton, Thomas, 140
Isabella, queen of England, 109, 123, 133

Joan of Navarre, queen of England, 134
Joice, Gilbert, 188
John of Gaunt, duke of Lancaster, 11, 14, 15, 17, 20, 23, 49, 56, 57, 65–9, 79, 80, 120–22, 124, 127, 130, 132, 140, 141, 143, 159, 180, 197
John of Lancaster, third son of Henry IV, 137, 146, 149, 152–5, 159, 161, 164, 170

King, Andy, 85
Kirby, John L., 95, 117, 128, 185
Knayton, Thomas, 147
Knighton, Henry, 56

Lamplugh, Sir Robert, 154, 180
Langley, Thomas, bishop of Durham, 101, 192, 194
Lionel of Antwerp, duke of Clarence, 20
Lisle, Robert, 148, 149, 158
Louis, duke of Orleans, 19
Lucy, Maude, 123
Lumley, Lord Ralph, 126

Markele, Robert, 100
Maudeleyn, Richard, 40
McFarlane, K. B., 3, 55, 185
McNiven, Peter, 124, 128, 129, 162, 163, 185
Middleham, John, 147, 149, 150, 152
Mindrum, John, 146
Mitford, John, 140, 144, 145, 147, 148, 149, 158
Mitford, William, 158
Montfort, John, duke of Brittany, 126
Mortimer, Roger, earl of March, 20, 21

Mowbray, Thomas, duke of Norfolk, 7, 14, 63, 144
Mowbray, Thomas, earl of Nottingham, 161, 162, 165, 166, 169, 171, 182, 183
Musson, Anthony, 78

Neville, Cynthia J., 121, 127, 129
Neville, Ralph, earl of Westmorland, 2, 7, 76, 85, 87, 88, 90–2, 104, 119, 124–6, 130, 131, 134–7, 145, 149, 150, 159, 161, 162, 164, 169, 170, 180, 181, 182
Neville, Robert, 131
Neville, Lord John, 122, 125, 132, 181
Neville, Thomas of Halomshire, 153, 158
Neville, Thomas, Lord Furnival, 134, 147
Newark, Master Alan, 87
Norbury, John, 70, 71, 118, 119
Norton, John, 99

Ormrod, W. M., 78

Panetrie, Richard, 99
Parliament: 'Good Parliament' of 1376, 13, 197; of 1386, 112; 'Merciless Parliament' of 1388, 13, 21, 31, 141; 'Revenge Parliament' of 1397, 4, 21, 27; of 1399, 3, 9, 10, 11, 19, 21, 23, 24, 27, 28, 33, 100, 196; 'Record and Process', 10, 25, 50, 164, 165, 166, 167, 168, 196; of 1401, 5, 27, 96, 99, 108, 110–13; of January 1404, 7, 96, 181, 188; of October 1404, 96, 104, 183, 188, 201; 'Long Parliament' of 1406, 1, 6, 27, 28, 96, 105, 185–202
Pelham, Sir John, 102
Percy, Henry 'Hotspur', 26, 75, 76, 82, 88, 90, 91, 121,128, 129, 134, 139, 140, 141, 142, 143, 144, 146, 149, 156, 159, 161, 181
Percy, Henry, earl of Northumberland, 2, 17, 19, 32, 75–88, 90, 92, 102, 106, 121, 122, 123, 124, 126, 129, 130, 133, 135, 141, 149, 150, 151, 162, 163, 164, 165, 168, 169, 171, 174, 179, 181, 184, 188, 202
Percy, Henry of Atholl, 141, 147, 148
Percy, Thomas, earl of Worcester, 2, 102, 105, 109, 126, 128, 133, 144
Persay, Sir Robert, 165, 180
Plumpton, Sir William, 162, 165, 180, 181
Pollard, A. J., 186, 187

Preston, John, 151
Prophet, John, 97, 101, 102, 107
Putnam, Bertha Haven, 78

Reid, Rachel, 75, 77
Redman, Matthew, 142
Rempston, Sir Thomas, 70, 107, 119
Repington, Philip, 183
Repton, Philip, 21, 24, 26, 29, 30, 32
Richard II, 3, 4, 13, 27, 29, 32, 79, 87, 89, 97, 103, 117, 131, 132, 141, 184, 196; Scottish campaign of 1385, 73, 86; crisis of 1388, 14, 15, 21, 193; Irish expedition of 1395, 63–5; peace with France, 57; 'Revenge Parliament' of 1397, 33; appointments to wardens of northern marches, 81–3, 121–4, 126; his deposition in 1399, 9, 10, 16–20, 22–4, 28, 31, 133; his death and rumors of his survival, 26; his reburial, 35–53
Robert III, king of Scotland, 83, 84, 87, 88, 189
Roddam, William, 147, 152
Rokeby, Thomas, 149, 150, 153, 159
Roos, Lord William, 104, 119, 132, 133, 191

Savage, Sir Arnold, 28, 100, 102, 105, 174
Scarle, John, 102, 113, 119
Scrope, Richard, archbishop of York, 2, 7, 8, 9, 17, 19, 29, 47, 104, 134, 137, 161–74, 177, 183, 184
Scrope, Lord Richard, of Bolton, 33
Shirlock, John, 99
Shrewsbury, battle of, 74, 145, 146, 147, 148, 187
Skirlaw, Walter, bishop of Durham, 102, 122, 134, 136, 143
Stafford, Edmund, bishop of Exeter, 102, 113
Standon, William, 188
Stapleton, Sir Miles, 125
Steele, Anthony, 91
Storey, Robin, 75, 91, 121
Strohm, Paul, 51
Stubbs, William, 3, 12, 25, 30, 32, 185
Swinburne, William, 140, 141, 146, 154, 157
Swinhoe, Robert, 143, 149, 152, 158
Swinhoe, Walter, 143
Swynbourne, Thomas, 61

Thirning, Sir William, 22
Thomas of Woodstock, duke of
    Gloucester, 13, 14, 56, 57, 63, 67, 69, 194
Tiptoft, Sir John, 28, 189, 190
Trevenant, John, bishop of Hereford, 102
Trullop, Andrew, 146
Trullop, Harvey, 146
Tuck, Anthony, 80, 86, 123, 130
Tuttebury, Thomas, 40, 119

Umfraville, Robert, 142, 144, 147, 152,
    156, 158, 169
Usk, Adam, 15, 19, 22, 56, 73

Visconti, Gian Galeazzo, 62, 63
Vergil, Polydore, 162

Walker, Simon, 119

Walsingham, Thomas, 18, 21, 43, 73, 161,
    167, 168, 172
Warkworth, John, 151
Waterton, Hugh, 70, 144
Waterton, John, 70
Waterton, Robert, 70, 100, 165
Watts, John, 29, 201
Wenceslas, king of the Romans, 60, 62
Widdrington, John, 147, 159
Willoughby, Lord William, 104, 119, 131,
    132, 133, 191
Worthington, William, 147
Wotton, Nicholas, 188
Wylie, James Hamilton, 74
Wymundeswold, William, 99
Wyndale, John, 147

Young, Richard, bishop of Bangor, 102